Plain Folk and Gentry
in a Slave Society

Plain Folk and Gentry in a Slave Society

White Liberty and Black Slavery
in Augusta's Hinterlands

J. William Harris

Wesleyan University Press
Middletown, Connecticut

All inquiries and permission requests should be addressed to the
Publisher, Wesleyan University Press, 110 Mt. Vernon Street,
Middletown, Connecticut 06457.

Distributed by Harper & Row Publishers, Keystone Industrial Park,
Scranton, Pennsylvania 18512.

Library of Congress Cataloging in Publication Data

Harris, J. William, 1946–
  Plain folk and gentry in a slave society.

  Bibliography: p.
  Includes index.
    1. Slavery—Georgia—Augusta Region—Public opinion.
  2. Slaveholders—Georgia—Augusta Region—Attitudes.
  3. Augusta Region (Ga.)—Economic conditions.   4. Augusta
  Region (Ga.)—Social conditions.   5. Public opinion—
  Georgia—Augusta Region—History—19th century.   I. Title.
  E445.G3H37   1985   975.8′6   85-7108
  ISBN 0-8195-6163-0 (alk. paper)

Manufactured in the United States of America

First printing, 1985
Wesleyan Paperback, 1987

For My Parents

Louise Pollard Harris

and

Jack W. Harris

CONTENTS

🍀 TABLES

❦ ILLUSTRATIONS

✹ MAPS

✸ ACKNOWLEDGMENTS

If I could remember his name, I would thank first a playmate of mine in Georgia many years ago. Much older and more knowledgeable than I (he was 10 and I was 7), he told me that southerners had owned slaves before the Civil War. Since I was myself a southerner I knew this couldn't be true, and I rushed home to get my mother to confirm my sense of self-righteousness. She didn't. In part this book is an outgrowth of my surprise and disappointment that day.

I owe many more specific debts incurred while researching and writing. The staffs at the Georgia Department of Archives and History, the Emory University Library, the University of Georgia Library, the South Caroliniana Library, the Perkins Library at Duke University, the Southern Historical Collection at the University of North Carolina Library, the Library of Congress, and the Harvard University Libraries, and the Boston Athenaeum were unfailingly kind and competent as I searched for sometimes obscure documents relating to the Augusta area. Virginia Shadron at the Georgia Archives was particularly helpful and led me to several items I would otherwise have missed. The Interlibrary Loan Division of the Johns Hopkins University Library helped me track down several sources.

Much of the research was undertaken as part of a dissertation, and during that time I received financial assistance from the Johns Hopkins Department of History, the Johns Hopkins Computer Center, and loan programs, some no longer in existence, subsidized by the Federal Government. A summer stipend from the National Endowment for the Humanities enabled me to complete research on the Civil War years.

Other scholars have shared ideas and their results. David Carlton, Drew Gilpin Faust, and Gavin Wright all gave helpful advice and lent copies of unpublished papers. Conversations with Edwin Bridges, Vernon Burton, Steven Hahn, and Robert McMath helped me puzzle out some of the mysteries of Georgia and South Carolina history. Commentators at meetings of the Social Science History Association and the Organization of American Historians made useful criticisms of preliminary presentations of my work.

I am most in debt to faculty members and fellow students in the History Department at Johns Hopkins. I undertook this project as a dissertation under the direction of Professor Willie Lee Rose. Her combination of friendly support, rigorous criticism, and intellectual honesty was both rare and inspiring. Her seminar in southern history offered the ideal forum for discussion and debate. She has always made her students feel the pleasure and responsibility of engaging with others in the common enterprise of historical scholarship. At an early stage of the research, Professor Rose had to withdraw from teaching because of illness. Professor William W. Freehling ably directed the dissertation to its finish, and has continued to offer support and advice. Professors Louis Galambos and Ronald Walters read early drafts of all or most chapters and offered many excellent suggestions. Laurence Shore and Fredrika Teute also read and commented on early versions of several chapters. Jack Censer, Jane Turner Censer, and Peter Wallenstein read later drafts, including the almost-final version, and their responses enabled me to improve the book at many points. Linda Merrell designed and drew the original versions of the maps.

One piece of advice from Professor Freehling was that Jeanette Hopkins would be a very tough editor, but a very good one. He was right on both counts. Her concern for everything from points of style to themes and organization have made this a much better book. Irene Pavitt's expert copyediting has helped make the book more readable and more accurate.

My greatest thanks go to my wife, Terry Kay Rockefeller. While writing her own dissertation and producing several documentary films, she found time to read and discuss the many versions of this project, from first proposal to final draft. There is scarcely an argument or a sentence which is not better for her thoughtful comments. All the while she managed to keep her good humor about my work even when I lost mine.

Finally, since sometimes I was too stubborn to take even the best advice, none of these people should be implicated in any errors of fact or interpretation that remain.

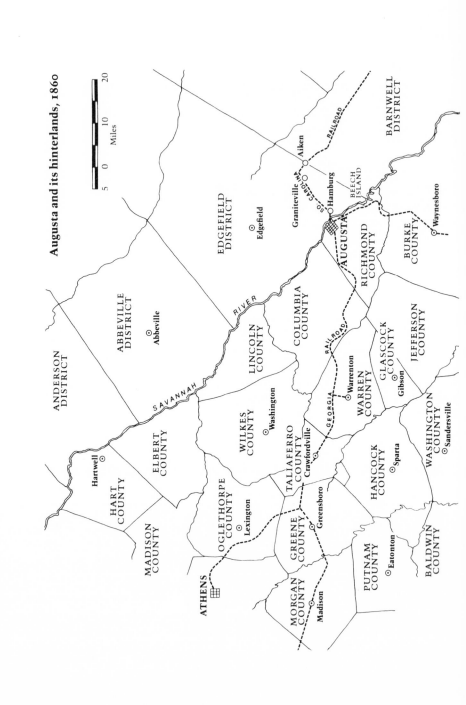

Augusta and its hinterlands, 1860

Miles
5 0 10 20

ANDERSON DISTRICT

ABBEVILLE DISTRICT
⊙ Abbeville

EDGEFIELD DISTRICT
⊙ Edgefield

BARNWELL DISTRICT

HART COUNTY
Hartwell ⊙

ELBERT COUNTY

SAVANNAH RIVER

LINCOLN COUNTY

COLUMBIA COUNTY

SO. CAROLINA RAILROAD
Aiken ○
Graniteville ○
Hamburg ○
BEECH ISLAND
AUGUSTA
RICHMOND COUNTY
BURKE COUNTY
⊙ Waynesboro

MADISON COUNTY

OGLETHORPE COUNTY
⊙ Lexington

WILKES COUNTY
⊙ Washington

TALIAFERRO COUNTY
Crawfordville ⊙

GEORGIA RAILROAD
● Warrenton
WARREN COUNTY

GLASCOCK COUNTY
⊙ Gibson

JEFFERSON COUNTY

ATHENS

GREENE COUNTY
● Greensboro

HANCOCK COUNTY
⊙ Sparta

WASHINGTON COUNTY
⊙ Sandersville

MORGAN COUNTY
Madison ●

PUTNAM COUNTY
⊙ Eatonton

BALDWIN COUNTY

Plain Folk and Gentry
in a Slave Society

Georgia and South Carolina

Introduction

In 1861, only about one-quarter of white southern families owned slaves, yet the vast majority of nonslave-owning whites followed southern planters into a long and bloody war to defend slavery. In doing so, they raised the obvious question: Why? What was it about the nature of class and race relations in the Old South that led them to such sacrifice?

The question (and it is, of course, many questions) has provoked some of the finest writing by American historians. They are still by no means agreed on the answer, or answers. The explanations of antebellum southern society are often subtle and complex, yet they can be divided into two broad categories.

One group of historians has accepted the basic premise of nineteenth-century opponents of slavery: that slavery inevitably divided the South into two classes of whites and that these classes had starkly opposing interests. Slavery, in this view, was inimical to the interests of most poor and middle-class whites, and slaveowners dominated this majority by keeping them ignorant, misleading them with false propaganda, and violently suppressing opposition. Hinton Rowan Helper, son of a North Carolina farmer, made this indictment in its most uncompromising form in 1857.[1] Historians who accept this view have been more subtle than was Helper in making their arguments, but in some interpretations, Helper's claim is still essentially intact. William B. Hesseltine, for example, in 1936 argued that planters invented and used the proslavery argument not chiefly to defend the South against abolitionists from without, but to "obtain unity within their section" and "substitute the sense of racial superiority for the mounting class consciousness of the nonslaveholders."[2]

Such a class approach is naturally attractive to Marxist historians. Eugene Genovese has produced by far the most impressive and subtle Marxist interpretation of the slave South.[3] While beginning with the assumption that slavery produced a class of planters with its own special interests, he explains their dominance with the concept of "hegemony." Their ideology grew not out of a conspiracy to defraud poor whites, but rather out of the complex but antagonistic relations between master and slave. According to Genovese, this ideology was fundamentally paternalistic and hierarchical, not liberal or capitalist, although planters' dependence on the world market introduced elements of liberal capitalism into their world view. Planters were able to dominate the South politically, despite the potential opposition of nonslaveowners, because they successfully convinced both themselves and most white southerners that their hegemony was based on reason and nature rather than on mere political and economic expediency. Genovese has argued further, although briefly, that concrete relationships between planters and poorer whites mitigated and helped disguise the long-term negative consequences for nonslaveholders of living in a slave society.[4]

A second group of historians has seen the South's white population as fundamentally united, despite the obvious distinction between slaveowners and nonslaveowners. These historians, however, have emphasized a variety of sources for whites' common values. Most often stressed is racism. In the most famous statement of this argument, Ulrich B. Phillips asserted that white southerners were united by "a common resolve indomitably maintained—that the South shall be and remain a white man's country. The consciousness of a function in these premises, whether expressed with the frenzy of a demagogue or maintained with a patrician's quietude, is the cardinal test of a Southerner and the central theme of Southern history."[5] A recent and more comprehensive restatement of this view is the analysis of racial thought in the South by George Fredrickson. While laying more stress than did Phillips on at least potential class conflict, Fredrickson argues that a common attachment to "*Herrenvolk* democracy," or democracy within the ranks of a master race, formed the key to unity among antebellum white southerners.[6]

Other historians, beginning with the undeniable fact that most southern men were farmers and landowners, have stressed the South's common agrarian economy as the most important basis for white unity. According to the agrarian interpretation, the South must be understood as an essentially middle-class or yeoman society, in which large slaveowners formed a small and relatively insignificant minority. Avery Craven, for example, wrote that most southerners were united above all by adherence to a "rural way of life capped by an English gentleman ideal" and that slavery in itself "played a rather minor part in the life of the South and of the Negro."[7] A similar argument was made in even more uncompromising form by Frank Owsley and his students. In his most important work, Owsley largely ignored slavery altogether.[8]

These historians often have insisted that the South was much like the North in its economy and ideals and that it shared with the North the American commitments to liberal democracy, capitalism, and Christianity. Because of this commitment to liberal democracy, Fletcher M. Green argued that "by 1860 the aristocratic planter class had been shorn of its special privileges and political power."[9] Such an interpretation makes it clear why non-slaveowners would unite with slaveowners in case of war, but makes it difficult to explain why there should have been a war in the first place. Craven and others have interpreted the South's secession as an irrational mistake, born of guilt over slavery or of emotions whipped up by a few fanatical extremists.[10]

Wilbur Cash, in 1941, proposed a third explanation for southern unity. According to Cash, southerners shared a "fairly definite mental pattern" that arose out of the frontier conditions of early settlement and was perpetuated by the frontierlike conditions of a plantation economy. This pattern, or temperament, was intensely individualistic, hedonistic, and essentially democratic in that it was shared by both planter and yeoman.[11] Cash's argument, too, has recently been restated in impressive form. Bertram Wyatt-Brown traces a southern ethic of "honor" to European, specifically Celtic, roots. Like Cash, he believes that frontier conditions and plantation slavery helped perpetuate and spread among all classes this sytem of honor, which in its details resembles much of Cash's description of the southern "mind."[12]

In sum, a large group of historians has accepted to a greater or lesser degree the claim of most antebellum southern spokesmen that white men in the South were united on fundamental values, and some have accepted the argument that most white men had the same fundamental interests. While emphases differ, most tend to agree that race, agrarian values, and frontierlike conditions were more important in uniting white southerners than slavery was in dividing them.

In this study, these questions will be pursued by an intensive investigation of a local area, and through an examination of how slaves, masters, and nonslaveholding whites interacted in their daily lives. The methods and approach are grounded in beliefs shared by historians who are known sometimes, and somewhat inaccurately, as "new social historians." Among these is the belief that generalizations about societies must be based at some level on actual knowledge about many individuals and that some of the sources containing crucial information about them—such as censuses and tax records—are best analyzed quantitatively. Only with such sources and methods can historians get a sound grasp of the typical in society and of the many possible variations from type. Another assumption important to the procedures is not always found among "new" social historians: that human actions must be interpreted in terms of what people themselves think they are doing. This is not to deny that their motives, knowledge, and interpretations of reality are profoundly affected by economic interests, social conflicts, institutions, channels of communication, or psychological strains of which they may not be fully conscious. It is to deny that interests, conflicts, or institutions in themselves provide explanations of human acts. The assumption is that people act on the basis of what they know and how they interpret what they know.

In short, the social historian ought to work toward a kind of bifocal vision: one focus on the reconstruction of "objective" circumstances and realities such as race, sex, wealth, or political office; the other on the reconstruction of perceptions, ideologies, and available knowledge. The sources for the latter kind of reconstruction are those long used by historians, such as letters, diaries, and newspapers.

The dual focus presents formidable practical problems in selecting, gathering, and analyzing evidence. To avoid some of the problems inherent in microstudies, this book analyzes the hinterlands of a commercial city. Within the economic reach of Augusta's cotton factors were many communities in two states, but all were loosely joined by a common past, a similar economy, and a flow of people, goods, and messages to and from the central city. Within this area, four communities are studied intensively: Glascock, Hart, and Taliaferro counties in Georgia, and Edgefield district in South Carolina. (For some purposes, Warren and Hancock counties in Georgia were added to this list.) The emphasis throughout is on rural society rather than on Augusta itself. These local communities differed somewhat in soil type, racial balance, wealth, and political heritage and institutions. The advantages of conducting the study this way were that the total area was small enough to study intensively with quantitative data and to survey all the major and many minor literary sources, large enough to include some variety in the communities studied, yet unified enough to make meaningful comparisons among the different communities.

The limitations of this approach are clear enough. Augusta and its hinterlands included about 220,000 people in 1860, or about 2 percent of the population of the entire South. I believe that this area is in most regards a representative slice of society in the cotton-growing Piedmont, but I would expect the rice-growing coast, the Chesapeake, the Mississippi delta, and other southern regions to be different, often quite different. I cannot claim to have exhausted all the possibilities for studying even the relatively small area around Augusta, and certainly not everyone will agree with the conclusions presented here. I am convinced, however, that a better understanding of antebellum southern society will be achieved after we have asked about other places some of the questions asked here about Augusta's hinterlands. My interpretation of society in the Augusta area draws from both major streams of interpretation of the South. White men there were divided by slavery. I argue, like Genovese, that these divisions were partly overcome by the personal relationships between planters and their poorer neighbors.

On balance, however, I find myself more in accord with those who have emphasized white agreement on fundamentals. The common experience of landownership and, equally significant, the common participation in the commercial cotton market gave planters and farmers similar economic values. And, like those historians who have emphasized southern racism, I believe that rich and poor southern whites shared a profound fear of and contempt for black people.

Yet I also found that this unity was precarious, not least because whites in the Augusta area had a remarkably ambivalent view of themselves and their society. The dominant public ideology held up the South as almost an ideal type of society, in which black slavery allowed liberty for whites without the dangers of anarchy. This ideal, which white Southerners called republican, had as one important facet a strong commitment to an agrarian economy in which most white men were independent producers, and in which most menial labor was performed by a degraded and dependent race that was excluded from the political community. Racially based slavery, therefore, guaranteed white liberty. This ideal was shared by owners and nonowners of slaves, and liberty was as important as slavery in the hearts and minds of even large planters.

This republican vision, however, was far more pessimistic than is modern democratic liberalism. Republicans thought that men were always liable to corruption and decadence and that liberty was always threatened by the loss of equipoise. It might be overturned, on the one hand, by excessive concentrations of political power, especially national political power; or, on the other, by excessive democracy, which in the long run must lead first to anarchy, then tyranny. Slavery, even while it supposedly guaranteed republican liberty for white men, simultaneously created grave threats to that liberty. As a public badge differentiating slaveowners from nonslaveowners, it reminded whites that political equality did not translate into economic equality. Rumblings of poor-white discontent frightened planters, especially because they depended on nonslaveowners to keep slaves under control. Planters could never be sure that the bridges between the rich and the poor in the South would be strong enough to withstand the assaults of an increasingly powerful threat from northern abolitionists and free-soilers.

Secession was an attempt by planters to protect what they saw as their liberties, including the liberty to own slaves, from future internal and external threats. The resulting war produced, in one of the many ironies of southern history, exactly what they had most feared. Before the Civil War, southern slaveowners had contained white class divisions sufficiently well to ensure continued control over black people unwilling to accept slavery on any terms but force. But the basis of that containment—an ideology of liberty, a potential for social mobility, and a web of personal relationships between classes—could not withstand the strains of war.

Slave resistance increased dramatically; the support of non-slaveholders, at first enthusiastic, withered away and even turned at times to outright opposition; the republican fear of power was turned—in the supreme irony—on the Confederate government itself. Many slaveowners felt faced with a choice they had always considered a logical impossibility: either liberty *or* slavery. By the end of the war, the bonds of community had so far dissolved that Confederate victory was impossible. Ultimately, the South's conquerors would seek to extend their own version of republican liberty to freed slaves, and the attempt, however unsuccessful, would change southern society forever.

Part I

A Slaveholding Republic

Domestic slavery, therefore, instead of being a political evil, is the corner-stone of our republican edifice.

GEORGE MCDUFFIE
Governor of South Carolina
1835

I say that, putting the cruelties of the system out of the question, we cannot be made to understand how any man can hold another man as a slave, and do right.

JOHN BROWN
Runaway Slave
1855

✺ Prologue: The Land of Cotton

In 1773, William Bartram traveled from Philadelphia to the backwoods village of Augusta to witness the cession of a vast tract of Creek and Cherokee land to the royal government of Georgia.[1] In the thirty-five years since its founding, Augusta had become a center for Indian traders in Georgia and much of South Carolina. These traders journeyed far to the west in search of furs and skins to send to merchants in Savannah or Charles Town.[2] The Creeks and Cherokees signed over the New Purchase, as the 1773 cession was called, to settle their large debts with some of the traders. It added more than 2 million acres to the colony of Georgia, the largest part of which was drained by the Broad River to the north of Augusta.[3]

Not all the Indian warriors, especially among the Creeks, were happy with the deal their chiefs had made. Bartram wrote to his English patron that the British Superintendent of Indian Affairs "thought it not altogether safe to go then into the Indian countries." But Bartram, a naturalist, had come precisely to see Indian country, and, undeterred by the warning, he set off immediately with the team chosen to survey the new boundary line between Georgia and Indian country, which would cross the Savannah River some eighty-five miles north of Augusta.[4]

Bartram wrote a glowing description of this northern part of the New Purchase. He told how the survey party first headed for Wrightsboro, settled by North Carolina Quakers in 1768, thirty miles west of Augusta and just inside the old boundary. Past Wrightsboro, they "entered an extensive fertile plain, bordering on the river, and shaded by trees of vast growth, which at once spoke its fertility."[5] Shortly afterward, they passed through what Bartram called "the most magnificent forest [he] had ever seen," full of huge oaks set in an otherwise open plain. At the end of the survey, Bartram wrote to England that the new country promised "plenty & felicity." Its riverine lands "are generally rich & those of its almost innumerable branches agreeable and healthy situations, especially for small farms, every where little mounts & hills to build on & beneath them rich level land fit for corn & grain with delightful glittering streams of running water through cane bottoms, proper for meadows, with abundance of water brooks for mills."[6]

This land contrasted sharply with land south of Augusta. Augusta itself was on the fall line, so called because at this point, rivers and streams were typically broken by rapids or waterfalls. Below the fall line, at one time the eastern edge of North America, stretched the coastal plain, uncovered thousands of years before by the receding ocean. Between the coastal plain and the hilly uplands (known as the Piedmont) lay a narrow band of sandy hills, a legacy of the ancient shoreline. The geological history of the area could be read in its contours and soil. The coastal plain was flat and sandy, and, except in river bottoms, it supported mainly pine trees. Its low value for colonial farmers is captured aptly by the name they gave it: the pine barrens. The "sand hills," too, had poor soil, although their higher elevation made their climate a little cooler than that of the plain. The Piedmont was a rolling, fertile country broken by many watercourses. There, a shallow surface mold covered a thick layer of mixed sand and red clay, formed by the gradual erosion of once gigantic mountains. Because of its contours, the Piedmont was subject to rapid erosion once the forest cover of oak and hickory was removed. The bottom land immediately adjacent to Piedmont rivers and creeks was often the richest of all, although its alluvial soil was subject to flooding.[7]

As Bartram noted, it was a rich land, one that could support grain and fruits. He pictured on it a happy world of small farms, no doubt much like those of the industrious Quakers he saw in Wrightsboro. Farmland the Piedmont did become, but neither the crops nor the farms were the kinds envisioned by either Bartram or the Quakers.

When Bartram visited Augusta in 1773, a few thousand white settlers at most lived nearby in upcountry Georgia or across the Savannah River in South Carolina. With them were already a few hundred black slaves. By 1792, when Bartram's account was published in his *Travels*, the population had exploded to more than 80,000. Most of the new people had come from Virginia and North Carolina on the wagon road that stretched to Augusta all the way from Pennsylvania.[8]

During the Revolution, which saw vicious backwoods guerrilla warfare around Augusta, migration temporarily came to a halt; but by the 1780s, it had reached ever higher levels. Among small farmers were such newcomers as George Mathews, a Virginia planter who settled with a few friends and many slaves in the Goose Pond district of Wilkes county, and was promptly elected governor of Georgia.[9] Mathews and his friends did not share the vision of Bartram and of Wrightsboro's Quakers. They planned, not small farms, but large fields of tobacco or other staple crops that would be tended by their slaves. They sought to reproduce the world of the Virginia gentry as they had known it.

The Georgia and South Carolina legislatures, eager to encourage men like Mathews, established tobacco-inspection stations in Augusta, Vienna, and other places. A flourishing little commercial center grew up in Petersburg, where the Broad River entered the Savannah, the site of another inspection station.[10] When the first United States census was taken in 1790, three years before a cotton gin was perfected, slaves already made up about one-quarter of the population of the upcountry near Augusta.[11] Within the confines of this still new frontier, a plantation society was struggling to be born. Eli Whitney and his cotton gin ensured that it would be.

If ever a crop and a place seemed well suited to each other, they were short-staple cotton and the lower Piedmont. The loam-covered clay contained many nutrients and held just the right amount of water. The pattern of rainfall—gradually increasing from spring to midsummer and gradually decreasing through autumn—spurred growth at the right time and left dry bolls to pluck. The growing season was long, as it had to be; it was, on average, at least 200 days.[12] By 1790, upcountry planters knew that they could grow cotton and knew that they could sell it, and many were experimenting with devices to remove the last bottleneck—getting the seeds from the lint—in the chain of production that led to England's textile mills. Young Eli Whitney, a visitor from New England, turned to the problem at the suggestion of a number of planters from the Augusta area and invented a gin on Nathaniel Greene's plantation near Savannah.[13]

Between 1790 and 1800, the production of cotton in the United States soared from 3,000 to 73,000 bales. White farmers and planters, with their slaves, poured into the South Carolina and Georgia Piedmont to take up new land, and, during the 1790s, the slave population near Augusta increased twice as rapidly as did the white population.[14]

Augusta became a thriving center for the cotton trade. Its cotton factors, wholesale merchants who sold cotton on consignment and provided planters with credit and supplies, drew in cotton from much of the Georgia Piedmont and from substantial areas of South Carolina. They then sent the cotton down the Savannah river to Savannah or on to Charleston, South Carolina, to be reshipped to Europe or the North. By 1826, one visitor complained that because "a valuable commodity" was "brought in abundance" to Augusta, the city showed "more . . . idolatry of money" than any other place he had seen.[15] To ensure their continued access to Augusta's cotton market, the merchants of Charleston, between 1828 and 1833, financed one of the first railroads in the United States; it ran from the coast to Hamburg, South Carolina, just opposite Augusta on the Savannah river.[16] By the 1850s, Augusta was the principal cotton and wholesale market for most of Georgia's eastern Piedmont, and for much of Edgefield, Abbeville, and Barnwell districts in South Carolina.[17]

The cotton economy ensured a continuing powerful dependence on slave labor, and most whites accepted slavery gladly. Even before the rise of cotton, William Savery, a Quaker visitor, had noted that Augusta was "a truly trying place to lodge" because "they can scarcely tolerate us on account of our abhorrence of slavery."[18] In 1805, the last of Wrightsboro's Quakers, disgusted by the rise of slavery all around them, headed for the free territory north of the Ohio River.[19] Augusta and its hinterlands had become by then one of the first duchies in cotton's kingdom.

Chapter 1

Slavery and Liberty

Alexander H. Stephens was a popular speaker, so it was not surprising that on July 2, 1859, a vast crowd gathered to hear him in City Hall Park in Augusta. Stephens was retiring from politics after eight terms as a United States representative from Georgia's Eighth Congressional District, and this was his farewell. It might be his last great public address.[1]

Stephens began with a review of his years in Congress—tempestuous years, he told his listeners, but fruitful. The United States, and Georgia, had seen great progress in the past sixteen years. Colleges had been founded; railroads, laid; territory, acquired and settled. Great disputes over slavery had arisen and subsided; in every case, the South had won on points of vital principle. African slavery had not been weakened by the assaults on it, but was, on the contrary, "greatly strengthened and fortified."

Would the present quiet in the country last? No one knew. Change is eternal, said Stephens; all things must die; and governments "are subject to the same law." Whether our own would die soon, or later, depended on whether the Union could be maintained without any loss of constitutional rights: "The Union on this basis, can be and will be preserved just so long as intelligence, virtue, integrity, and patriotism rule your national councils. How long this will be, will depend upon the people themselves."

Slavery rested "upon principles that can never be successfully assailed by reason or argument." It was stronger than ever because people had come to realize the great truth, written, Stephens said, in nature's laws and God's decrees, that subordination "is the normal condition of the negro." The failure to recognize this truth had been the downfall of the republican ideals of Aristotle and the other great philosophers of ancient times. "If our system is not the best, or cannot be made the best for both races, it is wrong," Stephens conceded. But if it was the best, then "we stand upon a rock as firm and impregnable as truth. And with union and patriotism amongst our own people, we have nothing to fear from any quarter—either in the Union or out of it. We hold our destiny in our hands, and in pursuing it to the end, we shall be but fulfilling a great mission in advancing a new order and a higher type of Christian civilization."

Stephens's farewell address offered his listeners no new ideas. He was expressing and reinforcing the elements of a familiar ideology, which had fastened itself on the area almost as surely as had cotton and slavery. Liberty and slavery were the keys to the ideology; although seeming opposites, Stephens and many others insisted, they were interdependent. The insistence that slavery perpetuated republican liberty was partly intended to reassure the audience that the most fundamental institution and the most fundamental ideal of southern society were consistent with each other.

The need to reconcile liberty for some with slavery for others was a legacy of the American Revolution. Planters, with other Americans, had fought to avoid being "enslaved" to British tyranny. Aside from the obvious suggestion of hypocrisy, the concept of liberty was contagious, and revolutionary ideology had been one spur to the abolition of slavery in the North.[2] Nevertheless, the dilemma of reconciling slavery and liberty had not become truly acute until the upsurge of abolitionist sentiment in the 1830s. Abolitionists insisted, often at the tops of their lungs, what many in both North and South had never been entirely willing to face: that black slavery was an egregious violation of the rights proclaimed in the Declaration of Independence and thus a violation of the cherished principles of the Revolution.

The southern response was to develop and systematize defenses of slavery that had been largely unspoken or unacknowledged. As a proslavery polemic published in Augusta in 1860 claimed, southerners had not thought much about slavery until the abolitionists had begun to attack it: "Our fathers left it to us as a legacy, we have grown up with it; it has grown with our growth and strengthened with our strength, until it is now incorporated with every fibre of our social and political existence."[3] The abolitionist challenge to slavery had sparked an examination of this pervasive and powerful institution; the polemic concluded that southerners were entirely confident that slavery was consistent with their ideals.

South Carolina had had, in the 1830s, a greater economic and social stake in slavery than had any other state, and South Carolinians had been prominent in developing the new proslavery ideology. One result had been an intense opposition to any hint of outside interference with slavery, the most spectacular instance of this opposition having been the nullification movement of 1828 to 1833, when South Carolina had attempted to defy the national government by "nullifying" the new high tariffs. As William W. Freehling has persuasively demonstrated, anxieties about slavery had underlain nullification; the point was to resist *any* "unconstitutional" exercise of national power, lest some future exercise of illegal power seek to abolish slavery.[4] On top of the nullification controversy had come the newly militant abolitionism of William Lloyd Garrison and other northern reformers. South Carolinians (and other white southerners) had reacted with outrage and horror to this attempted interference with slavery, and spokesmen had begun to defend slavery as compatible with progress, Christian morality, and republican liberty.

Southern arguments had been directed at the South as well as at the North. John Bauskett of Edgefield, South Carolina, in 1851 had reprinted in pamphlet form a proslavery essay by Baptist minister Iveson L. Brookes, a local planter, because Bauskett had feared that "there [was] some danger of the fanaticism of the north spreading among and infecting the consciences of the weak minded good Christian people of the South, upon the question of Right in the whites to maintain the existing relation with the Africans amongst us."[5] Many believed that the arguments had succeeded in convincing at least most white southerners that slavery was a good institution. Soon after Stephens's 1859 address, Henry C. Cleveland wrote to congratulate him for his comments on slavery. He agreed with Stephens that slavery was stronger than ever in the southern mind. "[T]en years ago," Cleveland thought, "many of our Southern men would say Slavery is an Evil, but such remarks cannot be heard now."[6]

Stephens's speech, with its reference to the republican philosophers of antiquity, is an excellent example of the southern attempt to place slavery in the context, not of tyranny, but of liberty. He found no contradiction between his defense of slavery and his love of liberty, for he believed that true liberty was neither unbounded nor suitable for all peoples. In this belief, he and many in his audience were conservative heirs to a complex pattern of thought that dated from the age of the American Revolution. Eighteenth-century Americans and these nineteenth-century southerners called this pattern "republicanism," since it was tied to elected, representative government.

The supreme republican civic value was a liberty distinguished from license by reason and law. People were happiest and most fully human when free, and thus republican government was best because it was the most free. Yet if liberty was the most precious political value, it was also the most fragile, because the liberty of the many was so easily destroyed by power—whether of one, as in tyranny, or of a few, as in oligarchy. And not even pure democracies were safe preserves for liberty. In democratic polities, the people as a whole were likely to turn to the unrestrained pursuit of purely selfish ends, a liberty that degenerated first into license and finally into an anarchic war of all against all. Ultimately, order could be restored only with the establishment of a tyranny based on raw military power.[7]

Republicanism had at bottom a pessimistic view of human nature, and republicans believed that even the best societies were always threatened by corruption and decay. In an 1850 letter to his half-brother Linton, a wealthy planter and politician in Hancock county, Stephens wrote that, in his opinion, politics and government "have in the main, since the formation of human society, been at war with the best interests of man." Men with strong passions and mean propensities, in whom the "animal and brutal qualities" triumphed over "the refined and intellectual," had always struggled for "government, place, and power." A politician for almost all his adult life, Stephens insisted nonetheless that "politicians are enemies of mankind. . . . They corrupt, debase, and degrade the people." The only hope for the future of liberty, Stephens continued, lay in "the virtue of the great mass of the people." As in his 1859 address, he argued that only their "virtue, intelligence, and patriotism" could hold corruption at bay.[8] This "virtue" and "patriotism" were other names for political virtue: the pursuit not of the personal, but of the common, or public, good. Only virtue could resist the passionate and corrupt pursuit of power. The contest between liberty and power, or liberty and license, was thus at the same time one between virtue and corruption.[9]

Not simply liberty, then, but ordered liberty, was the key to public happiness, and virtue, the key to ordered liberty. The classical republican "science of politics" had sought to ensure the stability and preservation of republics against corruption and decay by carefully balancing what were thought to be the contending orders of every society. A "mixed" republic should include elements of monarchy, aristocracy, and democracy (or the one, the few, and the many) so that no single order could assume full power and inevitably develop into its corresponding evil—tyranny, oligarchy, or anarchy. The American Revolution and the "contagion of liberty" that it had set off had made this classical ideal obsolete. America, with neither monarch nor titled aristocracy, had inevitably moved toward a more fully democratic republicanism, in both the South and the North. All government rested firmly on the sovereignty of the people, as manifested in popular elections.

Yet in the area around Augusta, much of the vocabulary, underlying assumptions, style of argument, and force of appeal of the old classical republicanism survived. Political debate was still concerned with the quarrel between virtue and corruption. Many southerners were convinced that the South was uniquely blessed to preserve republican liberty. Its agrarian economy was one blessing. Slavery was another. Cotton and slaves, they thought, would make it possible to preserve liberty.

April 15, 1858, was a beautiful day for farming. The sun shone in a clear blue sky as Benton Miller walked with his slaves Harry and Clark to field number four of his farm in Washington county. For more than a month, they had plowed Miller's farm almost every day, throwing up ridges a few feet apart in each field intended for cotton. This day, finally, they opened up the middle of the ridges with a scooter plow, dropped in cotton seed, and covered it. "It is the first time," Miller noted with evident satisfaction that evening in his journal, "that I ever planted cotton for myself. I am making a commencement in life." [10]

Neither Miller nor any other man was typical of all farmers in Augusta's hinterlands. But Miller's journal of 1858 and 1859 records a life similar in its daily concerns and yearly cycle of work to that of many men in the area. Like most white men in Piedmont Georgia and South Carolina, he was a farmer and the head of a family. He had to see that the work got done, from rail-splitting in January through hog butchering in December, with plowing, planting, weeding, harvesting, and a hundred smaller tasks in between. Like the large majority of farmers in Augusta's hinterlands, Miller had staked his hopes on cotton. From the time the seed went into the furrows until the final bale was sold almost a year later, he shared the many anxieties of dependence on cotton: late or early frosts, too much or too little rain, infestations of bugs, gin-house fires. More than once during 1858, he feared utter ruin from hail, rain, or drought. Even a bumper crop could lose money if prices fell too low. Success depended ultimately on demand in distant Liverpool.

Miller owned slaves, and in this, too, he was typical of farmers in the Augusta area. He owned few, however, and on most days he was in the fields working next to them. Slave ownership brought its own rewards and vexations: a man did not have to work so hard if he could force others to work for him, but no other property could be as troublesome and independent minded as a slave. So Miller shared, if in a lesser way, the satisfactions and the burdens of the great slaveowners.

Miller had indeed made "a commencement" in the way of life most respected in his society. As a young Georgian wrote in 1849 to the *Southern Cultivator*, published in Augusta, "I desire above

Table 1. Occupations of Household Heads in Augusta's
Hinterlands, 1860

Occupation	Glascock County (N = 326) (%)	Hart County (N = 346) (%)	Taliaferro County (N = 338) (%)	Edgefield District (N = 3006) (%)
Farmer	66	78	70	66
Overseer	3	3	5	4
Farm laborer	12	4	2	4
Nonagricultural	7	10	17	17
None, at home, other	13	4	7	8

SOURCES: Vernon O. Burton, "Unfaithful Servants? Edgefield's Black Reconstruction: Part I of the Total History of Edgefield County, South Carolina" (Ph.D. diss., Princeton University, 1976), 206; Georgia counties from samples from the manuscript returns of the United States Bureau of the Census, 1860.
NOTE: See Appendix A for detailed description. Percentages may not add to 100 due to rounding.

all things to be a 'Farmer'. It is the most honest, upright, and sure way of securing all the comforts of life."[11] In an overwhelmingly agricultural society, most white men wanted to farm, and most did (see Table 1). The allure of farming was moral as well as economic, for "independent" farmers happily considered themselves to be the best republican citizens.

In republican thought from seventeenth-century Englishman James Harrington to Thomas Jefferson, an agrarian society with widespread landholding was especially suited to republican institutions because the farmer was peculiarly independent and virtuous. The most famous American expression of this idea was Jefferson's, written in 1785:

Those who labour in the earth are the chosen people of God, if ever he had a chosen people, whose breasts he has made his peculiar deposit for substantial and genuine virtue. . . . Corruption of morals in the mass of cultivators is a phenomenon of which no age nor nation has furnished an example. It is the mark set on those who, not looking up to heaven, to their own soil and industry, as does the husbandman, for their subsistence, depend for it on the casualties and caprice of customer. Dependence begets subservience and venality, suffocates the germ of virtue, and prepares fit tools for the designs of ambition.[12]

Dependence—whether of political toady on patron, of merchant or tradesman on the whims of the market, or of tenant and laborer on landlord and employer—begat "subservience and venality." Dependent people served ambitious people; dependence and ambition in combination produced faction and conflict. Thus the most stable republics were composed of the only truly independent citizens—landowning farmers. Arthur Simkins, Edgefield planter and newspaper editor, told the State Agricultural Society of South Carolina in 1855 that "farmers and planters of the country are truly the bone and sinew of our bodies politic." Their natural independence and instincts of freedom had won the Revolution and had made the "experiment of Republican rule" a "dazzling reality." For "the largest Louisiana planter" or "the humblest Connecticut farmer," landownership in America was "full and absolute." Other governments, based on landlords and tenants, engendered "a feeling of dependence, if not inferiority." By contrast, the commonest American cottager "looks upon the little possession around him as his own without reservation, in the enjoyment of which he is safe from intrusion so long as he discharges his obligation to the community in which he lives." With their "instincts of freedom," such men had been the first to produce "the daring thought of a political revolution for Liberty's sake."[13]

As farmers had created American liberty, so they also could preserve it. In a speech to the Greene county Agricultural Society, Colonel R. H. Ward acknowledged that corruption had been the downfall of all previous republican governments, but he hoped that the demise of American freedoms, might still be staved off indefinitely by a "virtuous and enlightened yeomanry."[14]

Yet many of Simkins's and Ward's contemporaries in both North and South did not see the South as a republic of freeholders. They envisioned the southern landscape as dominated by huge plantations. Such a picture entered popular consciousness through countless novels, and received further expression through the work of such writers as the British economist J. E. Cairnes, author of *The Slave Power* (1861). In any slave society, according to Cairnes, were "three classes broadly distinguished from each other and connected by no common interest—the slaves on whom devolves all the regular industry, the slaveholders who reap all its fruits, and an idle and lawless rabble who live dispersed over vast plains in a condition little removed from absolute barbarism."[15]

In reality, however, most southerners knew that there was no such simple and sharp distinction between an elite of slaveholders and a mass of lawless and rootless poor whites. In 1860, most white family heads in Augusta's hinterlands were landowning farmers. In some counties, as many as two-thirds of all white families lived on their own farms.

In 1860, to be sure, the census takers counted 311 plantations of at least 1,000 cleared acres in Augusta's hinterlands, and another 800 plantations of at least 500 cleared acres. Examples of such large holdings are the two plantations owned by James Henry Hammond in the Beech Island area of Barnwell district, just southeast of Augusta in South Carolina. In 1850, Silver Bluff, the home plantation, had 385 acres planted in cotton and 400 acres planted in corn, and the field labor force was counted at sixteen plow hands, thirty-four full hoe hands, and nine three-quarter or half hands; nearby Cathwood had seventy-one hands cultivating 678 acres in crops. Hammond also kept thirty-five ditchers working most of the time reclaiming swamp land. At least fifteen other slaves did more specialized work.[16] Yet such large estates were exceptional. Almost nine in ten farms in the region had fewer than 500 improved acres, and about four in ten had fewer than 100 improved acres (see Table 2).

The mix of small and large holdings varied from community to community, even within Augusta's market area. Most of Hart county, for example, lay far enough north that the growing season averaged fewer than 200 days. Since this was too short for a good cotton crop, Hart county had more small farms and fewer plantations than did areas closer to Augusta, such as Taliaferro and Hancock counties or Edgefield district in South Carolina. Glascock county had a long growing season. But it lay almost wholly in the "sand hills," and its soil was poor for cotton. So Glascock, like Hart, had more small farms and fewer plantations than was typical for the entire hinterland area (see Table 2).

Small farms had many of the characteristics of large plantations. Most important, small farmers in the Augusta area were drawn fully into the commercial market for cotton. Despite Glascock county's poor soil, 70 percent of its smallest farms grew at least one bale of cotton in 1859. The vast majority of all

Table 2. Farm Size and Cotton Production in Augusta's
Hinterlands, 1859

Improved Acres	Glascock County (N = 200) (%)	Hart County (N = 523) (%)	Taliaferro County (N = 239) (%)	Edgefield District (N = 1,696) (%)	All Counties* (N = 8,904) (%)
FARMS BY SIZE, 1860					
3–49	29	48	23	23	19
50–99	37	29	23	22	21
100–499	31	21	48	45	47
500–999	3	1	4	9	9
1000+	1	2	2	2	4
FARMS PRODUCING AT LEAST ONE BALE OF COTTON					
1–24	70	45	64	40	
25–49	89	75	86	71	
50–99	89	79	90	87	
100–249	98	94	94	98	
250+	100	100	100	95	

SOURCES: U.S. Bureau of the Census, "Agriculture," in *Eighth Census, 1860* (Washington, D.C., 1865);
Farm Sample from the manuscript returns of the United States Bureau of the Census, 1860.
  NOTE: See Appendix A for detailed description.
  *Includes all counties and districts in the hinterland area; see Appendix A for list.

farms of at least twenty-five improved acres grew cotton in every
county sampled (see Table 2). Since cotton determined the yearly
rhythm of work on farm and plantation, the lives of farmers large
and small had a great deal in common. The patterns of work described in Miller's journal were similar to those recorded in the
yearly diaries of David C. Barrow, one of the area's largest land-
and slaveowners: plowing in spring, cultivating in summer, picking in autumn. Barrow and Miller grew more than cotton; like
almost all farmers there, they also planted corn and raised hogs,
basic foods of the South for whites and blacks.[17] Corn and other
food crops—wheat, sweet potatoes, turnips—contributed directly to the farmer's vaunted "independence." If he could feed
his family, slaves, and work animals, his cotton income was almost all profit.

If a farmer counted on only cotton, a bad year would leave him
short of both cash and food. His options then would be to buy on
credit, sell property, or draw on savings. Augusta cotton factors
regularly financed credit purchases by large planters, and small
farmers usually could get corn from their neighbors or from

country merchants by signing a note. In the long run, this was a dangerous course, for a man who was too much in debt might lose his farm. There was good economic reason for farmer and planter to hedge by growing adequate food—chiefly corn—to get his family and stock through the year. Then, as a contemporary put it (with some exaggeration), "He is independent in prices. The fluctuations of the market affect him slightly." This appeal blended moral with economic arguments: "The farmer who never buys corn or meat is generally thrifty, his household is the abode of abundance and peace, and the corn famine such as now prevails, never troubles him, but on the contrary fills his purse."[18]

Small farmer and large planter alike thus were pulled between cotton, with its possibility for maximum income, and corn, with its promise of relative security. The balance for each depended on the farmer's or planter's soil and resources, personal circumstances, and willingness to take risks. Those with the smallest farms were least likely to concentrate on cotton, partly because they simply did not have enough land to plant both cotton and a minimally sufficient amount of corn (see Table 3, p. 26). In Edgefield district, South Carolina, for example, cotton made up only about one-fifth of a small farmer's output, but more than one-half of a big planter's. Even this relatively small commitment to cotton, however, was enough to keep many small farms from growing enough provisions. In 1859 in Taliaferro county, more than one-half of all farms of fewer than fifty improved acres were not self-sufficient in food crops. In every county sampled, at least one-quarter of small farms were not self-sufficient. The Augusta area was predominantly agricultural and prosperous because of cotton, and widespread devotion to this purely commercial crop made farmers there as dependent on "the casualties and caprice" of customers in distant markets as were the merchants, manufacturers, or artisans suspected by Jefferson.

Such devotion to cotton among small farmers stands in contrast to the yeoman economy in the northern Piedmont, recently described by Steven Hahn.[19] There, Hahn has argued, small farmers rather than planters dominated agriculture, and throughout the antebellum period, yeomen continued to engage primarily in mixed farming. Food came first; cotton merely provided cash for

Table 3. Share of Cotton in Total Value of Farm Product by Size
of Farm, 1859

Improved Acres	Glascock County (%)	Hart County (%)	Taliaferro County (%)	Edgefield District (%)
0–24	23 (N = 11)	14 (N = 41)	34 (N = 15)	19 (N = 5)
25–49	38 (N = 37)	22 (N = 63)	43 (N = 28)	27 (N = 27)
50–99	36 (N = 66)	21 (N = 63)	40 (N = 51)	39 (N = 41)
100–249	40 (N = 44)	28 (N = 37)	45 (N = 73)	50 (N = 49)
250+	46 (N = 24)	47 (N = 5)	48 (N = 38)	56 (N = 40)

SOURCES: Outputs and sizes from Farm Sample from the manuscript returns of the United States Bureau of the Census, 1860; values as in Roger Ransom and Richard Sutch, *One Kind of Freedom: The Economic Consequences of Emancipation* (New York: Cambridge University Press, 1977), Appendix A.
NOTE: See Appendix A for detailed description.

necessary expenses or perhaps capital for original purchases or modest expansions of acreage. This same tendency can be seen among farmers in Hart county, at the northern reaches of Augusta's market, where the shorter growing season made cotton a truly risky crop. Small farmers were less likely than those nearer Augusta to grow it.

As Hahn also shows, many upcountry farmers resisted the trend toward greater commercialization of agriculture. Railroad development met surprising opposition from yeomen farmers and from the village merchants who served them. Still, with the rising cotton prices of the 1850s, the lure of the market reached even such relatively remote areas as Hart county. At a public meeting in 1858 to promote a railroad link to Augusta, one speaker "pointed out . . . that it would be a link in the iron chain that would girdle the world—that the electric wire would follow the line, and that the pulses of Europe and the British Isles might be felt to throb in the quiet town of Hartwell." Land values would increase when absence of good transportation no longer "confine[s] our home products to home consumption."[20]

The ideal solution to the opposite pulls of cotton and cash or corn and self-sufficiency would have been the development of a diversified agriculture based on marketable food crops. In the

1840s, the whole Piedmont area had seen the birth of an agricultural reform movement with just that goal.[21] Farmers had been reeling as a result of years of low prices; thousands had been migrating to more fertile soil in Alabama, Mississippi, and Texas. Observers had seen about them "evacuated and dilapidated mansions—worn out and exhausted plantations[, f]ields . . . disfigured with gaping hillsides, chequered with gullies, coated with broomstraw and pine, the sure indices of barrenness and exhaustion."[22] During the two decades immediately preceding the Civil War, farmers' organizations, such as the Planter's Club in Hancock county and the Farmers Club in the Beech Island area southeast of Augusta, at club meetings and in publications like the *Southern Cultivator*, advocated experimenting with new crops, raising more grass and oats, improving stock, growing fruit and vegetables for sale to cities and the North, and, above all, improving the soil with manure, ditching, and better tools and techniques for plowing and cultivating.

Discussions recorded in the minutes of the Beech Island Farmers Club show the wide range of social, moral, and economic benefits presented as incentives to diversify crops. Hammond rejoiced that "it is delightful to have everything around us the product of our soil and labor." More practically, he insisted that local farmers could easily replace northern suppliers of onions, apples, and Irish potatoes in Augusta's markets.[23] Another member argued that raising more stock would mean that planters "could feed better, live better keep clear of debt and improve our soil"; most agreed that improvement of the soil was the key to reducing the regrettable "spirit of emigration" so rife in the area.[24] Economic reform could make individuals and communities self-sufficient and truly independent.

Despite the vigorous movement for reform, cotton was never challenged as the prime commercial crop. The Augusta area as a whole even experienced a net shortage of corn and pork; basic foods had to be purchased each year from the upper South and the Northwest.[25] Some historians have blamed the "excessive" concentration on cotton and the failure to pursue reform more seriously on slavery itself. Eugene Genovese, most prominent among them, has argued that slaves had neither the incentive nor the education required to use sophisticated tools or to manage improved stock. Further, he contends that while planters were acquisitive enough, the social logic of the master–slave relationship led them away from the purely rational, profit-maximizing behavior typical of true capitalists, and toward "prebourgeois" or "nonbourgeois" ideology and psychology that emphasized the primacy of personal relationships.[26] The issues are complex, but certainly many slaveowners were as calculating and profit minded as any capitalist. David Dickson, of Hancock county, built a huge fortune with his shrewd management of slave labor, even conducting time and motion studies of picking and planting. Hammond similarly conducted elaborate experiments with seed, fertilizers, and land-improvement techniques, keeping careful records of results and substantially increasing the large estate near Augusta that he had acquired through marriage.[27] Such men were far from averse to agricultural reforms, including diversification.

Indeed, slavery in some ways encouraged certain kinds of diversification. A planter who owned his labor force, rather than hiring it only at peak labor times, had a natural incentive to keep workers busy growing corn, wheat, and other crops when they were not occupied with cotton.[28] Perhaps because of this incentive, large slaveowners in Augusta's hinterlands grew a greater variety of crops than did small farmers; they also grew more food per capita on the farm, and hence were more likely to be self-sufficient in food (see Table 4).[29] And if most planters did not invest heavily in machinery, this was partly because they always had the option of increasing production simply by buying more slaves—an option not available to northern farmers.[30]

Climatic and market factors, rather than slavery in any direct sense, discouraged greater crop diversification in the lower Piedmont. The climate was not conducive to the pattern of reform followed in the New England and the Middle Atlantic states, a pattern based on production of soil-conserving forage crops and concentration on dairy products. Heavy annual rainfall leached the soil of the Deep South, making it acidic, a condition difficult to correct before the advent of cheap commercial fertilizers. The combination of heat, humidity, and rainfall lowered yields of

Table 4. Diversity and Food Production on Farms by Size in
Augusta's Hinterlands, 1859

Improved Acres	Glascock County	Hart County	Taliaferro County	Edgefield District
MEAN NUMBER OF DIFFERENT CROPS PRODUCED*				
1–24	4.5	5.1	4.3	5.6
25–49	4.9	5.8	5.7	5.9
50–99	5.3	6.4	6.2	7.2
100–249	5.9	6.9	6.9	7.2
250+	7.0	8.0	8.2	7.9
BUSHEL-EQUIVALENTS OF FOOD CROPS PRODUCED PER PERSON ON THE FARM †				
1–24	21	17	15	27
25–49	26	21	19	24
50–99	33	23	27	27
100–249	51	37	32	31
250+	46	44	34	35

SOURCE: Farm Sample from the manuscript returns of the United States Bureau of the Census, 1860.
   NOTE: See Appendix A for detailed description.
   *Total number of different crops produced among cotton, wheat, rye, corn, oats, barley, peas, Irish
potatoes, sweet potatoes, orchard products, garden produce, butter, and hay.
   † Food crops converted to calorie-equivalents of bushels of corn. See Appendix A for detailed
description.

those grasses best suited for hay, reduced milk yields in cattle,
and made wheat subject to attacks of devastating fungus. If hay,
cattle, and small grain did not flourish in such conditions, certain insects did, and among them was the tick that spread Texas
fever and made it impossible to import susceptible purebred
cattle from the North to improve stock.[31]

These climatic constraints reinforced a second major cause of
the absence of diversification: the absence of markets for new
products.[32] Given the Northwest's superior ability to produce
grain and meat, only local markets could have provided a basis
for further diversification. Yet except for Augusta itself, local
markets scarcely existed in this overwhelmingly rural area. Most
of the towns in the countryside could more accurately be called
villages; none had 1,000 white inhabitants in 1860.[33] That a substantial local market might have spurred the movement for diversification is demonstrated by the behavior of farmers close
enough to supply Augusta's 12,000 people (and their many
horses). Richmond county was full of small farms growing fruit,

vegetables, hay, and oats for the city markets. With 2.5 percent of all the improved acreage in Augusta's hinterlands, the county raised 5 percent of all the area's livestock, 14 percent of all hay, 20 percent of all orchard products, and 85 percent of all garden products—and only 1.5 percent of all cotton.[34]

Nathan B. Moore's Richmond county farm shows how a small slaveowner could respond to the opportunities provided by an urban market. Moore fertilized his fields with manure he picked up in his own carts from city streets. On his "very neat" farm, he raised oats, wheat, millet, clover, grass, and peas. In 1859, he sold almost $5,000 worth of produce in the city, about three-quarters of it hay.[35]

Another Richmond farm was owned by William Eve, whose August barbecues were famous enough to receive mention in local newspapers in most years. Eve owned 133 slaves in 1856, and according to one visitor, he produced "not one bale" of cotton in the years just before the Civil War.[36] Eve told Solon Robinson, an agricultural writer and reformer, that he obtained yields of twenty-five bushels of wheat and eighty bushels of corn to the acre, which he sold in Augusta along with "tremendous amounts" of meat, fodder, and wood.[37]

A third farm near Augusta was the twelve-acre plot of George Walker, who in 1854 was growing asparagus, broccoli, carrots, raspberries, okra, plums, quinces, and more than twenty other kinds of vegetables and fruit.[38] The pull of the Augusta market reached down the Savannah river to the Beech Island area on the South Carolina side. In 1853, Hammond decided to switch one of his plantations entirely to corn ("A new idea," he wrote with obvious satisfaction in his journal). In 1858, his son, then overseeing the plantation, sold more than $3,000 worth of corn in Augusta during April alone.[39]

Indirectly, of course, slavery did have a profound impact on the crop choices of farmers near Augusta. Slavery allowed farmers to respond to their fullest ability to the worldwide demand for cotton, and gave them little incentive to find ways to get around the climatic constraints on what they could successfully grow. Slavery, too, helped create an essentially rural economy; the absence of urban markets was partly a consequence of slave-based cotton culture. Still, within the larger institutional constraints of a slave system, planters and slaveowners were highly attuned to international markets; in this, they were much like commercial farmers elsewhere in the United States. It was not the particular "nonbourgeois" psychology of slave masters that made cotton the king of crops near Augusta. Rather, the interplay of technological and market conditions, together with personal circumstances and attitudes, led each farmer to plant cotton or corn or, for that matter, clover or peaches. The Augusta market was simply not big enough to influence strongly the decisions of farmers without immediate access to the city. Instead, they watched for the news from Liverpool's cotton exchange, flashed by telegraph to Augusta's daily newspapers as soon as each steamer from England reached a North American port. They counted mouths to feed, guessed about future prices, and, each in his conservative or speculative fashion, decided how to allocate land and labor.

During the 1850s, more and more of those decisions resulted in planting cotton. The increasing tendency toward cotton is evident among yeoman farmers as much as it is among big planters. In Hancock county, for example, the largest farmers (with more than 250 improved acres) grew about thirty-six bushels of corn for every bale of cotton in 1849, and only twenty-four bushels for every bale in 1859. Meanwhile, farmers with less than fifty improved acres grew ninety-one bushels of corn for every bale of cotton in 1849, and forty-seven bushels for every bale in 1859. Planters continued to concentrate more on cotton, but small farmers were switching to cotton at a faster rate.[40] During the 1859 growing season, the overwhelming majority of farmers— even those with very small farms and even those in Hart county, at the northern reaches of the cotton belt—chose to grow at least one bale of cotton. Unlike most yeomen in the upcountry, many of them grew cotton even though they were not growing enough food to feed their families and animals (see Table 5, p. 32). They were, often enough, like Wilkes county planter Adam Alexander, whose wife wrote of him in 1850 that he was "busy & harried," opening up new fields for planting. "I have

Table 5. Cotton Growing and Food Self-Sufficiency on Farms in
Augusta's Hinterlands, 1859

Improved Acres	Glascock County (%)	Hart County (%)	Taliaferro County (%)	Edgefield District (%)
FARMS PROBABLY NOT SELF-SUFFICIENT IN FOOD*				
1–24	20	45	57	40
25–49	33	45	50	21
50–99	24	43	41	23
100–249	18	27	29	21
250+	4	0	24	16

Category	Glascock County (N = 46) (%)	Hart County (N = 102) (%)	Taliaferro County (N = 42) (%)	Edgefield District (N = 29) (%)
COTTON AND SELF-SUFFICIENCY ON FARMS WITH FEWER THAN FIFTY ACRES				
Growing cotton	85	64	79	66
Not self-sufficient	30	45	52	24
Growing cotton and not self-sufficient	26	31	40	17

SOURCE: Farm Sample from the manuscript returns of the United States Bureau of the Census, 1860.
NOTE: See Appendix A for detailed description.
*Self-sufficient farms grew the food-equivalent of at least fifteen bushels of corn per adult on the farm, after deducting allowances for seed and animal feed. This is a low estimate of the number of bushels needed to feed an adult in one year. See Appendix A for detailed description of calculations.

used all my influence to prevail upon him to sell negroes & all,"
she continued, "but the high price of cotton is so tempting, that
he cannot resist the trial."[41]

A broader approach to diversification might have stressed a
more diversified economy as a whole, rather than simply more
diversified output on farms. Manufacturing towns could have
absorbed marginal farmers, captured a share of northern and English profits, and provided more markets for food crops. Colonel
R. H. Ward pointed out in his agricultural address in 1850 that
"the most obvious imperfection" in the South's economy was
the "undue absorption of its productive wealth in the culture of
cotton." He urged his listeners to develop true "agricultural independence," not only by growing more grains, but also by build-

ing more factories and manufacturing more of their own implements.[42] James Henry Hammond stated this argument more
pointedly in a private letter: "I am beginning to think our Southern people are after all poor set of devils," he wrote to his friend
William Gilmore Simms. "If we cannot infuse more of the manufacturing & commercial spirit into them[,] more of vigor in
every thing they are gone."[43] Republican ideology, however, with
its archaic ideals of individual, rather than community, independence, contributed to the resistance to industrialization in the
South.

According to the manufacturing schedule in the 1860 census,
about 3,000 hands were employed in manufacturing in the Augusta area. Most worked in small mills or shops with one or two
fellow employees and are more properly classified as skilled
workers. Only about twenty establishments in the whole area
had a labor force large enough—twenty employees or more—to
be considered factories in the modern sense. About ten were in
or near Augusta. Most rural factories were cotton mills: two in
Greene county, one each in Hancock, Hart, and Warren counties,
and two in Edgefield district, South Carolina, including the famous mill town of Graniteville.[44]

For good reason, farmers and their children found working in
textile mills unattractive. Graniteville was touted by promoters
of industry as a great boon to the poor (and unproductive) of the
area. Graniteville and its president, William Gregg, were celebrated far and wide for their benevolent treatment of employees;
the village, which had been built for workers, included two
churches and a school.[45] In 1856, the Edgefield Advertiser carried a glowing description of the factory. "There is in this State
as impoverished and as ignorant a white population as can be
found in any other in the Union," wrote the correspondent, and
"the Graniteville factory is the first missionary in the work of
ameliorating their condition."[46] The picture drawn by one local
visitor who claimed to have spoken to many of Graniteville's
employees is less cheerful. The visitor was particularly appalled
by the long hours of work—from 4:45 A.M. to 7:00 P.M. in summer (with two forty-minute breaks for meals) and from 6:15 A.M.
to 7:30 P.M. in winter. Exposed to these conditions were many

eight and nine year olds, he claimed. The "manufacturing system improperly conducted," he concluded, thus has degraded
"the sons and daughters of proud South Carolina," and such evil
results "must eventually outweigh all the benefits that we shall
reap from [Graniteville's] manufactory . . . and do much towards
destroying that dignity and independence of character so peculiar to our beloved State. . . . If not arrested in its infancy, it will
prove more destructive than in the Northern States."[47]

The negative perception of factory labor was sharpened by
anti-North rhetoric, which often referred to the northern poor as
"factory slaves" or as "slaves of the rich in all but name." Graniteville's critic argued that "there is indeed a condition of slavery
[in factories] and while we denounce the institutions of the
North, we are steadily marching on in her footsteps." One can
imagine the effect of such rhetoric on the poor. Even the "benevolence" of Gregg, who forbade liquor in Graniteville village and
was chief snoop as well as chief operating officer, would have
been intolerable to most independent-minded southern men.

Not only the poor wished to avoid factories. In their own way,
most planters also shunned them, although local planters sometimes did invest in mills. According to Dun Company Reports,
the stock of the Madison Steam Mill Company (a cotton manufacturer) was mainly held by "wealthy farmers" in 1852, and Hancock county planters and slaveowners invested at least $150,000
when the Hancock Manufacturing Company was organized in
1851.[48] More often, though, major investors were merchants and
bankers from Augusta or other cities. Graniteville, by far the
largest cotton manufacturer in the Augusta area, was financed
chiefly by Charleston merchants, factors, and bankers; Joel Smith
of Abbeville District, South Carolina, was the only local planter
among the ten largest shareholders when the company was char-
tered in 1846.[49]

There were good reasons for planters' reluctance to invest. The
Madison Steam Mill Company went bankrupt in 1855 and disappeared before 1860. The Hancock Manufacturing Company col-
lapsed in 1854 and was sold to a group of merchants and professional men.[50] Yet risk alone does not explain slaveowners' low
level of investment in manufacturing enterprises. A recent com-

prehensive study by Fred Bateman and Thomas Weiss of antebellum manufacturing in the South found that, on average, manufacturing probably was three times as profitable as cotton growing—more than enough to compensate for the greater risk involved. At the same time, the study concluded, relatively little manufacturing capital in the South came from planters.[51] Surely, some planters stuck to cotton because they shared the convictions of the editor of the usually procommerce Augusta *Chronicle* that Lowells and Manchesters were "great sores on the body politic" and that southerners should therefore avoid "becoming a manufacturing people to any great extent."[52]

This kind of opposition to manufacturing was part of a more pervasive distrust of urban places and urban workers, a distrust that formed the other side of the glorification of farming expressed by Arthur Simkins.[53] This rural society suspected that men not firmly attached to the soil siphoned off wealth from the more honest toil of the farmer. In one exchange published in the Edgefield *Advertiser* in 1856, a letter from "Many Farmers" called the law "a profession that [has] reduced lying and immorality to a perfect science" and declared that "the estimation in which [lawyers] are held by honest yeomen [is such that] our language has no term of reproach, . . . which has not been happily applied to them."[54] Similarly, an Augusta *Chronicle* correspondent worried about the growing tendency of southern "country farmers" to move to cities and live without manual labor. "A sufficient number of merchants and professional men are essential," he wrote, "but every one you add beyond that number is a drone in the hive."[55]

Suspicion of urban people and urban values was heightened because many slaveowners equated those values with opposition to slavery. Cities and towns were full of free blacks and quasi-free slaves who set an unwelcome example for plantation slaves. The Beech Island Farmers Club had been founded as the Agricultural and Police Society, one purpose of which was to keep slaves away from Augusta and Hamburg, South Carolina.[56]

Urban whites, too, might threaten, or at least seem to threaten, slavery. Too many of them were foreigners or northerners, such as Tom Burch, an Irish bricklayer expelled by vigilantes from

Edgefield district, South Carolina, in 1859 for having used "seditious language"; such men were liable to do "very great injury among our negroes."[57] White mechanics in cities were already trying to keep slaves out of skilled jobs; maybe this was only the first step toward stronger opposition to slavery. This appeared as a real possibility to Christopher C. Memminger of Charleston, who in 1849 urged Hammond to speak out against "those who are agog about manufactures." If the South were to drive out black mechanics and operatives from its cities, their place would be taken by "the same men who make the cry in the Northern cities against the tyranny of Capital . . . and would soon raise hue and cry against the Negro, and be hot Abolitionists—and every one of those men would have a vote."[58]

The actual dependence of cotton farmers on the market could be obscured somewhat in rhetoric about virtuous and independent yeomen. An agricultural society must be better than an urban, "mobocratic" one. Furthermore, the institution of slavery guaranteed the South a special stability.

In the late 1830s, in response to abolitionist attacks, southerners had fashioned a potent republican defense of black slavery that had added immensely to the appeal of republican ideology. Edmund S. Morgan, in his study of colonial Virginia, was the first historian to point out the ways in which black slavery may have been, not incompatible with, but crucial to the rise of ideas of republican liberty in America.[59] Yet it seems that colonial Virginians themselves never openly spelled out any connection.

It remained for South Carolinians to make that connection explicit. As early as 1829, Governor Stephen D. Miller had argued that slavery produced important political benefits, since, in a slave society, the poor had no vote and so could not be bribed by corrupt politicians to disturb the property of wealthier men.[60] This somewhat vague formulation had been sharpened and strengthened in the aftermath of nullification by another South Carolina governor, George McDuffie of Edgefield district. McDuffie had laid out the many political benefits of slavery in his address to the state legislature in 1835, climaxing it with the declaration that slavery, far from "being a political evil, is the corner-stone of our republican edifice."[61] By the 1850s, such arguments were commonplace among politicians and writers in Augusta and its hinterlands. Slavery, their logic went, bolstered the stability of republican government in a way that complemented widespread landownership. Landowning ensured the virtue and independence of most citizens; slavery ensured that the poorest and most dependent people were permanently kept out of any role in government. Baptist minister and planter Iveson L. Brookes expressed the point clearly: so far from slavery being "incompatible with the genius of Republicanism," no republican government could long exist without slavery. Where the "lower orders of society" were enfranchised, they would come to control the government, and "knavish demagogues will soon find the means of rearing a despotism upon the ruins of such a democracy."[62]

The problem was the passionate nature of man; where the people are rulers, they must have independence, intelligence, wisdom, and virtue. Except in the case of "a general acquisition of knowledge never yet attained," Joseph Abney told one Edgefield audience, "a Democratic Republic cannot exist among men" without slavery; indeed, slavery "is the safe guard and very bulwark of Republicanism."[63]

Slavery also promoted stability by preventing the dreadful conflicts between capital and labor so evident in the North, those "gatherings of infuriated artisans to protest against the tyranny of capital," as Arthur Simkins noted in his agricultural speech in 1855.[64] The antagonism between capital and labor, according to Brookes, "contains the elements of agrarianism [that is, division of land among the landless] and anarchy" in republics because "whenever the lower stratum of society is entitled to the elective franchise . . . and should become, or suppose themselves oppressed by the holders of capital they can . . . by the ballot box control, through demagogue leaders, the legislative counsels of the state." This, Brookes concluded, meant that only "a monarchical or military despotism can ultimately control the populace, and secure the rights of property holders, where slavery is not the basis of society."[65] In almost identical terms, the editor of the Augusta *Chronicle* described the Lynn, Massachusetts, shoe strike in 1860 as a sign of the "irrepressible conflict" between capital and labor in the North. No law could prevent it, since the people made the law; the inevitable result must be the establishment of a stronger government, whether a military despotism or a limited monarchy with limited suffrage.[66] Slavery, by contrast, made possible progress without conflict.

A republican defense of slavery was not, it should be emphasized, inconsistent with a racist defense. On the contrary, racism was an integral and necessary part of the argument.[67] Every defender of slavery as a stabilizer of republicanism drew attention to God's providential wisdom in having stamped Africans as (again, the words are those of Reverend Brookes) "doomed, to perpetual servitude." Ancient slavery had died out by intermarriage, Brookes said, but this was impossible in the South, where masters never would marry slaves of an inferior race. Further, since blacks were happy and contented with their degraded status, they had no desire to change it. They would not rebel.[68]

This was what Alexander H. Stephens meant when, in his farewell address, he referred to the failure of ancient republican philosophers. They had not realized that subordination, necessary in all societies, must be based on race. Otherwise, degraded slaves eventually would bring down the state. Or, as James Henry Hammond told northern senators, "Your slaves are white, of your own race; you are brothers of one blood. They are your equals in natural endowment of intellect, and they feel galled by their degradation." The fortunate South, though, found "a race inferior to herself, but eminently qualified in temper, in vigor, in docility, in capacity to stand the climate."[69] They never would become a political threat.

A further result, also favorable to republican stability in the South, was that black slaves automatically made whites feel more equal to one another—and equality among citizens was a vital republican principle. Slavery "places the whites to themselves in the upper stratum of society, and upon a greater equality of social and political intercourse, than known in the civilized world."[70] And Hammond claimed that even poorer whites without land were still "elevated far above the mass . . . higher toned and more deeply interested in preserving a stable and well-ordered government, than the same class in any other country." [71]

Alexander H. Stephens covered all these points in his most famous speech, which he gave in Savannah shortly after secession. Stephens, now vice president of the new Confederacy, reviewed the many benefits of slavery in the new nation. He summarized in the words used first by George McDuffie twenty-five years before, declaring slavery to be "the 'real corner-stone' in our new edifice." [72]

Yet the fortunate nature of the combination of slavery and liberty was less obvious to all than Stephens and others sometimes pretended. Slavery had provoked a growing condemnation from the outside world, especially in the North and in England, which hypocritically (to southerners) depended on the staples grown by slaves. Slavery also created, by its nature, the possibility of a slave revolt. The potential combination of fanatical outside agitators and black rebels seemed increasingly menacing during the antebellum period. John Brown's raid on the government arsenal in Harper's Ferry, Virginia, in 1859 pointed up the dangers, which were radically increased by a further circumstance seldom discussed in public: a sizable and growing number of white farmers did not own slaves.

To be sure, most farmers in Augusta's hinterlands did own at least a few slaves, although the proportion varied greatly from county to county. In areas most suitable for cotton, more than three-quarters of farmers held slaves, while in less suitable areas, as few as one-quarter owned any (see Table 6). The ownership of even one or two slaves gave a small farmer a considerable community of interest with his big-planter neighbors. It might also have led him to share some planters' anxieties about his non-slaveowning neighbors. [73]

Yet the trends in slaveownership were not encouraging to those with doubts about the ultimate loyalties of nonslaveowning whites. Within Augusta's hinterlands, as in the South as a whole,

Table 6. Distribution of Slaves Among Farmers in Augusta's
Hinterlands, 1860

Slaves Owned	Glascock County (N = 213) (%)	Hart County (N = 253) (%)	Taliaferro County (N = 238) (%)	Edgefield District (N = 191) (%)
0	63	68	17	25
1–5	22	18	32	21
6–19	10	12	37	34
20–49	5	2	12	15
50+	0	0	2	6

SOURCE: Farm Sample from the manuscript returns of the United States Bureau of the Census, 1860.
NOTE: See Appendix A for detailed description. Percentages may not add to 100 due to rounding.

the proportion of slaveowners among family heads was slowly
declining, and this was true despite a gradual decline in the total
white population in the Augusta area (see Table 19, p. 203). The
sharply rising prices of slaves in the late 1850s seemed likely to
accelerate this trend by placing slaves even farther out of reach of
poorer farmers.

As sectional conflict intensified during the decade, loyalty
among nonslaveowners seemed more important and, to some,
less reliable. Uneasiness about nonslaveholders' loyalty led to
several proposals designed to spread slaveholding more widely
among white families.[74] These plans never got anywhere, but
their existence shows that more than one master feared that dis-
torted descriptions of their society by such writers as J. E. Cairnes
contained, perhaps, a core of political reality. Slave masters suffered from one dependence as troubling as any. In a republican
society, they needed the support of all white men, not just slaveowners. Without that support, slavery would collapse. And at the
bottom of the slaveowners' worry was their knowledge that their
slaves did not suffer bondage willingly.

Chapter 2

The Underlife of Slavery

In June 1850, Lemuel Reid of Abbeville district, South Carolina, hired a slave carpenter, George, from his neighbor Reverend Robert C. Grier. One afternoon soon afterward, Reid heard George talking to the other slaves. He told them that they "ought not to be discouraged on the account of their difficulties. There was no reason why they were in the situation they were, only that God permitted it to be so. That God was working for their deliverance. He was working by secret means, and would deliver them from their bondage as sure as the children of Israel were delivered from the Egyptian bondage. That the question had been in agitation for the last fifty years. That those who were working for them did not know exactly how long it would be before they would be set free. There was no doubt that it would be soon. That they ought to pray for [it], and their prayers would go up before God and be answered."[1]

Reid angrily interrupted this conversation and, despite George's attempts to apologize, sent him away. Reid raised an alarm in the neighborhood, and an informal investigative committee, composed of two men chosen by Grier, two chosen by Reid, and one chosen by these four, gathered to take testimony. They could not question George, since, frightened, he had run away. The committee and several bystanders heard Reid's story and questioned Grier. Some observers interpreted Grier's rather testy replies as "fully endors[ing] the language of the slave." Grier reporter later, in a letter to the editor of the Abbeville *Banner*, that he had merely expressed his opinion that slavery was one of many evils visited on man because of original sin. He doubted that George

41

had said anything truly seditious, and, in any case, if a slave wanted freedom, it was better for him to pray for it than to fight for it.

An angry exchange of charges followed in the columns of the *Banner*. Among others, James Fair and Allen T. Miller, both substantial planters in the neighborhood, accused Grier of secretly opposing slavery. They were especially upset because Grier, who was president of Erskine College, was in a position to influence young white people against slavery. Grier laid their charges to a conspiracy to oust him from Erskine, blaming a totally unrelated disagreement (either Fair or Miller apparently was on the board of trustees of the college). Whatever the cause, Grier was able to hang on at Erskine.

George was taken before a local magistrate's court later that summer. The records do not show whether he had been caught or had surrendered. A six-man jury found him guilty of having used seditious language, and the magistrate sentenced him to thirty-nine lashes, provided he was sent out of the state. If Reverend Grier did not send him away, he would receive another 300 lashes. George left South Carolina.

This story of slavery in Augusta's hinterlands reveals not only the well-known oppression that sought to crush the smallest efforts to resist or even the expression of hopes for freedom. It suggests also the slaves' conviction that freedom was good and would someday come. It shows, too, that white southerners could feel so threatened that, like Abbeville's citizens, they could punish slaves for mild and vague statements about freedom, and turn their suspicions on a prominent white slaveowner.

The story shows, finally, that plantation boundaries could not confine the slave community and that masters' values could not dominate it. Too many slaves had absorbed a Christian message of liberation; too many knew about abolitionism. Slave artisans like George helped spread the word from one slave quarter to another. In the eyes of Abbeville's white men, George's worst crime probably had been to remind them that their own idealization of slavery as a benevolent, paternalistic institution was a false one.

Georgian Thomas R. R. Cobb succinctly summarized the masters' idealized version in *An Historical Sketch of Slavery* (1858). Southern slavery, he wrote, "is a patriarchal, social system." The master, as head of his family, "cares for his slaves . . . avenges their injuries, protects their persons, provides for their wants, and guides their labors." In return, the slaves revere the master "as protector." Nine-tenths of masters, Cobb insisted, "would be defended by their slaves, at the peril of their own lives."[2] John C. Calhoun, a native of Abbeville District, had explained the relationship slightly differently. "Every plantation," he declared in 1838, was "a little community" and "perfectly harmonized."[3] Slaves were voluntary, although subordinate, members of their household community; they were members of the larger southern community only through the persons of their masters.

The work of many historians in the past two decades has clarified the nature of the plantation "community." Certainly, some masters tried hard to match reality to their vision and to convince themselves as well as their slaves that duty, morality, and reciprocal obligation, rather than force, lay at the foundation of the master–slave relationship. Yet it is clear that the slaves' view of their community was quite different from that of their masters. Slaves did not concede that their masters' dominance was always just, and slaves did not concede their masters' power over every aspect of their lives. Slaves were forced to work, of course; open resistance typically was repressed by the whip, and violent resistance might be suicidal. Yet slaves managed to forge considerable autonomy over some aspects of their lives. In some respects, especially in religious and family affairs, slavery was a kind of unacknowledged negotiated agreement, under which a partly autonomous slave community emerged.[4]

Evidence from the Augusta area confirms the existence of this slave community and demonstrates what has been overlooked in most recent historical work: that the slave community extended beyond the plantation quarters. It spilled over farm and plantation boundaries to become a kind of wider, underground spiritual and social community.

Most slave quarters in the Augusta area were simply too small to form isolated communities. Only one-quarter of the slaves, for example, lived on plantations with fifty or more slaves (see Table 7). The rest were about equally divided between farms with fewer than twenty slaves and plantations with from twenty to fifty slaves. The interests of owners and the desires of slaves coincided to ensure that slaves of different masters married each other, worked together, and worshiped together.

Benton Miller, who owned three slaves, regularly traded labor with his neighbors in Washington county. On March 16, 1858, he reported that for the first time, he "had a days work don by my friends." The friends were not the workers; the workers were his friends' slaves. Nine relatives and neighbors each sent one slave, and they joined Miller's own Clark and Harry to roll logs, repair fences, clean fields, and shuck corn. At the end of the day, Miller recorded who had sent help and noted that he now owed each of four friends a day's work.[5]

Miller borrowed or lent slaves many times that year. For two days in February, he traded Harry for Mr. Womble's Mance, so that Mance, a skilled artisan, could make some plow stocks. In March, he sent Harry to help Abb Haines roll logs and Clark to help "Uncle Kinnon" do the same. In April, "Mr. Brown's boy" helped Miller replant corn. In June, Harry and Clark cut wheat for two neighbors. In the autumn, Miller traded labor for picking and packing cotton, plowing in wheat, killing hogs, and hauling corn to the mill.[6] Other slaveowners, like Miller, traded slaves back and forth or hired them to nonslaveholders. Hired slaves might be the only extra labor available to poorer neighbors.

Slave artisans were especially likely to be traded or hired for short periods. Although there are no reliable and consistent labor records, and therefore no sure way to know how many slaves were skilled, the percentage of artisans among slave men in the South as a whole has been estimated to have been as high as 12 percent and as low as 2 to 7 percent.[7] Historians Roger Ransom and Richard Sutch have estimated that 10 percent of adult slaves in Georgia and South Carolina may have been skilled.[8] In 1870 in Edgefield county, South Carolina, however, only between 3 and 4 percent of black male household heads were skilled. In 1880,

Table 7. Slaveholdings by Size in Augusta's Hinterlands, 1860

Slaves Owned	Owners (N = 989)		Slaves (N = 13,771)	
	(%)	cumulative (%)	(%)	cumulative (%)
1–2	22.4	22.4	2.3	2.3
3–5	17.6	40.0	5.1	7.4
6–9	15.5	55.3	8.1	15.5
10–19	22.9	78.2	22.5	38.0
20–49	17.4	95.6	37.4	75.4
50+	4.4	100.0	24.6	100.0
20+	21.8		62.0	

SOURCE: Ten percent Sample from the manuscript returns of the census of slaves, 1860.
NOTE: See Appendix A for detailed description.

that percentage was about 2.5 in Edgefield, and less than 2 in three Georgia rural counties, while in Augusta, almost 18 percent of black household heads were skilled artisans.[9] In view of these levels of skilled black workers after the Civil War, it seems reasonable to take the Ransom and Sutch estimate of 10 percent as a maximum for the proportion of artisans among all slaves in Augusta's hinterlands in 1860. Since most masters did not own skilled artisans, they borrowed or hired from masters who did.

Bill Austin, a former slave from Greene county who was interviewed in the 1930s, remembered his father, Jack, as having been a "good carpenter, mason, and bricklayer." Jack's master, Thomas Smith, let him earn cash by working at jobs for neighboring planters.[10] William Stith, owned by W. W. Simpson of Hancock county, was also a skilled carpenter. According to William's son, James, Simpson "hired my father out to the other planters when he had nothing for him to do in the line of building on his plantation. . . . When he wasn't working for Simpson, he was working for the next big farmer, and then the next one, and then the next one." James Stith claimed that Simpson "couldn't afford to have [my father] handicapped in his going and coming. He could go whenever he wanted to go, and come back whenever he got ready, with a pass or without one."[11]

As the example of William Stith shows, artisans occasionally enjoyed a practical, if limited, freedom of movement. David C. Barrow's slave Daniel frequently worked for white neighbors. In

1855, Barrow sent his carpenters on their own to erect buildings at Blowing Cave, his plantation in far southwest Georgia. White artisans in towns and cities frequently complained about the competition from slaves whose masters allowed them to hire themselves out. These slaves paid their masters a stipulated sum per month, but otherwise were responsible for themselves.[12]

Because of their relative mobility, artisans served as links among slaves across plantation boundaries. They carried news and gossip about distant quarters and distant masters. Other kinds of work, such as the logrolling and corn shuckings mentioned in Miller's diary, also brought together slaves from different quarters. According to former slave Charley Hurt, "de neighbors all comes together, an' [went] to fust one place an' den de tudder an' husk de co'n."[13] Often, former slaves remembered huskings as the biggest of big times. Shucking was night work; masters served up special barbecues, often with whiskey or peach brandy. Estella Jones's description is typical of many. She wrote, "Dey wuz always glad when de time come for 'em to shell corn. Dey enjoyed dat better dan dey did Christmas, or at least jist as much. Dey always had to work durin' de day time and shell corn at night. De overseer wuz real good to 'em. . . . Most times slaves from other plantations would come over and help 'em. Dey used to put on dey good clothes 'cause dey wanted to dey best." The slaves shucked corn until ten o'clock, then danced and played games until midnight. She recalled similar parties after logrollings and late-night cotton picking.[14]

Hiring out artisans and holding corn-shucking parties benefited masters by introducing a useful and profitable flexibility into slavery. The same flexibility, however, produced cracks in the system of rigid control, cracks through which otherwise isolated slave quarters were joined into a larger black community.

Family life and religion, as well as work, joined slave communities across plantation boundaries. Most masters conceded to slaves the right to choose their own spouses, and thus marriage partners often belonged to different owners. Typically, advice to planters argued that "taking wives and husbands among their fellow servants at home, should be as much encouraged as possible," since intermarriage of slaves of different owners was "likely to lead to difficulties and troubles."[15] Owners of few slaves obviously could not insist on this. Two of Benton Miller's three slaves married blacks belonging to nearby masters. In practice, even large slaveowners did not enforce restrictions. In 1854, Linton Stephens bought Luke from George Culver, who was moving to Alabama; Luke's wife and child belonged to another master in Sparta.[16] In December 1850, two slaves of the wealthy Alexander family of Washington, Georgia, married slaves belonging to a Mr. Hester and a Mr. Holmes.[17] In 1860, Alexander H. Stephens tried to hire Jerry from his Wilkes county owner because Jerry planned to "take a wife on my plantation." Jerry had been visiting the Stephens plantation regularly for a year.[18]

In 1856, David C. Barrow tried to buy the wife and child of his slave Sam from another owner.[19] These cross-plantation marriages sometimes took place without the owners' knowledge. In 1864, one of Barrow's overseers discovered that the slave Munroe had been secretly married for several years to a woman on a nearby plantation. He asked Barrow to "let me know if I must let him [Munroe] gow" to visit his wife—as Munroe obviously had been doing all along.[20]

Evidence from former slaves reinforces the point that marriages tied plantations as well as individuals. Kizzie Colquitt's parents lived on opposite sides of the Broad River, "an mah father and mother had to cross the river to see each other."[21] Since Hannah Murphy's parents were owned by different men, her father had to "git a pass to come see us, and he come Sundays and twic't a week."[22] Claiborne Moss's parents lived on plantations "not far apart"; because they were "right there in the same neighborhood," they "would go visiting . . . from one place to the other."[23] About one-sixth of some 130 former slaves from the Augusta area interviewed in the 1930s mentioned that their parents had lived on separate plantations.[24] The husband usually visited his family every weekend, or more frequently if his master was lenient. These separations placed one more unwelcome burden on slave families. Marshall Butler, a former slave in

Wilkes county, described his parents, who had had different owners, as having had "one of dem trial marriages—they'se tried so hard to see each other."[25] At the same time, fathers' treks from quarter to quarter added more links across plantation boundaries. Family life, like work, helped break down isolation and create a more unified black community.

Perhaps one of the strongest links binding this community was the Christian religion. Many owners encouraged, and few discouraged, Christianity among their slaves. For example, Miller allowed Harry or Clark to attend services on alternate Sundays; Barrow encouraged his slaves to join his Methodist church; James Henry Hammond built chapels on his plantation. In slave-owners' eyes, religion both justified slavery as an institution and made slaves better, more obedient workers. Thus Robert Toombs, Wilkes county resident and United States senator from Georgia, claimed that the large number of slaves "enjoying the consolations of religion" was "striking evidence" that "interest and humanity cooperate[d] in harmony for the well-being of our laborers."[26]

More than one former slave remembered the message from white Christian preaching as "nothin' but you must be good, don't steal, don't talk back at your marsters, don't run away, don't do dis and don't do dat." According to former slave Charles Coates, one white preacher liked to add an admonition to "be sure and git all dem weeds outen dat corn in de field and your master will think a heap of you."[27] When C. B. Walker, the superintendent of Sunday schools at Trinity (Episcopal) church in Edgefield, South Carolina, boasted of his seventy-seven "colored scholars," he assured his planter church members that instruction was "*altogether oral*" and that the teachers were "wholly trustworthy."[28]

The records of the white-controlled Goshen Baptist church in Lincoln county show how religion could promote masters' interests among slaves. Most of the members of the church were slaves. The sixth rule of the church called for those "intending to marry" first to "make it known to their master, mistress, or overseer." Among church actions recorded in the minutes was the unanimous excommunication of Frank, belonging to Jacob Zellars, for "unChristian conduct in rebelling against the authority of his master."[29]

But just as clearly, the minutes also show that black members could exercise some control over their own affairs and that the church allowed them to act as a community. Black members regularly met (under the supervision of a single white) to consider charges against one another of adultery, dancing, drinking, profanity, or lying. The accuser usually was a fellow slave, and a committee of slaves investigated each accusation. Black members excluded violators of church discipline and welcomed back any who showed evidence of reform. White members showed some respect for their black fellow church members. In 1853, they permitted the slave Charles "to exercise his gift [of preaching] in publick."[30]

In one sense, undoubtedly, good Christian slaves—peaceful, honest, well-behaved—were profitable slaves. Yet slave membership in white churches had ambiguous consequences. In the first place, the weekly church meetings brought together slaves of different plantations and placed much slave behavior under the direct control of slaves themselves, acting as a community. Second, while the church emphasized masters' control over slave marriages, it brought those marriages under religious sanction, and perhaps served as a restraint on masters who wanted to sell slaves apart from their mates. The result was a diminution in some measure of the master's power. Third, conversion of a slave did not necessarily mean pacification. In 1850, Goshen Baptist church readmitted the slave Aaron to fellowship; he had been excluded for adultery. The next year, Aaron petitioned for liberty to preach. White members, after conferring with Aaron's owner, William Gulatt, rejected the application. In 1855, Aaron was charged with "insubordination & rebellion" against the authority of his master because he had run away; the church unanimously excluded him.[31] Aaron may have rebelled in spite of his conversion or because of it. Christianity had not tamed Aaron; on the contrary, it may have inspired him to resist and given him authority over other Christian slaves.

The slaves' Christianity was, in any case, never bounded by the rules or walls of white churches. Many slaves attended services led by slave or free-black preachers. Gertrude Thomas, wife of a large slaveowner, attended services led by black preachers at a church near her husband's Richmond county plantation. At one of these, led by Sam Drayton, a free black, her slave servant Amanda experienced a powerful conversion. As Mrs. Thomas described the scene, "After the sermon while Drayton was calling up mourners Aunt Pink after swaying to and fro fell perfectly flat upon the floor. Several women rushed to her assistance when she rose and commenced shouting. This had such an affect upon Amanda that she went up to the altar. I believe in her for she is not one to act from impulse so much as settled conviction. When she went up I noticed Lurany (her mother) fully expecting an out burst of feeling upon her part. I was unexpressibly touched by her manner, for her maternal affection is the most strongly developed feeling she has. Instead of shouting she raised her hands in such a perfect ecstasy of gratitude, that words were not requisite." The mood affected Mrs. Thomas as well. She described a "low moaning sound" that rose up during prayer, gradually growing to "a perfect wail." One after another, the slaves took up the sound until it became "the most awfully harrowing sound I almost ever listened to. I can not describe its effect upon me." [32]

Funerals, like Sunday services, were important community events for slaves. The dead man or woman was laid out on a "cooling board" while carpenters fashioned a coffin during the night. Men were dressed in suits; women, wrapped in sheets. Preferably, a black preacher led prayers over the coffin; then the body rode a cart or wagon to the graveyard. The slaves followed, carrying pine-knot torches to light the way on moonless nights. As the coffin was lowered into the grave, the gathered slaves were led in prayer and song; the favorite hymn was

> Hark from de tomb a doleful soun'
> My ears hear a tender cry
> A livin' man come through the groun'
> Whar we may shortly lie.
> Heah in dis clay may be you bed
> In spite of all you toil
> Let all de wise bow rev'rent head
> Mus' lie as low as ours. [33]

When Mary, a favorite servant of Linton Stephens, died, Stephens was deeply touched. He wrote his brother, "Her station was a humble and lowly one, but its vacancy is quite a void to me.—She was not only a most useful servant to me, but also a true and faithful friend. . . . There are not many people in this world whose deaths I would lament more than I lament poor Mary's." Yet when she was buried, the slaves failed to tell Stephens, and he missed the funeral. "I suspect," he wrote honestly enough, "that the negroes really preferred that I should not go. . . . My presence or that of any other white person would probably have embarrassed the officiating negro minister."[34] *Embarrassment* was probably not the word Stephens's slaves would have chosen. They just wanted to bury their own.

Informal prayer meetings, often held on weekdays, drew together blacks from several plantations. Former slave Claiborne Moss remembered that slaves had had "house to house" religious meetings "any time they felt like it."[35] Charley Hudson, from Elbert county, attended black prayer meetings at several different plantations.[36] Alec Pope of Oglethorpe county recalled that Saturday night prayer meetings sometimes had been broken up by patrollers.[37] Slave preachers, known as "chairbackers," led many of these meetings. According to Manuel Johnson, a former slave from Wilkes county, "chairback" preachers in his neighborhood had moved from plantation to plantation to lead services.[38] Slaves sometimes gathered together in the woods at "brush arbor" churches. Former slave Pierce Cody, of Warren county, described one such church, which had been constructed of felled trees and brush, with seats of rough slabs.[39]

Hammond recognized that independent formal or informal black congregations potentially undermined his own power. He built meeting houses to keep his slaves away from Augusta's black churches. He made sure that Sunday services were supervised by whites, and ordered that otherwise "no religious meeting is allowed on the plantation beyond singing & praying, & at such times as will not conflict with the plantation hours, & always with the permission of the Master or Overseer."[40] Despite Hammond's care, his slaves made their own use of and extended these religious privileges. In 1851, he complained in his diary of "religious troubles among the negroes. They are running the thing into the ground by being allowed to[o] much organization— too much power to the head men & too much praying & church meeting on the plantation. Have ordered all church meetings to be broken up except at the Church with a white Preacher."[41] Another master who became upset at slave prayer meetings was Dr. Byrd, owner of former slave Sarah Byrd. Master Byrd whipped two women from another plantation when he found them at a cabin prayer meeting on his plantation. "I reckon," Sarah Byrd reminisced years later, "he thought us wuz praying ter get free."[42]

In their own religious services, and in sermon, song, and story, slaves came to see themselves as a people of a God greater than any master. Above all, they found and expressed an identity with the Israelites, whom God had delivered. Many must have been like Andrew Moss's mother. She would sneak off to her own "prayer grounds," a "twisted thick-rooted muscadine bush. She'd go in dar and pray for deliverance of de slaves."[43] Others, such as Jacob Stroyer, heard as children from their parents that "God would free them before they died."[44] This was the message that Lemuel Reid's slaves heard from the slave carpenter George. A similar message lay behind the story that former slave Maria Callaway's grandfather told her: "We often waited until the overseer got behind a hill, and then we would lay down our hoes and call on God to free us."[45]

Complete control of slaves by masters required slaves to stay inside plantation boundaries, but achieving this proved impossible. Because of work, marriage, religion, or social life, every neighborhood saw a continual traffic of slaves. Some of this movement was legitimate; some, not; some, ambiguously in between. Especially alarming were the many occasions when slaves from different plantations joined in forbidden or even criminal acts.

Many whites complained about underground slave activity. "A Citizen" wrote to the Edgefield *Advertiser* about slaves gathering and drinking on Saturday nights.[46] Octavious T. Porcher and Alexander H. Stephens discovered that their slaves had slipped off to nearby towns on weekends.[47] Iveson L. Brookes's overseer repeatedly punished Daniel, who was "in disposed to say [stay] at home of nights and of Sunddays and never ask[s] for a pass at all."[48]

In the Beech Island area of South Carolina, southeast of Augusta, planters established the Agricultural and Police Society in 1851 because the "irregularities" of their slaves had become so "notorious" as "to affect our interests" and "to endanger the peace and tranquility of the country." The chief source of evils arose from "the unrestrained manner in which these people are allowed to ramble about the neighborhood and the free and unrestricted intercourse the[y] have with the cities of Augusta and Hamburg."[49] Discussion in the (renamed) Beech Island Farmers Club in 1859 demonstrates how effective the planters had been. Mr. Mills complained that "in this neighborhood negroes are in the habit of rambling about, & they think they are independent on Sundays . . . [and] think they have purfict liberty to walk any mans plantation." Mills, along with other members, urged a stronger patrol system.[50] He seemingly had forgotten his own remarks two years earlier: "We may talk about keeping them home at night—It cant be done."[51]

Theoretically, the slave patrol should have prevented such "rambling." All white adult males were subject to patrol duty; patrols policed roads at night and punished slaves who were found off their plantations without passes from their masters.[52] But the patrol system worked well only in times of general alarm. During tranquil periods—that is, usually—patrol duty was merely boring and so avoided. One Farmers Club member complained that not five patrols had passed near his plantation in seven years. Moreover, planters did not fully trust the patrol system. James Henry Hammond thought patrollers mostly drank and caroused; Dr. Cook of the Farmers Club agreed with him.[53]

The patrol often did not know whether slaves were where they were supposed to be. Masters allowed, or at least tolerated, much communitywide slave social life, especially on weekends. Former slave Ellen B. Warfield recalled that "we was free to go see the niggers on other plantations, as long as we got a pass."[54] Maria Clements and her fellow slaves in Lincoln county would "get passes and visit round on Saturday evening or on Sundays, jis mongst their selves."[55] According to Claiborne Moss, "when slaves wanted to, they would have dances . . . from one plantation to the other. The master didn't object."[56] Saturday was the slaves' "day to howl," as one former slave put it. Blacks on some large plantations organized weekly music and dancing.[57] Saturday night frolics on the William Eve plantation in Richmond county drew slaves from the Clayton, Phinizy, and Hammond plantations—all owned by members of the Farmers Club.[58]

Patrollers who broke up these extralegal gatherings sometimes did so at their own risk. The South Carolina Court of Appeals upheld one conviction of patrollers for having whipped slaves who had gathered at a quilting bee. The slaves had permission to be at the party, although technically they were violating the law because no white man was present. The editor of the Edgefield *Advertiser* approved the decision. "How many of us," he wrote, "have permitted our slaves the enjoyment of a wedding party and ceremony" or allowed slaves to help one another build a cabin or gather a crop. "[S]ocial relations and intercourse among themselves" are among the "humble virtues that may be consistent with [the slave's] condition," he continued. Masters should "concede something of the sacredness of the domicile" to slaves, even if patrols must overlook minor transgressions of the law.[59] The theoretically rigid system was, in practice, somewhat flexible. The flexibility was too much in the masters' interest for them to dispense with it, yet too easily exploited by slaves for masters to be happy with it.

From the masters' point of view, legitimate gatherings of slaves belonging to different plantations might lead to, or be indistinguishable from, illegitimate or illegal activities. At the parties described by Claiborne Moss, for example, the slaves usually managed to get whiskey, despite laws against drinking by slaves.[60] Julia Henderson's grandfather occasionally slipped off without a pass and, with other slaves, broke into neighbors' smokehouses to enjoy a forbidden feast.[61] Midge Burnett, who lived on a river, remembered that "on moonlight nights yo' could hear a heap of voices an' when yo' peep ober de dike dar am a gang of niggers a-shootin craps an' bettin' eber' thing dey has stold frum de plantation."[62] Another former slave, Samuel Andrews of Hancock county, remembered one party crowded with slaves without passes. When patrollers surprised the illegal party, Andrews's uncle threw hot ashes at them. In the confusion, the slaves escaped to their plantations.[63]

Such communitywide contacts and support made running away much easier for slaves than it otherwise would have been. Slaves ran away for long and short periods. They did so to reunite with relatives, to avoid or protest punishment, or to complain about decisions by overseers that they thought were unjust. Only rarely did slaves succeed in reaching the North and permanent freedom. John Brown was one who did. He escaped from a DeKalb county farm in the 1840s. After careful preparation, and with a combination of tenacity, intelligence, courage, and luck, he made it first to New Orleans and then to the North. His difficulties and narrow escapes explain why so few could duplicate his feat.[64] Many other slaves escaped for shorter times, or even permanently, by hiding in nearby woods and swamps. Samuel Andrews's uncle, for example, escaped with his brother and hid in woods close to their plantation. The two men killed hogs and would "slip the meat to some slave to cook for food." They survived until emancipation.[65] According to Isaiah Green, a slave from a Greene county plantation near his own escaped before the Civil War and successfully hid for seven years until freedom was declared.[66] Former slave Ellen Campbell knew of a slave who ran away because his master refused him permission to marry a woman from another plantation. He survived for three years around Augusta before being shot and killed.[67]

Interviews with former slaves and evidence left by whites show that runaways usually received assistance from other slaves, as did Samuel Andrews's uncle. Jacob Stroyer recounted the story of Isom, who ran away from a plantation close to his. When, after a short time, Isom failed to return as expected, Thomas Clarkson, the owner's son and also overseer, hired a slave catcher and his dogs. Clarkson, Clarkson's wife, and the hunter discussed the case at breakfast one morning and decided that Isom must have fallen in with more experienced runaways. The two men set out to find Isom, and Mrs. Clarkson went upstairs to her room—whereupon Isom came out from hiding and sat down to breakfast at the same kitchen table! Isom's audaciousness was unusual, but the help he obtained from other slaves was not.[68] As in the cases described by Ellen Campbell and Isaiah Green, this help could come from slaves belonging to other masters; most runaways left their plantations, but not their communities.

Individual runaways were not the most serious problems for the white community. Stroyer described escapes by several slaves who banded together in swamps with runaways from other plantations. It "made it very difficult and dangerous for slave hunters to capture those whom they were hired to hunt." These escapees sometimes killed both hunters and dogs sent after them.[69] In a study of court records in Anderson and Spartanburg districts, north of Abbeville District in South Carolina, historian Michael Hindus found that more than three-quarters of slaves convicted of crimes against property had been convicted with others in a group. As Hindus puts it, the court records reveal "the 'underside' of slave life—the gambling, carousing, fighting, and stealing that whites periodically and unsuccessfully tried to repress." Much of this crime involved slaves from different plantations.[70]

Because of ubiquitous illegal slave activity, including running away, slaveowners needed support from the entire community of white men including nonslaveholders. For good reason, masters were concerned when poor whites joined slaves in illegal activities, and many reacted strongly against any implication that white nonslaveholders accepted racial equality.

Sexual relations, including cohabitation and interracial marriage, raised that implication. Interracial sexual contacts, frequently casual and short lived, attracted little attention, but some counties diligently prosecuted fornication and adultery cases involving blacks and whites. The June 1858 term of the Glascock County Superior Court indicted persons in two such cases: one involving a white woman and a free black man; the other, a married white man and a free black woman. In the latter case, separate juries later found the man innocent and the woman guilty, a remarkable commentary on either the southern man's notions of justice or his knowledge of sex.[71]

Some whites openly cohabited with blacks. In a study of free blacks in Edgefield district, South Carolina, historian Vernon Burton identified at least seven instances of interracial legal or common-law marriages.[72] John H. Cornish in 1856 baptized four children of one Edgefield married couple, "[T]he Father white—Mother coloured."[73] The incidence of these marriages cannot be accurately measured, but at least some whites in the 1850s were concerned that miscegenation was increasing. In 1852, the Georgia legislature passed a law increasing the penalty for white men who lived with black women. A supporter of the bill argued that the law was needed to arrest a "degrading" practice "manifestly increasing in many portions of the state." Opponents chiefly objected that a new law would have no effect in preventing interracial marriages.[74]

Slaveowners were most disturbed when slave underground activities involved whites and blacks cooperating in crime. Only occasionally were these crimes as serious as the murder in 1852 of Mrs. Herring, of Columbia county, by two men—one white, one mulatto.[75] Nonetheless, scattered evidence in court records, manuscripts, and slave narratives indicates the existence of an informal underworld network of relationships between poor whites and slaves. As these records show, a key element in crimes committed jointly by blacks and whites involved slaves trading stolen goods for liquor. Selling liquor to slaves, although strictly illegal without a master's written permission, went on regularly. Individual distillers sometimes traveled at night from plantation to plantation with their product. Some Hancock county planters caught "Cock-eyed" Johnson selling liquor to a crowd of twenty or thirty slaves at Mrs. Small's plantation in 1860.[76] At other times, slaves traveled to the liquor. One of the complaints against "grog-shops" was that they attracted slave customers at night. As one protemperance correspondent of the Augusta Chronicle wrote, grogshops' "power for evil does not terminate with the day. At night the servants from the contiguous plantations, stealthily repair to them with their master's property and exchange it for less than its market value, and receive money or whiskey in exchange."[77]

Slave narratives sometimes describe more elaborate black-market activity. As a slave in South Carolina, George Ball regularly bartered with a white river trader; in exchange for pork, Ball offered stolen fish and one time stolen cotton. When Ball's master discovered that cotton was missing, he led a group of neighbors to the house of a nearby poor white man, whom they mistakenly blamed for the theft. They burned down the man's house, and later called a meeting "for the purpose of devising the best, surest, and most peaceful method of removing from the country the many white men who, residing in the district without property, or without interest in preserving the morals of the slaves, were believed to carry on an unlawful and criminal traffic with the negroes."[78]

The narrative of former slave John Brown recounts similar experiences from his life in Baldwin county in the 1830s and 1840s. "So it happens," Brown claimed, "that when these poor whites cannot obtain a living honestly, which they very seldom do, they get the slaves in their neighborhood to steal corn, poultry, and such like, from their masters, and bring these things to them; corn especially. . . . This system is carried on to a very great extent, and as the parties to it are interested in keeping the secret, it is not often the masters find out how much they are robbed."[79] In 1856, Long Creek Baptist church, in Warren county, expelled Thomas Kent, an overseer, who apparently had masterminded a similar scheme of corn thefts.[80]

Local courts regularly prosecuted whites for selling liquor to slaves, buying stolen goods from them, or generally carousing with them. A Hancock county grand jury in 1859 indicted Frances Arnold for selling gin, brandy, whiskey, and rum to Mat, a slave of Sarah Hall, and Stephen Jenkins for selling liquor to George, a slave of James Butts.[81] A year earlier in the same county, J. H. Ledbetter was indicted for receiving stolen goods from a slave.[82] In 1861 in Taliaferro county, Thomas Arnold (possibly the husband of Frances Arnold) and Bill Meadows were indicted for furnishing liquor to slaves.[83] Oglethorpe county grand juries indicted David Thomas for buying stolen cotton from a slave in

1839; George Maxey for selling liquor to several slaves in 1848; Harris Pace for the same offense in 1849; Charles Finch, William Drake, and Torbert Woodal for the same thing in 1850; and David Burnett for trading liquor for stolen cotton, also in 1850.[84]

Local citizens knew that occasional prosecutions exposed only the tip of an iceberg. Greene county authorities, for example, were quite active in attempting to prevent slaves and poor whites from drinking and trading together. In 1844, they broke up an illegal gambling parlor, and arrested several white patrons for gambling and the owner for selling liquor to slaves. In 1856, the grand jury indicted two men for selling liquor to slaves. Two years later, another grand jury indicted Robert Ward and Benjamin Ray for gambling with slaves.[85] Still, one Greene county grand jury noted that while only a few criminal cases had been brought to them, "we feel constrained to believe that illegal traffic with negroes is carried on to a considerable extent," especially in view of the large number of blacks who "are frequently seen drunk both in town & country[,] and notwithstanding our efforts been specially exerted to ferret out the violators . . . they have been unavailing." Jurors concluded that the patrol law was, in effect, "a dead letter." Ten years later, another grand jury made the same complaint, deploring "the great laxity and inefficiency in the proper execution of our present Patrol laws."[86] Other county court records paint a similar picture. Columbia county's grand jury in 1850 recommended "to the proper authorities to have the Patrol law rigidly enforced and particularly [laws for] the suppression of negro meetings contrary to law." The 1858 jury felt it their "duty to recommend particularly the enforcement of the Patrol law as we have reason to believe there is neglect in this matter." Apparently, things did not improve, since another jury in 1861 again urged enforcement of the patrol law, so that the county might "ferret out . . . the scamps that are corrupting our negroes by trading with them and furnishing them with spiritous liquors."[87] Burke county grand juries similarly decried in 1838 "the total disregard of the law forbidding the sale or furnishing of spirits to slaves," and recorded in 1851 that "we regret very much that though the laws [governing traffic with slaves] are very strict . . . under the present regulation the evil is not supprest."[88] One Burke resident, in 1858, wrote to the Augusta *Constitutionalist* complaining about one Anthony Bines, who, nominally a slave, operated his own wagon business using hired slaves. Worse from the writer's point of view, Bines's house had become the rendezvous of "all the mean white people and negroes of the county" and a center for traffic in stolen goods.[89]

White farmers near Augusta often expressed their concern about thefts of meat met at Molasses Branch in Edgefield district, South Carolina, to encourage prosecution of "certain white about thefts of meat met at Molasses Branch in Edgefield District, South Carolina, to encourage prosecution of "certain white men" of the neighborhood who were "leagued with the negroes in this rascality."[90] A striking expression of these complaints appears in the preamble to the regulations of the Savannah River Anti-Slave Traffick Association, formed a few miles south of Augusta in 1846. According to the preamble, slaves formerly had been "essentially members of the family to which they belonged," and relations with masters had been "simple, agreeable, easily maintained, and mutually beneficial." Now, however, "Masters and Slaves are beginning to look upon each other as natural enemies," with "harsh yet inefficient discipline on the one hand, and sullenness, discontent, and growing depravity upon the other." The cause of the change was said to be "the extensive and growing traffick unlawfully carried on with slaves by white persons and chiefly by Retailers of Spiritous Liquors." Slaves were "plundering" barns, storehouses, and even crops still in the fields; hundreds of slaves were scouring the countryside at night, "picking up every article of value"; poultry had disappeared from the area, except for the "waggon loads" sent to Augusta by liquor retailers. Worst of all, slaves' "minds are fatally corrupted," and they are being "directly taught to regard their owners, and especially their overseers, as unjust and unfeeling oppressors." The black "becomes a serpent knawing at [society's] vitals or a demon ready with knife and torch to demolish its foundations." Those who traffic with slaves, the preamble concluded, are "more potent than the abolitionist" as a threat to slavery, and if not stopped, the current state of things "must speedily put an end to agriculture or to negro slavery."[91]

As the preamble demonstrates, concern with slave thieving and trading went far beyond the natural reactions of individuals angry about slave drunkenness or the loss of property. Superior court justice Iverson L. Harris articulated the most fundamental concern in a charge to the grand jury of Greene county in 1860. Strongly denouncing illegal trading with slaves, Harris declared that "the great object that should be kept in view by us, is to keep the slave in subordination. That the white man should not *stoop* to equalize himself with the slave, nor suffer the slave to rise above what he naturally is, if we wish to perpetuate the institution." Harris cataloged the whole range of restrictions on slaves and free blacks, and the laws prohibiting each of the "many . . . ways by which we might raise a slave above his status quo," laws enacted "for no other purpose, but the keeping of the slave in subordination to the master."[92] For if slaves were to become equal to some white men, how could masters prevent them from becoming equal to all white men?

Judge Iverson Harris's charge exposes the greatest weakness of slavery: that slaves themselves rejected masters' patriarchal definition of their condition. The illegal underlife of slavery was simply the most blatant expression of this rejection. In the cracks of the peculiar institution, slaves found room to define their predicament in their own terms. Fugitive slave John Brown made this point when he wrote that "we cannot be made to understand how any man can hold another man as a slave, and do right."[93] Former slave Rachel Adams made the same point when she reflected in old age that "it's mighty good to do jus' as you please, and bread and water is heaps better dan dat somepin t'eat us had to slave for."[94]

True, slaves usually hid their sense of injustice, as they hid much else. When Master Singleton died, Jacob Stroyer and Singleton's other slaves gathered around the body, "shed false tears," and told the mistress that old Colonel was surely in heaven. Then they went outside and told one another, "Thank God, massa gone home to hell."[95] Many other slaves could have fitted

Brown's description of himself: "I had an instinctive knowledge of character which I had acquired from a long habit of studying the expression of the countenance . . . I had been forced to watch the changes of my master's physiognomy, as well as those of the parties he associated with, so as to frame my conduct in accordance with what I had reason to believe was their prevailing mood at any given time."[96]

Most slaveowners in turn hid their own secret: that they knew in their hearts that slaves had rejected the legitimacy of slavery. This is why masters were often so uneasy. Not that they constantly feared for their lives, or always expected revolt. Whites knew that the sheer military balance in their favor made successful rebellion virtually impossible, and nothing approaching one appeared in Augusta's hinterlands during the 1850s. Yet the unease showed through time after time. Tennessee suffered an insurrection scare in 1856, and concern spread immediately to the Augusta area. Looking back on that scare two years later, Gertrude Thomas wondered that she had felt no special alarm at the time: "I sometimes think that we are like the inhabitants at the foot of Mt. Vesuvius, remaining perfectly contented among so many dangers."[97] James Henry Hammond tried to keep his slaves away from Augusta because he was sure that there were "more abolitionist[s]" there than "took Harper's Ferry." Black churches in Augusta, he reasoned, might easily be converted into military organizations.[98] The editor of the Augusta *Chronicle* tied these issues to the larger question of white control. He complained that too many slaves were allowed to hire themselves out. Discounting fears of insurrection, he admitted to "uneasy feeling" among slaves at times. He blamed this on the easy availability of liquor, on whites who traded for stolen goods, on black preaching, and on public discussion of the slavery issue.[99] In Warren county in 1851, a vigilante committee expelled Nathan Bird Watson, a white mechanic, on grounds that he was spreading abolitionist ideas among slaves.[100]

Underlying all these anxieties was the knowledge of a shadow community of blacks with their own ideas about slavery. Most slaves did not accept the masters' definition of the plantation as a patriarchal community. Master and slave both knew the truth:

that a white community held down a black one by force. Slave-owners knew, therefore, that they needed support from the whole of white society to keep slavery viable. They needed legal sanction to whip slaves. They needed the patrol, however much it rankled them to need it. They needed to be able to bring the law down on men who "tampered" with their slaves. They needed political support to help them defend the institution of slavery against the attacks of northern abolitionists. Hence the fears of men such as Christopher C. Memminger, who had urged Hammond to warn the South against the introduction of potentially abolitionist mechanics and operatives.[101] Indeed, some feared that the South was already full of secret abolitionists. They were not always without evidence for their fears.

Chapter 3
Portents of Class Division

On a winter's day late in 1859, in Hancock county, young John Pool, son of an old shingle maker, was on his way home from Sparta when he met Mr. Long, overseer on Judge James Thomas's plantation. Long asked for news from town. Everyone in town was excited about the news from Virginia, Pool said. John Brown was in prison, awaiting execution for his occupation of the Harper's Ferry arsenal, and abolitionists were threatening to break him out.[1]

According to an account of the incident by local planter and politician Linton Stephens, Pool told Long that the result would be *"a war."* Because there were so many more blacks than whites, Pool continued, *"he was going to take care of himself by joining the strong side,"* adding that he wished *"'there weren't no niggers, nohow,'"* for then he could get paid more for his labor. (Whites outnumbered blacks in the South, but Pool assumed that Hancock county, with its majority of blacks, was typical.) When Long asked how he would manage to join the abolitionists, Pool answered that he would *"black himself and go to them."*

Pool was a poor man, a farm laborer who told the census taker in 1860 that all his property was worth less than $100.[2] He had been born in the mid-1830s in Hancock county, where his father had eked out an existence as a tenant farmer and shingle cutter. In his candid comments to Long, Pool probably took for granted that an overseer would share some of his own resentment against the rich slaveowners who dominated Hancock county's economy and local politics. He was mistaken. Long reported what Pool had said to some of those wealthy men.

Jack Smith and other Hancock slaveowners formed a "vigilance" committee and hauled Pool before them to be tried for "uttering abolition sentiments." Pool denied everything, swearing that he "was as good a friend of slavery as any man who owned a hundred niggers." No one believed him. Smith asked Stephens, who was not one of the vigilantes, for advice on the case, and Stephens replied that Pool was just a "poor, simple native" who was hardly worth punishing. The only people who could be "annoyed" if Pool were punished were "a few other simple people of his own class," who might look on Pool as a "martyr." Pool himself, Stephens thought, was "not a *dangerous* man, whatever his wishes might be; for there wasn't a negro in the county with so little sense as to be fooled into trouble by such a fellow." Fortunately for Pool, the committee took Stephens's advice, and let him go with a stern lecture.

The only known source for this episode is a letter from Stephens to his half-brother, Alexander. Newspapers often failed, as in this instance, to report such cases: whether because they were considered trivial or potentially inciting is not clear. Many slaveowners, however, feared what Pool might represent. It was frightening enough to contemplate the dangers of a slave uprising, the possibility that some new Nat Turner or some abolitionist like John Brown might lead blacks in violent revolt. What if other whites, like Pool, secretly harbored dangerous thoughts and resentments? Did northern fanatics have thousands of potential allies in the very heart of the slave states themselves?

Proslavery writers held that black slavery enhanced, rather than impeded, a sense of equality among whites. Georgia's Thomas R. R. Cobb, in *An Historical Sketch of Slavery*, wrote that "every citizen feels that he belongs to an elevated class. It matters not that he is no slaveholder; he is not of the inferior race; he is a freeborn citizen; he engages in no menial occupation." Socially, Cobb argued, rich and poor whites were part of the same ruling class, which was marked by "republican equality." The poorest white "meets the richest as an equal; sits at his table with him; salutes him as a neighbor; meets him in every public assembly, and stands on the same social platform." A democracy of manners based on race compensated for less important inequalities in wealth.[3]

Cobb was not entirely wrong, as can be seen from what Gertrude Thomas called in her diary a "singular little circumstance." A man came to her front door and told Mrs. Thomas that her husband had met him on the road and sent him on to wait there at the plantation. Mrs. Thomas thought the strange man looked so much like a mulatto that she "was in a quandary" as to "what to do with him." Fearing to insult a white man, however, she "invited him into the fire," where he stayed until Mr. Thomas returned.

At dinnertime, Mr. Thomas invited the stranger to the table. "When he took his hat off," Mrs. Thomas wrote, "he looked more suspicious than ever." Mr. Thomas's suspicions were now aroused, and he began to ask the guest questions, including "*where they voted* around here?" The man replied that he was not a voter. " 'You are not of age?' 'Yes, sir, but the law does not allow me to vote.'" Mrs. Thomas added that "the temptation to reply to him that the law 'that did not allow him to vote did not allow him to sit at a white ladys table' was almost irresistible." The intricate dance of politeness during this incident and Mrs. Thomas's indignation when she learned that her visitor was indeed a mulatto demonstrate the significance of racial consciousness and racial mores. A nonwhite was *not* a proper dinner guest for a white lady. Equally important, a poor white was, literally, a proper guest—if perhaps not entirely welcome at the table of this rich planter family. Mrs. Thomas did not like slavery; but race, not class, was the fundamental social division she perceived.[4]

The same point was made by William Thomson, a Scottish artisan who traveled in the United States. In the 1840s, Thomson visited a large planter, Judge Schley, who lived eight miles from Augusta. Thomson, who wanted a job in Schley's mill, was pleasantly surprised when Schley "treated me with perfect equality, called me 'Mr. Thomson,' said 'Yes, Sir,' or 'No, Sir' just as I would do, in speaking to a gentleman."[5]

Still, even profound racism on the part of wealthy planters did not destroy consciousness of class differences among whites.

James Henry Hammond's complex (and not always consistent) attitudes illustrate this point. Hammond's racism is beyond question; it is apparent in both his private and his public statements. In a public defense of slavery, for example, he declared that blacks simply lacked "the capacities and qualifications of an anglo-norman, anglo-saxon, or even a celt."[6] To abolitionist Lewis Tappan, he wrote that he and "all observant persons" could see that "in their mental structure [Negroes] differ from us almost as much as in color & features. Amalgamation or equality of any kind between the two races are on account of these circumstances, *utterly & forever out of the question*. . . . It is an instinct."[7] Hammond's letters to his intimate friend William Gilmore Simms echo these sentiments. In 1854, when he discovered that many of his slaves had been consistently working less than required, he fumed to Simms that "after nearly a quarter of a century of experience," he had finally come to realize "the utter *treachery & stupidity*" of Negroes, and that "the negro race differs as much from ours as that of swine from dogs to say the least—that they are Baboons on two legs gifted with speech." A few weeks later, he wrote to Simms that "there is no such thing as securing the fidelity of a negro except to your mere person."[8]

Yet Hammond was far from a democrat in manner or belief, despite (or perhaps because of) his own quite humble origins. In one of his letters to Simms, he classed "hirelings" with black slaves as capable of only "treachery & stupidity," and added that "of our own race among the low bred & uneducated class, from whom our overseers come, not one in ten is in *morale* a whit superior to a negro."[9] Once a year, Hammond invited all his neighbors, rich and poor, to a grand feast. One guest described her amusement as many of the "stiff and prim" plain folk, many of whom were of the "quaint religious class," wandered ill at ease through Redcliffe's parlors. She described Hammond on this occasion as "like a great feudal landlord."[10] This kind of personal contact was designed to display Hammond's superiority to, not his equality with, the plain folk.

As Thomson himself remarked, despite the respectful conduct of employers to their workmen, all men were not "upon an equality—far from it;—for if a man is poor, there are a hundred and fifty ways in which he will feel it."[11] Such feelings included, at times, fear and resentments among both poor and rich whites.

Some resentments were a result of concrete experiences, as when James Darnal's three-year-old daughter was run over and killed by a neighbor's wagon, driven by a slave. "I am poor," Darnal wrote to Alexander H. Stephens, "and not able to contend with him and that is the reason he has not made me any recompence."[12] A seamstress in Augusta once complained to Gertrude Thomas about the way some of her customers treated her. She "mentioned some instances," Mrs. Thomas wrote in her diary, "showing how carelessly her feelings had been trampled upon by people who altho' wealthy—had no higher sense of honor than herself—I had never seen Sarah's feelings apparently so outraged."[13] When slaveowners formed the Savannah river Anti-Slave Traffick Association in 1846 near Augusta, they admitted, in order to try to refute the charge, that "it has been said ours was a combination to oppress the poor."[14]

As in Hammond's case, the resentments sometimes appeared at the upper end of the social scale. Spann Hammond, a son of Hammond, complained in his diary about the "worthlessness & obstinacy" of a local wagoner who was destroying fodder. "White laborers," Hammond thought, "are the hardest to get on with."[15] An even more striking complaint is recorded in the minutes of the Beech Island Farmers Club. When the club was discussing how to make the local slave patrol system more effective, one wealthy member declared, "There is a class of white men about here that a patrole would do good in katching those Hunting Fishing & Steeling rascals; the patrole could not chastise them, but they could take them up & prosecute them & this should be done."[16]

Class issues entered at times into local and state politics. A letter in the Edgefield *Advertiser* in 1856 urged that property taxes be partly replaced by a poll tax, so the *"loafing vagabond* and *idle drone"* would have to contribute to the public till. The writer dared candidates to "defy" the *"Pauper Vote."*[17] When Governor Joseph E. Brown of Georgia vetoed a law passed to help banks during the Panic of 1857, the Augusta *Chronicle* denounced the veto as "the low and miserable effort of a most contemptible demagogue, to array the prejudices of the poor against the rich."[18] The brother-in-law of David C. Barrow reminded him in the midst of Barrow's campaign for a state senate seat from Oglethorpe county that "a man of your wealth & decency must expect to be opposed by agrarianism's sons, on such occasions; to be charged with lack of sympathy for the poor;—but the hands of society have to look after this always."[19]

Worries about the white poor surfaced during the temperance movement, briefly popular in Georgia and South Carolina in the 1850s. Temperance advocates, who first concentrated on passing local and state laws to banish "grog-shops," blamed demon alcohol for the crime, violence, and poverty that at times seemed to pervade white society. As early as 1851, the Edgefield *Advertiser* urged local voters to outlaw taverns, which one correspondent blamed for a spate of recent killings in Edgefield.[20] When the town did elect a prohibition ticket in 1852 and closed down taverns, the district grand jury praised the decline in crime and drunkenness.[21] (Either the law or its effect must have been temporary, for in 1856, George D. Tillman, then representing Edgefield district in the South Carolina state legislature, shot and killed a bystander during a quarrel after a faro game in a village tavern.)[22]

In Georgia, the movement peaked in 1853. The Augusta *Chronicle* supported a state temperance law in strong editorials. Delegates to antiliquor meetings passed resolutions urging the state to allow local communities to regulate the liquor traffic, with the justification that the people in each county "are compelled to provide for their own poor, and to pay the expenses of . . . criminal investigations."[23] Ultimately, a state temperance convention met and memorialized the legislature. Among the evil results of the liquor traffic, according to its memorial, were that "pauperism of every form is rendered familiar to a people blessed of God with the means of honorable independence above any other people on earth. . . . Taxes are levied upon the sober . . . to support in drunkenness, indolence, and waste a large portion of the population."[24]

Temperance was, in part, a response to a real and visible problem, for much personal violence did grow out of drunken encounters. At the same time, the movement was a local manifestation of a national reform impulse that already was more than two decades old and heavily influenced by Baptist and Methodist churches, which dominated southern religion. At a third level, temperance was a way for southerners to deflect more general fears and anxieties raised by what, from the point of view of the respectable, seemed to be antisocial behavior among poor whites. By blaming liquor for crime and poverty, temperance advocates were acknowledging these problems while shifting responsibility for their existence away from the structure of society and placing it squarely on the poor themselves.

One wing of temperance was openly political. The temperance convention memorial itself argued that "the purity of our popular representative government is tarnished, and the entire system is endangered, since the grog-shop has become the center of power to unscrupulous demagogues." The movement in Georgia ultimately sprouted an independent campaign for the governor's office; but its candidate attracted few votes, and the issue subsided in importance.

Other issues also were connected to class divisions. In newly formed Hart county in 1854, the first order of business for the county's first elected officials (the members of the inferior court) was the choice of a location for the county seat, to be named Hartwell. The court chose a site nearer to the Savannah River, where the wealthiest planters lived, than to the geographical center of the county.[25] Many inhabitants of the poorer western part of the county regarded the location as rank discrimination against them. In May 1854, some dissidents met publicly to complain about the new site, on the grounds that it was "ineligible, inconvenient, and destructive to the permanent interest of the people." The meeting passed resolutions condemning the inferior court for having acted against the clear interests of the majority, asking that the site be changed to "Center of the World" (so named by Indians), calling on the members of the inferior court to resign, and appointing a committee to circulate petitions on the subject.[26] On June 19, a similar meeting supported the court's choice of a site. The gathering not only backed the court and site, but also condemned the "factious and disorganizing tendency" of the movement of "part of our fellow citizens in the western portion of the county." Some speakers at the second meeting were more direct, accusing the leaders of the anticourt meeting of preferring a site near their own properties, and their followers as being, among other things, "a few malcontents," "a miserable squad," and "a small mob."²⁷ The dispute continued throughout the summer. Westerners claimed signatures of the majority of the county's voters, and argued that the inferior court was merely upholding the interests of "those who live on the soil in proximity to the Savannah River." They were supported by one of the five members of the court but eventually lost a court battle, and the original choice of Hartwell remained.²⁸

In the dispute over the location of the county seat, geographical and property interests overlapped. Western dissidents were no simple collection of poor yeomen. Their leader, Job Bowers, owned $6,000 worth of real estate in 1850. At least six of eleven persons who can be identified as anticourt activists (speaking or circulating petitions) were slaveowners in 1850. But the procourt group was almost certainly wealthier. Of nine identifiable procourt activists, seven were slaveowners in 1850, and the average values of both their slaveholdings and their real-estate holdings were greater than those of their opponents.²⁹ The dispute over the siting of the county seat and its important legal functions, therefore, represented in part a clash of larger planters against smaller farmers. The losers were convinced that the Savannah river interests had subverted majority rule with an exercise of "unjust and despotic power." The losers resemble those yeomen in the upcountry who, according to historian Steven Hahn, fought wealthy patrons of railroad and commercial development on the grounds that the benefits of development would largely favor commercial planters.³⁰

These scattered expressions of conflict show that class issues could surface in white political life. They do not necessarily mean that resentment against wealth or privilege ever advanced so far as to threaten an institution so fundamental to southern society as slavery itself. That could have happened only if the poor whites and "yeomen" farmers had come to see their poverty or lack of greater success as somehow directly connected to slavery. At times, slavery's defenders in the Augusta area had their doubts about the ultimate political loyalty of nonslaveholders. "Sweet Home," a correspondent of the Edgefield *Advertiser*, revealed perhaps more than he intended when he complained that local slave masters exhibited signs of "luxury, ignorance, and degeneracy" and that their "lordly pride and haughty disdain" affected relations with poorer neighbors and drove away small farmers and mechanics.[31] The editor of the Augusta *Constitutionalist* charged, in 1851, that Union party candidate Howell Cobb owed his election as governor to votes of nonslaveholders who secretly opposed slavery. His counterpart at the Augusta *Chronicle* vigorously disputed the charge, but admitted that "slavery is indeed a 'doomed institution' when an anti-slavery party exists in the heart of its territory."[32]

To many slaveholders in the 1850s, one of the most alarming aspects of the growing antislavery agitation in the North was a political appeal by abolitionists to southern white nonslaveholders. The most famous abolitionist appeal to nonslaveowners in the South was *The Impending Crisis of the South*, published in 1857 by Hinton Rowan Helper, son of a middling North Carolina farmer.[33] Helper bitterly denounced slaveowners. Buttressing his case with elaborate statistical comparisons of northern and southern states, he declared that slavery had blighted southern society and had allowed the North to progress far in advance in all the arts of civilization. The result was "unparalleled illiteracy" and "degradation" among the great majority of southern whites, who often were worse off than slaves. The slaveholding "oligarchy" had kept power in the South only by their "demagogical manoeverings" and "intrigues and tricks of legerdemain." Nonslaveholders were granted only a "cunningly devised mockery of freedom"; for "all intents and purposes they are disfranchised, and outlawed." As a result, the "lords of the lash" were "the oracles and arbiters of all non-slaveholding whites, whose freedom is merely nominal."[34]

Helper proposed a detailed plan for nonslaveholders to organize politically and make sure that "no slavocrat should, in the future, be elected to any office whatever." The new parties would proscribe slaveholders socially and would immediately lay a tax of $60 on every slave, which would be used to colonize blacks in Africa, Central America, or the West. Helper suggested an immediate convention of nonslaveholders to organize their party.[35] His shrewd coupling of abolition and colonization was designed to appeal precisely to men such as John Pool, who despised both slaveholders and slaves.

Helper's argument seemed potentially effective to some southerners. In 1860, on the eve of Abraham Lincoln's election, the New Orleans *Daily Delta* editorialized that should a Republican be elected to the presidency, his party would soon have "followers and sympathizers" in every southern state, and "the arguments of Helper's infamous book" would be "reproduced in the South. . . . Let us beware of the day when the struggle shall be transferred to our own land; when the slavery question shall . . . become a domestic question; armies of our enemies shall be recruited from our own forces."[36]

Helper's appeal was only the most famous, not the first, made to nonslaveholders. Eight years before, at the height of the national conflict over the disposition of territories won in the Mexican War, a pamphlet with a similar theme had appeared over the pseudonym "Brutus" in Edgefield district and elsewhere in South Carolina. (The Spartanburg *Spartan* attributed the pamphlet to William H. Brisbane, formerly a Baptist minister in the state, who had gone north about ten years earlier.)[37]

"Brutus" championed South Carolina's white poor against the "favored aristocrat," and never mentioned slavery; but his message was plain enough. "This state is said to have a republican form of government. It may be the *form*, but the substance is wanting. . . . [T]he great mass of the people are virtually disfranchised." This inequality in political power served to protect the interests of the large rice and cotton planters at the expense of those who "have to work with their own hands." "What can the poor man do here?" "Brutus" asked. "He can make nothing to lay up for his family. He cannot get his children educated. He and his family are doomed to poverty and ignorance, and to the contempt of the favored aristocrat."

Like Helper, "Brutus" called for a popular political movement to "teach the masters of overgrown plantations that we cannot always endure this state of things." The goal of the movement, he concluded, must be to force the adoption of a new state constitution, "in which the interests of the *free* laborer shall be provided for."

Politicians, orators, and editors in Augusta's hinterlands were quick to deny the claims of such writers as Helper and "Brutus." As a Wilkes county legislator put it in 1850, on the subject of slavery, "the people knew no party distinctions."[38] Or, as the editor of the Augusta *Chronicle* argued, "Away with the idea that the interests of slaveholders and nonslaveholders in the South are not identical. They are so in fact, and in the feeling of all classes."[39]

At the same time, southern leaders attempted to respond to such charges by showing poor whites that slavery promoted their economic well-being—demonstrating, in the process, that the threats of Helper were taken seriously. Francis W. Pickens, for example, appealed to the poor of Edgefield district in a speech in 1851. He said, "Mr. Chairman! has any man thought seriously of the terrible effects of abolition when brought to our homes and to our firesides? Three millions of black slaves, turned lose [loose] upon the community . . . would work for little or nothing—a bottle of rum and twist of tobacco; what would become of the free artizans, enterprising mechanics, and industrious laborers of our country?"[40]

As slaveowners recognized, however, nonslaveholders did not always see the logic of this argument. Slaves, after all, were already competing with white artisans and laborers. Perhaps other whites would turn their anger about competition with slaves into anger about competition with slave masters, as did Pool. Anger based on competition did produce at least the germ of an antislavery movement among the whites most directly threatened by slave competition—the skilled artisans. In Georgia, as in other southern states, "mechanics' associations" in several places, including Augusta, agitated for laws that would severely restrict the rights of free blacks, and even slaves, to work as artisans.[41] The associations never went so far as to attack slavery itself, but individuals did. Their bitterness is evident in a letter to Alexander H. Stephens from B. C. Warner, a former resident of Macon. Warner wrote in 1861 from an army camp in Mississippi, objecting forcefully to that part of the new Confederate constitution that allowed slavery into territories without restriction. According to Warner, the constitution should read instead, "In All Such territory the Institution of Negro Slavery Shall Exist and Be used as Meneals and For Menial Labor only[;] That Negro Slaves Shall Not Be alowed to work in the Arts of Mechanism." There were thousands of mechanics willing to defend the Confederacy, Warner told Stephens, but slaveowners must not make mechanics of their slaves: "We want A Stop put to it peaceably if we Can Forcebly if we Must. . . . the poore Man Has the same Right to protect Life Liberty and property as the Rich Man." To make the implication of his complaint perfectly clear, Warner added that "white Men is Free and Equal in this Country[,] or at least the Constitution and Laws sayes so[,] this Being the Case we Must Not Make the Negro Equal to one portion of white Men Without Making them Equal to All."[42]

Slaveowners recognized that it was not always obvious to non-slaveholders just how their own interest was involved in the system. Hence they emphasized a purely racist argument for slavery. "It is African slavery," according to a Georgia newspaper editorial quoted in the Edgefield *Advertiser*, "that makes every white man in some sense a lord. . . . Here the division is between white free men and black slaves, and every white is, and feels that he is a MAN."[43] The *Advertiser's* editor added his own comment. If slavery were abolished, the poor would be degraded into a condition of equality with blacks. "Insolent free negroes would thrust themselves into [poor whites'] society and make proposals of marriage with their sons and daughters."[44]

Sexual contact was one thing for poor whites to fear; and, as Pickens insisted, violence was another. Abolition, he told his 1851 Edgefield audience, would "convert this land of happiness into scenes of universal blood, and then finally, into a barbarian wilderness. Let no man hug to himself the fatal delusion that he is too poor to feel the withering blight of that dreadful curse, if it should come."[45]

Racist arguments tapped a deep well in white southern culture. The racism of men like James Henry Hammond lent authenticity to their appeals to poor whites for support. Yet slaveowners did not always welcome the ways in which racism appeared among the poor, for example, as interracial violence, including attacks by nonslaveowning whites on slaves. It is one of the many ironies of southern slavery that such attacks, fostered by a racism crucial to the system, sometimes appeared to slaveowners as attacks on their own interests and prerogatives, and even on their claims about the essential benevolence of slavery.

Racial violence was common enough, but the motives behind it are rarely so apparent as in a case brought to the attention of Linton and Alexander Stephens in 1854. William Schley, Jr., of Augusta, wrote to the Stephens brothers to ask their help in a "vigorous prosecution" of John Raley and his father, both of Warren county. (This was probably the John Raley listed in the 1860 census as a twenty-seven-year-old farmer, with a farm worth $1,000 but no slaves.) London, a slave belonging to a Mr. McAlpin, had been sent on an errand to recover two stray mules, one of which belonged to William Schley's relative, Robert Schley. Although London had a proper pass, the Raleys had brutally beaten and whipped him. William Schley enclosed a letter written by John Raley to defend his actions. London, wrote Raley, "acted more like a white man and him Drunk than a negro—I ordered him to strip and he said that he did not have to do that for his Master, let alone other people, beside a great deal of other talk[.] he had acted very improper indeed, and so upon these grounds I taken the liberty of whipping him, for his misconduct, he was very impudent."[46]

Such behavior was not simply an economic threat to a slaveowner's property, nor even just a threat to his self-esteem as a benevolent master. More significantly, it raised the specter that many poor whites might turn their racial resentment of blacks against the owners of blacks. The gravest threat from Helper's appeal was that it married racism and class resentment in just this way.

The opinions of mechanics such as B. C. Warner carried little weight in an overwhelmingly rural and agricultural society. Far more important were the attitudes of white laborers and yeoman farmers. Their political importance hinged on their numbers, in the first place, and on their opinions, in the second. Their opinions, in turn, depended partly on how they saw themselves in a society with masters and black slaves. To Hinton Rowan Helper, nonslaveholders were a vast majority living in abject and degrading poverty. An examination of the divisions of wealth and the structure of opportunity in Augusta's hinterlands can reveal the raw demographic potential for an antislavery "party" there.

If we take as a rough indication of a poor family one with no real property, about 30 to 40 percent of all white families in Augusta's hinterlands were poor in 1860. Probably a more reasonable guide is the ownership of little or no property of any kind. By this criterion, if we take $250 worth of property as a cutoff point, somewhat fewer families—ranging from 19 to 38 percent in four counties sampled—would be classified as poor (see Table 8).

Laborers, tenant farmers, and women in factory or other semi-skilled work accounted for most of the household heads among the poor. David Lewis, a Hancock county planter, who wrote in 1859 that it was "a boast among the common people that they did not have to hire out in order to make a living,"[47] was wrong. John Pool was not the only white man in Hancock county who earned his keep by simple manual labor. In 1860, more than 150 whites, or almost one-sixth of all working adults, were farm laborers there.[48] Many lived with parents. After marriage, they became farm operators themselves. Although many eventually bought or inherited land, many other manual laborers had to support families on meager and uncertain earnings. In some counties, such as Taliaferro, only a few were in this difficult

Table 8. Household Heads by Property Owned in Augusta's Hinterlands, 1860

Value of property ($)	Glascock County (N = 325) (%)	Hart County (N = 346) (%)	Taliaferro County (N = 336) (%)
	REAL ESTATE		
0	42	40	29
1–249	5	4	3
250–1,499	33	35	30
1,500–9,999	20	20	34
10,000+	1	1	4
	ALL PROPERTY		
0	14	21	10
1–249	22	16	9
250–1,499	29	27	19
1,500–9,999	28	31	37
10,000+	8	6	25

SOURCE: Household Sample from the manuscript returns of the United States Bureau of the Census, 1860.
NOTE: See Appendix A for detailed description. Percentages may not add to 100 due to rounding. Household head is the first person listed for each dwelling.

position, but in Glascock county, one out of eight white households was headed by a laborer (see Table 1, p. 21). White farm laborers worked much like black slaves—plowing, chopping, and picking on someone else's land. They could not, of course, be whipped for poor work or disobedience, but they could be summarily dismissed. They were not economically independent.

One of the few documents that offer a glimpse of a white farm laborer is the farm journal of Benton Miller. In 1859, Miller hired Joseph Renfrow as a live-in laborer. In the daily entries of farm work for that year, Renfrow cannot be distinguished from Miller's slaves on the basis of work performed. Renfrow plowed and planted alongside Harry and Clark in the spring, and picked cotton with them in the autumn. On May 6, Miller wrote that "Jo pretended to split out middles [with the plow] in No 5 all day. Jo is doing badly now."[49] Nowhere in his journal did Miller criticize his slaves so strongly.

Many farm operators were propertyless tenants. The importance of antebellum tenantry has been obscured by the growth in tenant farming after the Civil War.[50] Even before the war, tenants worked a significant proportion of all farms—one-tenth in South Carolina's Edgefield district, for example, and almost one-quarter in Hart county.[51] Like laborers, some were tenants only temporarily, working portions of parents' or in-laws' plantations and ultimately coming into a share of the family property. (Miller was technically a tenant, since the land he worked belonged to his father-in-law, although Miller paid no rent on the farm.) But many other tenants had no such prospects.

A revealing letter from a poor renter in Taliaferro county to Alexander H. Stephens shows how trapped a tenant could feel. "Dear Sir," wrote Wilie Poortwood, "I am determ to try to make som outher Way of trying to liv and aultho I hav not pade you all that I owe yet I intend to doo it[.] [I] cannot make eney thing[;] I am on a nother man['s] land and cannot hav eney thing only what he ses and Whare he ses." Poortwood asked Stephens to sell him on credit "a little cornor of land the som of thirty achors [acres]. . . . I Will pay you for it and I Want you to hold it until I pay you for it."[52] Clearly Poortwood was feeling some of that "dependence, if not inferiority" that Arthur Simkins had blamed on "the relation of landlord and tenant."[53] In a poignant closing comment, he wrote, "I Want a home for my Wife and little babys to have that no one can run them a Way from and to hav land enuff to bery them on Without intruding on mine or her connections in eney Way."

Emily Burke in the 1840s visited a poor woman "in the interior of Georgia," probably Burke county.

> I found this woman living in a small log house, very neat, but there was nothing belonging to it, to which the term comfortable could be applied. She had a bed, a table, two or three benches that were used instead of chairs and a very little crockery. The kitchen was a separate little building, of course scantily supplied with cooking utensils. The entertainment she prepared for me, while I sat with her in her little kitchen on a stool, consisted of coffee without sugar, fried bacon and corn bread mixed with water only. She had neither vegetables, butter, or any other condiment we consider essential to any repast. In the course of the afternoon she showed me a roll of cloth she had just taken from the loom, which she told me, was all the product of her own hard labor, commencing with the cotton seed. On inquiring if she could not pur-

chase cloth much cheaper than she could manufacture it, she replied, "she could if her time was worth anything, but there was no labor she could perform that would bring her any money."[54]

The diary of John H. Cornish, the Anglican minister in Aiken, South Carolina, includes several portraits of poor families. In January 1849, he visited the Blalock family, whose daughter was "very sick." "The family," Cornish wrote, "has a bad reputation. The Mother loves the Bottle—all of them are totally ignorant." The daughter told Cornish that she could not read, had never prayed, and did not know the Lord's Prayer. Six years later, Sarah Blalock—perhaps the same daughter—was dying. Cornish visited her frequently, and in February, he baptized her. On April 23, a week before Sarah died, Cornish gave her communion and wrote that "many very poor people were gathered around the head of that poor sick girl in the hovel where she is lying. The scene was awfully solemn."[55]

Gertrude Thomas's diary provides another glimpse of the life of the poor. In 1856, she visited her cousin Eliza Anthony Thomas, who had run away and married without her mother's permission. "We found Cousin Eliza living in one of the rudest huts with a mud chimney to it, Not near so good a house as our kitchen. The house had one room in it, very plainly furnished. . . . She evidently felt mortified at the extreme plainness of everything."[56]

Visiting Swedish actress Fredrika Bremer left a happier portrait of a poor "clay eater" she visited in Richmond county in 1850. Mr. G., as she called him, lived in a newly built "shed" in the piny woods with a "pitifully thin" wife and several "beautiful" children. To Mrs. Bremer, this "freeman in the wild forest" seemed "proud as a king" and "delighted with his world, with himself, his children, and in particular with his wife."[57]

It is not clear from Bremer's description whether Mr. G. owned land. If so, his status was already one step above that of the poorest whites. Even educated and perceptive northerners, such as the traveler Frederick Law Olmsted in the 1850s, argued that propertyless families formed the majority of all whites in the "plantation districts."[58] This contention was untrue for the Augusta region. Farm owners' families made up the solid majority of the white population. It is difficult to divide them into ranks, and it seems doubtful that southerners had clear criteria for doing so. If slave ownership marked true prosperity or success, the successful would have included a substantial majority of families in the Black Belt county of Taliaferro, a small majority in South Carolina's Edgefield district, and about one-quarter of those in Georgia's Glascock and Hart counties. Another substantial proportion of families owned land, but no slaves. Or, if we use an arbitrary criterion such as the ownership of at least $1,500 worth of property in all forms to rank families, then about one-quarter to one-third of families owned at least that much, and about the same proportion owned between $250 and $1,500 worth of property (see Table 8, p. 78).

These respectable, if not prosperous, families included most skilled artisans and owners of small farms. Cornish visited several of these "plain folk" near Aiken, South Carolina. Among them were Joshua Barton, his wife, and their five children. None of the seven was baptized, and none could read or write "distinctly." Yet, according to Cornish, "Tho' poor, they seem to be in comfortable circumstances, cleanly, neat & tidy & industrious." Another was John Plunkett, a miller. When Cornish preached at the funeral of Plunkett's son William, the fifty or sixty persons present enjoyed "a feast in its way," with pork and beef, potpie, peach pie, turnips, corn- and wheat bread, coffee, and persimmon beer.[59] Most small farmers lived in plain frame houses, with perhaps two rooms on the ground floor, a shed extending behind, and, for large families, two more rooms upstairs. Inventories of property taken at their deaths usually list a horse or a mule, a few farm implements, a few pieces of furniture, and perhaps a feather bed and a Bible.[60]

Some accumulated more. In his farm journal, Miller listed (with some pride, we might imagine) 163 items in an "Inventory of what is in B. H. Miller's Plantation for the Year 1858." Besides Mary, Clark, and Harry, the list included two "feather Beads," one silver caster, one "watches (gold)," numerous items of furniture, dishes, tools, and, among several drugs, a bottle of "stricknine."[61] Benjamin Paschal, of Wilkes county, was also relatively prosperous. He sold fifteen or twenty bales of cotton in 1856. In letters to his sister-in-law Martha Shank of Alabama, he mixed farm news with social notes, describing a muscadine and candy-pulling party, a serenade, and a husking party in the neighborhood. Paschal may have been an important member at social gatherings, since he also had the time and the money ($6) to invest in attending a local "fiddling school."[62]

The southern "gentry" was not mythical, although numbers were small. Again, no clear dividing line separates the gentry from the rest of white families. If $10,000 worth of property is the dividing line, the gentry included about 25 percent of families in Taliaferro county. A more stringent criterion would be the possession of $10,000 worth of real estate; this group would include 1 or 2 percent of white families in poorer Hart and Glascock counties, and 5 or 10 percent in Taliaferro and Hancock counties or Edgefield district. In predominantly slave counties, in other words, the truly wealthy formed a significantly higher proportion of the white population. Ownership of that much land almost always meant ownership of many slaves. Hancock's fifty-six planters with more than $10,000 worth of real property in 1860 all owned slaves; the average number of slaves was fifty-five.[63]

The life of a rich planter's family was naturally quite different from the life of a small farmer's. The rich could travel north or to Europe; some filled their homes with luxury goods; all enjoyed the attentions of house slaves. Rich planters' children could be indulged with expensive clothing, expensive horses, and expensive educations. When James Henry Hammond built a new mansion, Redcliffe, as a suitable site for his library, sculpture, and aristocratic taste, the cost overrun alone was $2,500.[64]

Still, many wealthy planter families never knew aristocratic luxury. Their houses were rarely the Greek Revival mansions of myth. More often, they were ramshackle frame structures that had expanded along with incomes and family size, with perhaps an imposing set of columns added on one side in the prosperous 1850s. A wide central hall was usually the echo of an original two-room, double-frame house or log cabin with a breezeway down the middle. A visitor described Liberty Hall, the Alexander Stephens estate, as an "old wooden house" in a grove of original forest trees, surrounded by untrimmed weeds—and Stephens owned thirty-two slaves in 1860. Parker Callaway, who owned eighty-nine slaves in Wilkes county in 1850, lived with his family in an unpretentious four-room frame house. David Dickson, a famous agricultural reformer and by repute the richest man in Georgia, lived in a small, simple frame house on his Hancock county plantation.[65]

The gap between rich and poor whites in Augusta's hinterlands may have been no greater than it was elsewhere in the United States. The rich everywhere live well, and the poor do not. Southern apologists, while unable to deny altogether that some white southerners were poor, vigorously disputed northerners' claims that the South was filled with a huge number of miserable "white trash." The white masses in the South, they proclaimed, were infinitely better off than were what James Henry Hammond called the North's "hordes of semi-barbarian emigrants." "You meet more beggars in one day, in any single street of the city of New York," he declared in the Senate, "than you would meet in a lifetime in the whole South."[66]

Both critics and defenders could have pointed to certain statistics to back up their points. Certainly, wealth was divided unequally among white southerners. In the Augusta area, for example, the richest tenth of all household heads typically owned half the real estate (as measured by value) and more of the total property in each county (see Table 9). Furthermore, a substantial share of all families owned less than $100 worth of property of all kinds. Yet this skewed distribution was not very different from the distribution in some northern communities. According to one measure of the overall distribution of wealth, called the Gini index,* counties in the Augusta area had a distribution less

---

*This measure falls on a scale from 0 to 1. The Gini index of 0 for wealth holding would indicate perfect equality, with every family or individual owning an equal amount of property. The higher the index, the more unequal the property distribution. The index would be 1 if a single family or individual owned all

Table 9. Measures of Wealth Distribution in Augusta's
Hinterlands, 1860

Category	Glascock County (N = 325)	Hart County (N = 346)	Taliaferro County (N = 336)	Edgefield District (N = 3007)
WEALTH OF HOUSEHOLD HEADS				
Real Estate				
Mean ($)	987	997	2,009	3,519
Median ($)	300	500	1,000	809
With none (%)	42	40	29	38
Share of richest tenth (%)	53	53	51	*
Total Wealth				
Mean ($)	2,773	2,515	7,334	12,124
Median ($)	700	800	2,900	*
With none (%)	14	21	10	*
Share of richest tenth (%)	64	60	47	*

GINI INDEX OF INEQUALITY, TOTAL WEALTH

Glascock County	.76	Wisconsin farmers	.45
Hart County	.75	Ohio farmers	.44
Taliaferro County	.67	Wisconsin	.75
Augusta, Georgia	.85	Milwaukee, Wisconsin	.89

SOURCES: Georgia and South Carolina: Georgia counties from samples from the manuscript returns of the United States Bureau of the Census, 1860; Vernon O. Burton, "Unfaithful Servants? Edgefield's Black Reconstruction: Part I of the Total History of Edgefield County, South Carolina" (Ph.D. diss., Princeton University, 1976), 203. Wisconsin and Milwaukee: Lee Soltow, *Patterns of Wealthholding in Wisconsin Since 1850* (Madison: University of Wisconsin Press, 1971), 9, 63. Wisconsin and Ohio farmers: Gavin Wright, *The Political Economy of the Cotton South: Households, Markets, and Wealth in the Nineteenth Century* (New York: Norton, 1978), 26.
*Data not available.

equal than that in some rural areas of the old Northwest, but more equal than that in northern cities. Not surprisingly, antislavery advocates usually were comparing the rural South with their ideal images of the rural North—full of neat farmhouses, surrounded by neat fences, and dotted with neat small towns.[67] Southerners like Hammond, at the same time, preferred to identify the North with its cities, teeming with their "hordes of semi-barbarian" inhabitants. Hammond was correct that prop-

---

the property. For a fuller explanation of the Gini index and a description of the computer program used to calculate it here, see James P. Whittenburg and Randall G. Pemberton, "Measuring Inequality: A Fortran Program for the Gini Index, Schutz Coefficient, and Lorenz Curves," *Historical Methods Newsletter* 10 (1977): 77–82.

erty was distributed more equally among white southerners than among northern city dwellers.[68]

Differences in wealth and status may not seem the same to a man who feels trapped at the bottom and to another who expects to move up. Slavery's apologists insisted that white poverty in the South resulted, not from the structure of a slaveholding society, but from variations in talent and worth found among any group of human beings. South Carolina's William Harper, in a well-known proslavery essay republished in 1860 in Augusta, wrote that "among us, we know that there is no one, however humble his beginning, who, with persevering industry, intelligence, and orderly and virtuous habits, may not attain to considerable opulence."[69]

As young men looked around at their older neighbors, they could find evidence for Harper's assertions; the average wealth of household heads increased regularly with age, at least until late middle age. In Taliaferro county, for example, household heads in their twenties owned, on average, property worth $2,444 in 1860; those in their thirties were worth $4,782; those over fifty typically owned more than $12,000 in property. In Hart and Glascock counties, absolute levels of wealth were lower, but the pattern was the same. (See Table 10, p. 86. The drop-off in wealth at older ages was quite probably due to the transfer of slaves and land to children as gifts when the children married or reached adulthood.)

This is only one measure of what was, in fact, a remarkable social fluidity in Augusta's rural hinterlands. The fluidity is clearest when we examine the careers of individuals. Of a sample of about 500 household heads in three Georgia counties in 1860, more than one-quarter had moved into their current counties since 1850, even though the area had experienced a substantial net outmigration during the decade. These newcomers were most often poorer than their more stable neighbors, and more likely than those neighbors to be laborers, artisans, or professionals.[70] Many undoubtedly had moved in search of greater economic opportunity; studies of mobility in nineteenth-century America have shown consistently that the poorer a man was, the

Table 10. Mean Wealth of Household Heads, by Age, in Augusta's
Hinterlands, 1860

Age of House- hold Head	Total ($)	Real ($)	Slaves
Glascock County			
20–29	1,263	464	.5
30–39	1,977	818	.9
40–49	4,394	1,864	3.0
50–59	2,810	933	1.9
60+	9,775	2,706	7.7
Hart County			
20–29	829	397	.5
30–39	1,589	802	.9
40–49	4,079	1,579	3.1
50–59	3,813	1,778	2.3
60+	3,797	1,014	3.1
Taliaferro County			
20–29	2,444	462	3.0
30–39	4,787	1,271	5.0
40–49	8,254	2,196	8.6
50–59	12,508	3,819	10.1
60+	13,391	4,075	13.2

SOURCE: Household Sample from the manuscript returns of the United States Bureau of the Census, 1860.
NOTE: See Appendix A for detailed description.

more likely he was to be a migrant.[71] Many of these migrants
never found success. Gertrude Thomas's diary records one visit
to a cousin who since her marriage had moved "once in Georgia.
Then to Alabama and back again to Georgia." Each time, Mrs.
Thomas recorded, "they have worsted themselves."[72]

The difficulties of tracing such people precludes a detailed
analysis of their long-term successes and failures. Perhaps geographic mobility reduced the possibility that these people would
form the base of political opposition to a slaveholding regime.
In any case, newcomers in the three counties sampled were by
no means universally poor. In every county, some owned slaves;
in every county, newcomers owned, on average, at least $1,000
worth of property.

Among more permanent residents, social mobility (that is, a
change of occupation or wealth) was normal, and in the 1850s,
most of that mobility was up, not down. Most people did not
reach Harper's "opulence," but many did rise—to the ownership

of a farm, a few slaves, or even a large plantation. Among the approximately 353 household heads who could be traced back to 1850 census records, for example, were some 32 men who were overseers, artisans, or laborers, or who were the sons of overseers, artisans, or laborers. In 1860, at least 10 of these 32 were farmers. Ninety-five (or about one-quarter of the total) were either landless farmers or the sons of landless farmers in 1850; by 1860, 43 of these 95 were landowners. Twelve of the 95 owned at least $1,500 worth of land in 1860 (see Tables 11 and 21).

Slaveholding, too, was within reach of at least some poorer

Table 11. Social Mobility of Men in Augusta's Hinterlands, 1850–1860

| | OCCUPATIONS | | | | |
| | | Occupation, 1850 | | | |
Occupation, 1860	Farmer	Nonmanual	Manual*	Other	Total
Farmer	151	5	8	3	167
Nonmanual	1	6	1	0	8
Manual*	11	0	16	1	28
Other	2	0	0	1	3
TOTAL	165	11	25	5	206

| | SLAVE OWNERSHIP | | | | |
| | | Slaves Owned, 1850 | | | |
Slaves Owned, 1860	0	1–4	5–10	11+	Total
0	93	6	1	0	100
1–4	20	22	5	0	47
5–10	9	6	7	4	26
11+	0	1	9	22	32
TOTAL	122	35	22	26	205

| | REAL ESTATE ($) | | | |
| | | Real Estate, 1850 ($) | | |
Real Estate, 1860 ($)	0	1–1,499	1,500+	Total
0	40	9	1	50
1–1,499	26	49	4	79
1,500	11	29	40	80
TOTAL	77	87	45	219

SOURCE: Family Sample from the manuscript returns of the United States Bureau of the Census, 1860.
NOTE: See Appendix A for detailed description. Includes men from Glascock, Hart, and Taliaferro counties who headed households or who were boarders in 1850 and 1860. Numbers vary due to missing data.
*Manual workers include overseers, skilled artisans, and laborers.

men. Of the 353 persisting household heads, 166 owned no slaves in 1850. By 1860, 32 of these 166 were slaveowners. While most of them lived in Taliaferro county, nonslaveholders in all three counties had become slaveholders over the decade (see Table 20, p. 204).[73]

The paths to land- or slaveownership were many. Some men, no doubt, had simply come into an inheritance. Others had married well, and marriage frequently united slaveowning and nonslaveowning families. Benton Miller, for example, may have received his three slaves as a gift from his new father-in-law.[74] Hammond had successfully courted his future wife with an eye on the large fortune in land and slaves he stood to receive as her husband.[75] Still other men earned their opportunities. Alexander H. Stephens had been left an orphan, with a legacy of a few hundred dollars, in the 1820s. By dint of talent, hard work, and some timely assistance from local relatives and planters, he had by 1860 accumulated an estate of thirty-two slaves.[76] And every man who did rise served as an example of the possibilities open to whites in a slave society.

Yet if some rose, others fell—a point also demonstrated by the patterns of mobility. Sixteen farmers or farmers' sons in the 1850 sample were overseers, artisans, or laborers ten years later. Six of these sixteen had been tenant farmers in 1850; they had clearly failed to become independent farmers. An example of such a failed career is that of David R. Ware, a landless farmer who came to Hancock county about 1840. He rented land from wealthy Andrew J. Lane, and by hard work and clever management, he built up a thriving livestock enterprise. By 1850, he owned five horses, twenty-four head of cattle, and a hundred pigs and hogs. The year before, he had raised three bales of cotton in addition to large food crops. In 1852, Ware was forced off his land after a chimney spark set fire to his house. Lane, the landlord, observed that "he parted from the place with many regrets and much reluctance." By 1860, Ware had "moved to another place where there was no pasture and his livestock [had] dwindled to nothing"; the census taker that year listed him as a farm laborer.[77]

Aside from those falling in occupation, at least ten landowners in the 1850 sample had lost their land by 1860. Perhaps most sig-

Table 12. Social Mobility and Slavery: Slaveholdings of Men in 1860
Compared with Parents in 1850

Slaves Owned by Son, 1860	Slaves Owned by Parent, 1850			
	0	1–10	11+	Total
0	41	12	0	53
1–10	3	9	18	30
11+	0	0	1	1
TOTAL	44	21	19	84

SOURCE: Family sample from the manuscript returns of the United States Bureau of the Census, 1850 and 1860.

NOTE: See Appendix A for detailed description. Data from Glascock, Hart, and Taliaferro counties; see Appendix B for county-by-county tables.

nificant for its potential political impact, of forty-four sons of nonslaveholders in 1850, only three had become slaveholders by 1860. Meanwhile, 30 percent (twelve out of forty) of the sons of slaveholders in 1850 were nonslaveholders ten years later (see Table 12).

The mobility of wealth is especially striking when we examine changes in slaveownership during the depressed decade of the 1840s. In Taliaferro and Warren counties, 271 household heads in 1850 can be traced back to the 1840 census, which also lists slaveholdings. (See Appendix A for the hazards of using these sources.) In 1840, 119 of these men and women were nonslaveholders, and during the next decade, 20 of these had become owners of slaves. Over the same time, 24 slaveowners had lost their slaves. Thus the proportion of nonslaveholders in the overall sample of stable household heads had remained essentially unchanged.[78] Obviously, there was great fluidity at the margins of the slaveholding class—those owning one or two slaves. A bad crop year, an unfortunate death, or a simple lack of talent for farming could easily move a man from master of slaves to nonslaveowning farmer. Meanwhile, the average number of slaves owned had increased. The total population of slaves was slowly growing, but the population of *owners* of slaves remained steady. Most slaveowners could count on growing slowly wealthier just because of natural increase among slaves. Most nonslaveowners were likely to remain nonslaveowners.

The dynamics of social mobility indicated especially by these statistics on slaveholding means that class lines must have been remarkably blurred to the people behind the numbers, who lived, worked, hoped, despaired—and answered questions when the census taker came around. It was obvious to Wilie Poortwood that he and Alexander H. Stephens were of different "classes." But it was always difficult to know just where one "class" left off and another began. No hard and fast distinction could be drawn between landowner and tenant, for many tenants did become landowners. Nor did any sharp line divide slaveowner and nonslaveowner. Miller in his fields spent many days doing exactly the kinds of physical labor done by thousands of farmers with only sons or hired hands to help. Similarly, the line between farmer and planter, laborer and tenant, even artisan and farmer were not always clear, since people on either side of the line were often more alike than different, and may have spent some time on both sides.

At the same time, no southerner could deny that there were many poor whites among the plantations. And unlike a free-labor society, a slave society provided an unmistakable badge of success in the form of the ownership of black people. The clarity of this badge always left open the possibility that the white South might divide in some decisive way—not just into whites and blacks, but also into slaveowners and nonslaveowners—and that nonslaveowners might turn against those who had what they could not have. All the time, the proportion of nonslaveowners was growing in the heart of this plantation economy. In the face of ferocious attacks from outsiders, and an ever-present restlessness among slaves, it was no wonder that anxious members of the slaveholding elite listened hard for murmurs of discontent among their nonslaveholding neighbors.

Slave masters worried about two ways in which white class subdivisions and resentments might fuel opposition to slavery. On the one hand, racial antagonism—endemic in southern culture and encouraged by slaveholders—might turn into antagonism against those who owned blacks. On the other hand, whites might turn against slavery from a natural sympathy arising from overlapping ways of life. White laborers and poorer farmers already worked much like black slaves. If, in addition, they could sleep with slaves, drink with slaves, steal with slaves, and even murder with slaves, might they not someday join with slaves in overturning bondage itself? Sympathy for black slaves did appear occasionally among nonslaveholders. A Taliaferro county farmer, for example, was convicted in 1859 of harboring a runaway slave for three months.[79] In Greene county, according to "A friend" who wrote to Alexander H. Stephens in 1860, one William Freeman (who may have been educated at Stephens's expense) was "trifling" with local slaves. "[W]e have known of his being drunk," this anonymous correspondent began, "but we never intended to medle with it until other things come to light[.] he gives Negrows passes goes in the old fields and woods on Sundays and is teaching them to write and cipher[.] I do hope you will take him from this neighborhood."[80]

Some southerners thought that the occasional expressions of discontent portended greater trouble. J. Henly Smith, a young political protégé of Stephens (and not a slaveowner himself), wrote to Stephens several times in regard to his concerns about the ultimate loyalties of southern plain folk. If the Republicans ever won control of the national government, he wrote in 1860, "they will form a party and have adherents and supporters all over the South—in every state. . . . The nonslaveholders will very generally adhere to the new party, and slavery will be crushed out forever."[81] Smith worried that too many southerners were like "A Minuteman," who wrote to the Edgefield *Advertiser* on the eve of South Carolina's secession, suggesting that every large slaveowner sell one in ten slaves, on credit, to a nonslaveowning neighbor, and thereby "make *interest* supply the deficiency of patriotism." That he had joined a local prosecession vigilante group could not conceal the veiled threat in his letter: "Already I have seen it mentioned in Abolition journals that they have allies among the non-slave owners, of which class I am sorry to say I am; for reasons that I very much regret, I never was able to own one."[82]

Such fears were behind various schemes designed to spread

slave ownership more widely. In 1856, Governor J. A. Adams of South Carolina wanted the state legislature to exempt one slave from sale for debts to encourage poor whites to buy slaves. Others, including a vocal faction in Edgefield district, wanted to reopen the transatlantic slave trade, and argued in part that the resulting lower slave prices would help diffuse slaveownership among the poor and prevent dangerous immigration by more nonslaveholding whites.[83] As opponents of reopening the slave trade pointed out, however, more slaves might make poor whites even poorer. "If my labor is to be supplanted by that of negroes," wrote one man who described himself as "very poor," "how can I live?"[84] Nor did all of the slaveholding elite fear the plain folk. James Henry Hammond, in his enthusiasm for secession in 1850, wrote to William Gilmore Simms that "what faith & hope I have [on our southern people] rests entirely on the common people—on our non-slaveholders, much more than our political party leaders."[85]

Perhaps the role of white class divisions becomes plainer when we specify more precisely what the term *class* means. John Pool, after all, was a member of a class only in the most limited sense of the word—a convenient designation for a statistical group of the "poor" or the "nonslaveholders." A more narrow but more meaningful concept of class would restrict it to social groups based on not only a common interest, but also a common consciousness. In a famous exposition, historian E. P. Thompson has argued that a class is not a "thing" at all, but rather "class *happens* when some men, as a result of common experiences (inherited or shared), feel and articulate the identity of their interests as between themselves, and as against other men whose interests are different from (and usually opposed to) theirs."[86]

Thompson's definition allows us to see the common pattern behind Linton Stephens's complacency and Smith's anxiety about class divisions. Stephens told Hancock County's vigilance committee that "such fellows [as Pool] were to be watched and taken care of, when a conflict might be thrust upon us by a far different class of men, but that he never could *produce* the conflict nor start a first ripple towards the first wave."[87] Smith, in his letter to Alexander Stephens, argued that "if taken at the right time and under proper circumstances, the nonslaveholders of the South would come up as one man and drive back abolitionism at the point of the bayonet," a prediction that proved rather close to the mark in 1861.[88]

In Thompson's sense, and as Linton Stephens saw, Pool was not part of a class of nonslaveholders, because there was none. At the same time, as Smith saw, the poverty and anger of men such as John Pool, James Darnal, B. C. Warner, and others among "agrarianism's sons" might be the elements for creating such a class. What worried Smith and many others was that class might "*happen*," that nonslaveholders at the wrong time and under the wrong circumstances might no longer feel part of a community of all white men.

ぞ Chapter 4

Ligaments of Community

In 1857, David C. Barrow ran for election as state senator from Oglethorpe county. His first task was to win nomination by his own Democratic party. An open, mass meeting would ostensibly make the nomination at the county courthouse in May. Barrow's chief opponent was another wealthy slaveowner, Dr. Willis Willingham, one of many Whigs who had followed Alexander H. Stephens and Robert Toombs into the Georgia Democratic party after the demise of the Whig party. The 1857 race was Barrow's first, and his politically experienced brother-in-law William McKinley came north from Baldwin county to offer his advice. A revealing letter to Barrow summarizes McKinley's observations.[1]

Stating his conclusions first, McKinley urged Barrow "*at once,* to appear daily at the public centres," such as the courthouse, to make contact with men from other parts of the county. McKinley thought Barrow could count on fifty votes from his own neighborhood and several more from Methodists in other neighborhoods because Barrow was a prominent Methodist. Barrow should pay "immediate attention" to Archer Griffith of the "Shake Rag" neighborhood: "G's daughter boards at Willingham's but he is old panel Democrat & his district like yours is nearly unanimous & the two together form the Democratic stronghold of about 85 votes nearly 1/4 of the entire party." Hick Jackson, D. Pittard, and Griffith all hoped to win nomination to the Georgia House of Representatives. McKinley thought that Barrow's best bet would be a deal to support Griffith and Clarke, a former Whig, for the House, in return for their support of him against Willingham: "For such a concert if it please you no time

94

is to be lost. I should think it would be arranged with Clarke & yet not endanger you with Jackson & Pittard's friends, by simply *leaving Clarke & them to conflict on that point.* Keeping yourself aloof from them, but yet carrying in Wolfskin for Clarke."

"There is very active wire-pulling here," McKinley explained, and Barrow needed to nurse Lofton, one of the most powerful wire-pullers. Upson and Robinson would support Barrow; Sims was undecided; and "the Johnsons & G. Landrum I met only in mixed company & could get no satisfaction from them. . . . Jackson is now brother-in-law of the Johnsons but one of them was once son-in-law of Clarke."

This letter is interesting, not for its intricate details of political maneuver, but for its exposure of the underlying structure of local politics. Most striking is the small scale of the political arena. A few hundred voters determined the election. Success depended on a network of personal ties based on face-to-face contact. Barrow first had to rely on his neighbors, as his rivals did on theirs. Other personal ties—church membership, kinship, marriage—added to the neighborhood base. Barrow then had to gather support from the rest of the county—partly by personal campaigning, partly by striking deals with potential rivals. Here again, personal ties might be crucial—a friendship in one case, an in-law in another, an old party tie in a third. Victory finally depended on some combination of popular support and elitist ties. The balance between the two might vary; popular support might overwhelm elitist challenges, or the already powerful might propel unknowns into office. One way or another, personal ties were crucial. These ties were among the "social and political ligaments" that, one contemporary claimed, bound whites together and lent strength to slavery.[2]

One important personal tie between planters and plain folk was direct assistance in time of need. Wealthy neighbors, for example, lent food to small farmers during shortages. While historians used to describe southern planters as so highly specialized in the crops they grew that they bought food from nearby farmers, the opposite was more nearly the case. In 1855, for example, Nathan Gilbert, himself the owner of a slave, wrote to Alexander H. Stephens that he had "tried to buy Bacon every where that I thought I could possibly get [it] and have failed." His family was now "entirely without. . . . It looks like we are oblige to suffer if you do not help us. Please to do so and we will remember you in every thing."[3] A drought in 1860 badly damaged the corn crop near Augusta, and during the next winter and spring, many families faced distress. They turned for help to wealthy neighbors. In January 1861, R. B. Brodnax wrote to Stephens that because of the drought, he had "maid a short crop of corn." He asked for a loan of $20 "to help my buy sum corn and if you will I can make out to live. . . . help me if you Pleas and confer a lasting favour and will help a Poor man that is in want."[4] That same winter, David C. Barrow's overseer "let Mr Haughton have 140 Bushels of corne out of my last years crope . . . [and] I have let James H Glenn have 8 tubs of corne."[5] In May 1861, a member of the Smith family wrote to Barrow that his family was "suffering" because they "had no meat in three weeks and but little bread We have no money nor Cant get none We are all a bout to starve." Smith asked for a loan of "50 or 60 dollars if you will[,] if I dont make but just that much you shall have it. . . . if you Will lend us some money do it immediately and send it in a letter you Will oblige your suffering friends bye so doing."[6]

As this letter makes clear, much of the exchange between neighbors involved credit as well as barter. The credit might be a matter of waiting indefinitely for repayment, or it might involve signing a formal note and calculating interest. Large planters, through their ties to local banks and cotton factors, had a direct line to banks and merchants in New York, Boston, and Liverpool. They could pass credit along, either as large and small direct loans, or as credit sales to poorer men and women.[7]

The intricacies of the credit network are clear in another letter to Stephens. In 1852, Thomas Belk, a Sparta artisan, asked Stephens for a loan because he was having trouble collecting from his own customers. He was "Placed right now whare 25 dollars would Do me moore good than 50 would at the close of this year." He continued, "I have got notes and accounts a plenty if I had the money for them to serve me this year but the people say they cannot pay me for they have not made enough to feed their familys and to sue a man that is good for his contracts under those sucumstances I can not Do it with the right kind of feeling."[8]

When a Hancock county woman who worked in a textile mill needed money to buy a small house at a sheriff's sale, she went to Linton Stephens.[9] When Alex Allen was faced with a payment due on some property and was unable to collect money owed to him, he appealed to Barrow for help.[10] When Reverend E. H. Evans found himself $900 in debt to his church for advances in pay, he asked fellow Baptist—and very wealthy planter—Iveson L. Brookes to lend him that much, as his friends were "among the Baptists who are like myself poor."[11]

In Augusta's hinterlands, as elsewhere in the rural South, credit transactions were indispensable. Rural commerce would have dried up without credit because there was not enough currency, in either specie or banknotes. Notes given for purchases circulated as a substitute for money, passed from hand to hand when the debtor seemed to be a good risk.[12] These market transactions in goods, services, and credit were a form of social as well as economic exchange. Barrow, Stephens, and Brookes not only were making investments, but also were helping neighbors and friends. Payment might come in many ways, including the casting of a ballot.[13]

One indication of the social nature of some of these transactions was the slight chance of repayment. Every year, Alexander Stephens accumulated notes ranging from a few dollars to a few hundred dollars, and he often complained that he could not get people to pay up.[14] This was, no doubt, in part because he took legal clients like Edward L. Meadows, who asked Stephens to defend him in an assault case, even though he admitted that he had no money and would only try to pay Stephens later. Stephens also represented Mr. Belding, who felt obligated to defend his sister in a divorce case but was "poor . . . and not able to pay much if any fees."[15] Nor was it likely that Stephens would be repaid any money lent to Elizabeth Akins, who in March 1861 wrote him to "appeal to [your] ever readiness to relieve the distressed." Her husband had been fined $50 and jailed for thirty days for assault. "His business is neglected," the letter continued, and "without him in planning for a crop I do not know how I will be able to make bread for my children[.] I admit his falts you know his falts but be the case as it may be I wish in my heart it was otherwise[,] he is my Husband." The aid of a few dollars, she promised, "shall always be remembered by a grateful heart."[16] Linton Stephens probably did not expect to collect the money he lent to "Old Mr. Robert Bird," who, Linton wrote, was "a poor man but a working one and I never knew him to be so destitute. . . . I let him have 30 dollars to buy bread, tho' I could ill spare it."[17]

Although most planters fell short of the Stephens brothers' generosity, many lent money or services to friends and neighbors. Planters' papers mention many loans and credit sales, for amounts large and small.[18] The most systematic records of these transactions are in inventories of estates, made at death and copied into the records of county probate courts. In Glascock county, Georgia, two wealthy planters died in September 1860: the estate of John Cheeley included forty-four slaves and four notes (three from William Coleman and one from R. A. Beall), worth altogether about $1,000;[19] the estate of William Seals included twenty slaves and nineteen notes for amounts ranging from $4.55 to $450, ten for less than $30 each. Seals also left almost seventy "accounts," all but seven for less than $10 each, including one (with James Mathews) for fifteen cents. These accounts were probably with neighbors and others who had used Seals's cotton gin and press or his threshing machine.[20]

About two-thirds of the estate inventories in three counties between 1858 and 1863 included notes—individual debts owed to the estate. (See Table 13 for systematic data about debtor–creditor relationships from these inventories.)[21] Some inventories included one note, and others, almost twenty; six was average. Men and women who lent money or sold goods on credit were considerably wealthier than those who did not.

Debtors could be rich or poor (see Table 14, p. 100), laborers or artisans, small farmers or wealthy planters. Debtors tended to be wealthier than average in two counties, and poorer in one. The inventory records, however, clearly show a net flow of credit

Table 13. Notes for Debt in Estate Inventories in
Augusta's Hinterlands

Category	Glascock County (1858–1862)	Hart County (1862–1863)	Taliaferro County (1858–1861)
Number of inventories	19	21	20
Number with notes due	15	14	13
Mean debt due ($)	698	400	1,209
Mean debt due per note ($)	116	63	208
Mean debtors per inventory*	6.1	6.4	5.8
Mean wealth of creditors ($)	8,900	10,880	17,631
	(N = 12)	(N = 9)	(N = 13)
Mean wealth of those without notes in inventory	5,324	688	5,875
	(N = 3)	(N = 3)	(N = 7)

SOURCES: Records of estate inventories, GDAH; wealth from the manuscript returns of the United States Bureau of the Census, 1860.
NOTE: Excludes merchants.
*Sixteen debtors who owed notes to more than one estate are counted once for each estate.

from wealthy planters to small farmers, artisans, and the poor. Behind most notes was a face-to-face encounter, a bargain with more than economic import that often was a subtle interplay of dependence and independence. A person who asks for money, food, or favors is in some sense admitting dependence on another. When Alexander Stephens was a struggling young lawyer, he had to borrow a horse to go to a nearby town on business. After being turned down, he was "fill[ed] with mortification and a due sense of my humble dependence. There is nothing worse than to ask and be refused." He almost decided to walk rather than risk another rejection.[22] At the same time, to offer a note in exchange is to insist on ultimate independence, to demand an acknowledgment of long-term contractual equality.

To give credit may display generosity or liberality—and power. Along with payments of principal and interest, other, less tangible obligations gather around such transactions. Thomas Belk's letter (when he asked Stephens for a $25 loan) spelled out this sense of a generalized reciprocity: "If you will condecene to assist me that much this one time of need I will be under the greatest obligation to you at all times."[23]

The 1850s, to be sure, was an appropriate decade for generosity among cotton planters. Prices were high; creditors could

Table 14. Wealth of Debtors in Augusta's Hinterlands

Category	Glascock County (1858–1862)	Hart County (1862–1863)	Taliaferro County (1858–1861)
Number of inventories	19	21	20
Number of debtors*	91	84	64
Number with wealth data	48	47	42
Wealth of debtors			
Mean real estate ($)	786	1,486	2,879
Mean total wealth ($)	1,920	4,195	10,681
Mean slaves owned	1	4	9
Slaveowners (%)	27	47	76
Wealth of all household heads in county:			
Mean total wealth ($)	2,773	2,514	7,333
Slaveowners (%)	24	26	72

SOURCES: Records of estate inventories, GDAH; wealth from the manuscript returns of the United States Bureau of the Census, 1860.
*Sixteen debtors who owed notes to more than one estate are counted once for each estate.

expect to be repaid by most people eventually, and debtors could expect to carry their debts without trouble. In hard times, however, debt relationships might easily turn sour. Planters would be forced to press smaller creditors; liberality would be transformed into meanness; and small farmers would become more resentful of richer neighbors. In individual cases, this was already true in the 1850s. Courts were kept busy with suits over debts, and creditors complained publicly that they had not received "true value" in return for promises of payment.[24] Yet there is little evidence of widespread resentment or social protest by debtors in the 1850s. Most men repaid, and planters could afford to carry indefinitely the minority of notes that ended up in estate inventories marked "doubtful" or "insolvent." Prosperity thus underwrote neighborhood exchanges and helped bind together farmers and planters, nonslaveholders and slaveholders. That he lent his neighbors corn was one reason that Barrow could count on them when he asked for their votes.

In their own neighborhoods, farmer and planter met informally to exchange visits, work, tools, and money. In their churches, they met to worship. Evangelical churches had entirely dominated organized religion in the Augusta area since the Great Revival in the early years of the nineteenth century. Almost all practicing Christians were Baptist, Methodist, or Presbyterian.[25] The intensely individualistic theology of southern evangelical churches emphasized that each person must face his or her own sinfulness and stand alone before God in hope of salvation by God's grace. Among thousands of northern evangelicals, this sense of personal sin and responsibility had fed into the great reform movements, notably abolitionism. But in the South, social and economic pressures had squelched early Baptist and Methodist opposition to slaveholding, and by 1850, southern evangelicals had long since come to terms with slavery. The reform impulse had been channeled almost entirely into efforts to preach salvation to more individuals—whether unchurched whites, slaves, or foreign heathen. Neither churches nor individual Christians felt obligated to press for change in the area's political or social institutions.[26]

At the same time, each evangelical congregation was a real community, not a mere collection of individual worshipers. Members prayed together, gave comfort in times of sorrow and distress, and shared the joy of each converted sinner. Dolly Burge was one of many pious Methodists who attended not only Sunday services, but also revivals, prayer meetings, and weekly "love-feasts."[27] This sense of community can be seen nowhere more plainly than in each church's collective responsibility for its members' behavior. Baptists, Methodists, and Presbyterians insisted on strict adherence to church rules, which required temperance and held dancing, gambling, and swearing to be sinful. Each church also sought to keep its members at peace with one another and regularly intervened to help settle personal disputes.

In 1857, Thomas Glaze of Goshen Baptist Church in Lincoln County was "excluded" from membership for having offered "gross indignity" to a female member, amounting to "a direct challenge to her virtue."[28] In Warren County, Long Creek Baptist Church excluded Simon Harrell for drunkenness and fighting in 1850. In 1855 in the same church, one member complained that John Roberts and Robert Brinkley had been gambling on horses and cards and keeping "immoral" company, and that William Long had been drinking "too freely" and visiting places "unbecoming a Christian." Brinkley and Roberts, both of whom had joined the church during a revival in 1853, denied the charges but chose to resign from membership. The next year, Long Creek Baptist church excluded Thomas Kent, an overseer, for stealing his employer's corn and sending slaves to steal neighbors' corn.[29]

Members were not always expelled, even when they violated church discipline. In Sardis Baptist church in Elbert county, Thomas Bobo confessed to his excessive drinking and was forgiven. In 1850 in the same church, after Tinsley Powell accused fellow member John Powell of having used profane language, apparently during a quarrel, the church heard the case, and John Powell acknowledged his sin and asked forgiveness. The church voted to "retain" him in fellowship. Tinsley Powell disagreed with the vote, whereupon the church appointed eight respected members to a committee to investigate further. The next month, the committee reported that it had settled the difficulty.[30]

In some ways, church walls contained more equality than did any other public place. Since slaves had immortal souls, they could be accepted as full church members. So could women, white and black. Indeed, in most churches, women outnumbered men among whites, and blacks outnumbered whites. In 1860, for example, twelve white men and twenty-nine white women were members of Williams Creek Baptist church in Warren county. Only twenty-eight men were among eighty-nine white members of Long Creek Baptist church. In Goshen Baptist church, blacks far outnumbered whites.[31] White men nevertheless remained "more equal" than others, and they usually determined church policy by vote, while white women assisted ministers, helped run church affairs, and investigated complaints against other women members.[32]

In wealth or occupation, church members did not differ greatly from the white population as a whole. Most men were farmers or planters. They typically owned land, and their wealth reflected that of their counties and neighborhoods.[33] Differences in wealth apparently did not distinguish denominations—although the evidence is incomplete[34]—and persons of all economic ranks were numbered among professing Christians. David C. Barrow, Adam Alexander of Wilkes county, Gertrude Thomas, and Iveson L. Brookes of Edgefield, South Carolina—himself a prominent minister—were all wealthy and all devout church members. In 1860, both Adam Cason, who owned almost $50,000 worth of property, and landless farmers and laborers like Samuel Skelly and Wiley Allen belonged to Warren county's Long Creek Baptist church. Rich or poor, all alike were sinners, all were subject to church discipline.

Churches were not perfect communities. They sometimes were wracked with unsolvable internal disputes. One client of Alexander H. Stephens wanted to sue for damages after he was dismissed from his church for lying.[35] And while church membership cut across class and racial lines, the influence of evangelical Christianity in creating even an imperfect sense of community among whites should not be exaggerated. Some congregations were hardly communities at all. In his report for 1860, the clerk of Williams Creek Baptist church wrote that his congregation stood "greatly in need of help from on high, to aid us in this time of great weakness and cold and barrenness as a church for it really appears that we are in danger of becoming extinct as a church."[36]

The influence of churches was also limited because not all whites attended services, read the Bible, or took part in religious activities. John H. Cornish, Episcopal minister of Aiken, South Carolina, visited many of these people—such as Joshua Barton, who, with his wife and five children, had not been baptized, or the Blalocks, whose daughter Sarah had never prayed and did not know the Lord's Prayer.[37] Many whites, perhaps the majority, did not even belong to a congregation, although they occasionally attended Sunday services or summer camp meetings, or kept a bible at home. Some came into contact with a minister only rarely, as when Reverend Cornish preached to fifty or a hundred people in a Graniteville, South Carolina, warehouse.[38] In Wilkes county in 1859, church rolls swelled as many among the "almost hopeless" joined during revival season,[39] but after the excitement of the revival, some drifted into apathy. Poor roads and a shortage of ministers kept many people away from services.[40]

Sophia Chapin, an Edgefield teacher from New England, complained in letters to her father that bad roads and limited preaching meant that she could "attend church very seldom."[41] The editor of the Edgefield *Advertiser* drew attention to slim attendance at Edgefield churches, while confessing that he himself was rarely present because he lived four miles out in the country.[42] Small congregations gathered once or twice a month to hear an itinerant preacher.

Evangelical religion, despite such obstacles, brought together thousands of whites in fellowship. The shortage of qualified ministers and the small size of congregations in some ways encouraged people of different denominations and sects to mingle with one another, since devout Christians were likely to attend whatever services were held nearby. The first time that Cornish preached in Aiken, "all sorts" attended, "from Romanists to the most radical Presbyterians." Although Cornish's church had only thirty or so communicants, it was typically full for two Sunday services when nearby Baptist and Methodist churches had no preaching of their own.[43]

Churches controlled their members, but in a special way. Their only punishment was exclusion from fellowship. They held all white members, rich and poor, male and female, to the same standards of behavior. Above all, the evangelical churches promoted a compelling version of equality—the equality of every man and woman before the Lord. In doing so, they promoted as well a solidarity among whites that served in part to mask and override inequalities of sex, wealth, and status.[44]

In neighborhood and church, white men formed significant community ties. As citizens, they *were* the community. Their local governments kept order and provided necessary services. In elections, they chose representatives to decide on everything from the location of bridges to secession and war. Political leaders not only decided vital issues, but also embodied and expressed a community's ideas of itself.

These ideas were often quite different on opposite sides of the Savannah river. A stranger set down first on a plantation in Edgefield district on the South Carolina side, then on one in Hancock county on the Georgia side, might not be able to distinguish between the two. The soil would look much the same, as would the crops in the fields, the slaves at work, and the overseers or plantation owners. Were the stranger set down at the court houses, however, especially at election time, he or she might well notice differences between the two states, particularly in the behavior and language of their politicians. The editor of the Augusta *Constitutionalist* caught some of this difference during a visit to Columbia during the Civil War, when he noted that "Carolina politics are very different from our own," which he attributed to Carolinians' "Huguenot" blood and to the strong influence of family connections in the state.[45] More than traditional blood, it was traditional institutions and ideology that most characterized South Carolina's politics.

As measured by its political institutions, South Carolina was a state that time had seemingly forgotten. Its political structure had not changed significantly since its constitution had been ratified in 1808. That document embodied a major compromise between the South Carolina low country, dominated by enormous rice and sea-island-cotton plantations, and the upcountry, by then the heart of the newer, short-staple-cotton region. By the turn of the nineteenth century, the upcountry had far outstripped the coast in population, but the low country still controlled the state with its disproportionate share of representation in the legislature.

The constitution of 1808 had satisfied sectional claims by basing legislative representation on both numbers and taxable wealth. This left the coast, with its many slaves, with more power than its small white population alone could justify. At the same time, the agreement largely satisfied upcountry districts like Edgefield and Abbeville, which already were well on the way toward creating their own plantation-dominated economies.[46] Ties of kinship, friendship, and marriage between coastal and upcountry planters helped solidify the compromise in the fol-

Table 15. Wealth of Candidates for Office in Edgefield District, 1850–1860

Office sought	Date	Real Estate		Total Wealth		
		Mean ($)	Median ($)	Mean ($)	Median ($)	(N)
House of Representatives (S.C.)	1858–60	18,637	16,500	80,720	67,225	(16)
House of Representatives (S.C.)	1850–52	6,141	4,450	*	*	(24)
Local office †	1860	2,989	2,500	9,429	5,640	(18)
Local office †	1850	3,439	3,000	*	*	(23)
All Edgefield household heads	1860	3,519	809	12,124	*	(3,006)

SOURCES: Edgefield *Advertiser*, 9 January, 17 April, 24 October 1850, 20 October 1852, 20 October 1858, 18 January and 17 October 1860; wealth from the manuscript returns of the United States Bureau of the Census, 1850 and 1860; household data from Vernon O. Burton, "Unfaithful Servants? Edgefield's Black Reconstruction: Part I of the Total History of Edgefield County, South Carolina" (Ph.D. diss., Princeton University, 1976), 203–204.

*Data not available.

† Sheriff, tax collector, ordinary and clerk.

lowing decades. While sectional issues continued to intrude into state politics, the alliance of low-country and upcountry planters successfully prevented major changes to the 1808 system.[47]

The institutional arrangements of 1808 helped make South Carolina's politics among the most peculiar in the nation by 1850. Almost all power lay in the hands of the state legislators, who chose not only presidential electors (selected by the voters in all other states), but also the governor and all other state officers. Thus before the Civil War, no South Carolinian was able to cast a ballot in an election for a statewide office. This lack of focus for statewide organization is one reason that true political parties did not develop in antebellum South Carolina: every candidate for office ran ostensibly as an independent.[48] Since South Carolina's districts remained in some ways appendages of the state legislature, South Carolina's local politics were to that extent unique.

By far the most powerful local officials were district representatives in the state legislature. The legislature determined most tax rates. Each local delegation also appointed all nonelected local government officials, such as two boards of commissioners, to oversee roads and public buildings, and magistrates, who, among other tasks, heard most trials of slaves. Representatives were, in effect, a kind of ex-officio executive committee in each district.[49] Local voters chose Commissioners of the Poor (who had charge of paupers), a sheriff, an ordinary (judge in probate court), a clerk, and a tax collector. These jobs were largely administrative; incumbents were paid from fees.[50]

As measured by the wealth of candidates for the legislature, South Carolina deserves its reputation as an aristocratic state (see Table 15). Legislative candidates, in particular, were likely to be very wealthy.[51] Wealth was prestigious; it was often taken as a sign of ability. Wealth gave a man time to campaign. It was not, however, an absolute requirement for success. The typical candidate for local office, rather than for state representative, actually owned less property than did the average family head in Edgefield. At least one state representative elected in 1860, moreover, had no property at all, according to the census.[52] Furthermore, while Edgefield's representatives were usually wealthy, they were not necessarily "aristocratic," as their campaigns for office show. If held according to South Carolina ideals, of which John C. Calhoun had been both exponent and symbol, elections would have been quiet exercises of republican virtue. No political parties would stir up passions. Voters would choose men of merit purely on the basis of character and opinions; these men would be leaders, not merely voices of constituents. Reverend Iveson L. Brookes outlined the ideal in a letter of advice to his ambitious son-in-law. Concentrate on your profession (law) and avoid politics, went the advice. Wealth and honor will follow success, and then you may be "called" to serve "without condescending to the usual schemes of electioneering intrigues commonly employed by would be politicians."[53]

Polite announcements by a man's friends that he was a candidate for office were a bow to the ideal; they were occasionally accompanied by equally polite acceptances by the candidates.[54] At most, campaigning was to consist of exchanges of views at neighborhood barbecues sponsored by "disinterested and generous" citizens. Real elections were rather different, however, and had been at least since the turmoil of nullification. Between 1828 and 1833, ultraconservative nullifiers had created what was, in effect, a full-blown party in order to carry the state for their platform of resistance. Fearing excessive democracy, they had, ironically, stimulated it with their intensive campaigns for votes. South Carolina politics had never been quite the same.[55]

Consider, for example, the lament of the editor of the Edgefield *Advertiser* in 1852, who wrote, "Unfortunately . . . it has come to such a pass that a man, however deserving and capable, asks in vain the privilege of representing Edgefield, unless he can make up his mind to ransack every nook and corner of the District and court the favor of every man who lives at a Cross-Roads or keeps a dram shop."[56]

This is a fair description of electioneering in Edgefield. An Edgefield legislator painted a picture even more damning. George D. Tillman was an active supporter of one of the periodic campaigns to democratize state politics by expanding upcountry representation and allowing the voters to choose the governor and presidential electors. In a vitriolic attack on low-country control of the state, Tillman claimed that in politics "merit is with us generally ignored." A major cause of this evil was that, unlike (low-country) parish representatives, those of the (up-country) districts "have generally large constituencies, so turbulent, so hard to manage, so full of ambition, so conflicting in local interests, that but few members are reelected."[57]

An earlier speech by Tillman to constituents had elaborated his analysis. While urging division of Edgefield into at least two districts, he complained that the large size and population of the district "and the consequent lucrativeness of her district offices, was the cause of so many bitter contests for the offices of profit." At every general election, the field was crowded with candidates "who, after having obtained wealth, seek the honor of a seat in our Legislative assembly." Many "fierce and protracted contests" resulted, and the winners could scarcely take office before being ousted by some "demagogue."[58]

For his own district, at least, Tillman was accurate about the high turnover among representatives. The 1852 Edgefield delegation to the South Carolina House of Representatives was completely different from the 1850 delegation. In 1854, all six representatives were again different, although one had been elected in 1850. By 1858, none of the 1854 representatives was still in office, and the 1860 elections returned only one incumbent.[59]

Candidates' charges and countercharges confirm that Edgefield's elections were indeed frequently "turbulent" and bitterly contested. In 1853, S. S. Tompkins and J. C. Allen exchanged acrimonious letters in the columns of the *Advertiser*. Tompkins, defeated by Allen in a special election, charged that some of the poll boxes had been improperly opened and that Allen had lied about them, had cheated people by passing along bad notes, and, worst of all, had lowered himself to soliciting votes openly from a man who had impugned Allen's character.[60] The next year, Joseph Abney, defeated in his bid for reelection to the legislature, blamed the loss on false rumors that he favored division of the district and that he did not own the requisite amount of property for the office. Abney went on to attack excessive electioneering, which was inevitably corrupting both the people and their candidates.[61] In 1855, Edmund Penn defended himself against charges that he was bankrupt, charges that he claimed had caused his defeat in the recent election for clerk.[62] None of these men suffered quite the indignity as that suffered by W. L. Parks, who garnered only sixty-four votes in the 1852 election for tax collector. That, according to Parks, was because his opponents had spread a rumor just before election day that he was dead![63]

A candidate, to get elected, must get votes, and voters were anything but passive. All adult white men could vote and most did—in the 1858 legislative election, more than 90 percent of them. To appeal to voters on the basis of aristocratic pretensions, or to expect them to come to candidates instead of the other way around, was to ask for defeat.[64]

Martin W. Gary, a candidate for the state legislature in Edgefield in 1858, suffered this predicament. Gary had defended Representative Tillman in a celebrated murder trial. Tillman had killed an Edgefield artisan during a faro game. During the trial, local mechanics had interpreted some of Gary's remarks as insulting, and these "insults" came back to haunt him during his campaign. Gary tried to defend himself in a public letter. He denied that he had disparaged mechanics. He looked not to the calling, but to the man. Others charged that he wanted no poor man's vote. "I am," he insisted, "but a poor man myself, and it would be but natural that I should hope for their support." He countered by claiming that the "purse-proud rich" were saying that he lacked the property required for a seat in the legislature. Why, Gary indignantly protested, some of my best friends are mechanics![65] His strategy of self-defense did not impress. He lost the election, and even though he lived in the village of Edgefield, he finished seventh there in the field of eight candidates.[66]

The necessity of gathering support in a fundamentally democratic yet highly personalized political system pushed South Carolina toward the organization of true parties, despite strong antiparty ideology. After Calhoun's death, several state leaders worked to create what would be, in effect, a state branch of the national Democratic party. In the main, these leaders had opposed outright secession in 1850, when many South Carolinians had rejected the national compromise over slavery in the territories. In Edgefield, this party organization was led by Arthur Sim-kins, editor of the *Advertiser*, and Preston Brooks, who was elec-ted to Congress in 1852. Radicals organized behind secessionist Francis W. Pickens. Supporters of Brooks and Pickens tried to outdo one another in labeling each other a "party."[67]

Since party organization was still suspect throughout the 1850s, ambitious men had to cultivate voters all the more with intense campaigning. Every vote counted; every string in one's personal network had to be pulled. The extent of these networks is indicated in a letter from John L. Tobin to a friend, S. S. Evans. Tobin represented Barnwell District in the state legislature, but in the letter, he was concerned with an upcoming election for brigadier general of the militia cavalry. Tobin had been "traveling for the last two months . . . endeavouring to fish up votes" for that honor. After grousing about having been cheated when a deal with a potential rival had fallen through, Tobin got to his "principal object" in writing: having heard that a lieutenant in one troop was "a nephew of your father," he wished to suggest to Evans that "a letter from the old gentleman in my favour might have some weight with him."[68]

Since nephews of friends' fathers did not abound, every candi-date first had to establish a sound neighborhood base among men he knew personally. Direct influence with favors, friend-ship, and liberal displays of hospitality was ideal; barring that, support by the wealthy was a good substitute. From the base of a single neighborhood, a candidate might hope to attract votes, or other support, from relatives' and allies' neighborhoods. This truth was behind every candidate's claim to have been put for-ward by his "friends." The importance of neighborhood support can be measured in election returns. Map 3 on page 120 indicates residences of three legislative candidates and location of polling places where they ran best in the 1858 Edgefield legislative elec-tions in the 1850s. The vital role of neighborhood support is clear: every planter was politically in the hands of his yeomen neighbors.[69]

Georgia's counties, unlike South Carolina's districts, were largely autonomous in local affairs. An inferior court, with five elected judges, was the chief executive authority. The court levied local taxes and spent the money on roads and bridges, jails and courthouses, common schools and pauper support.[70] Other county officials, also elected, were an ordinary, a sheriff, a tax receiver, a tax collector, and two court clerks. Each militia district (a subdivision of a county) elected, in addition, two constables and two justices of the peace. Justices' duties reflected their titles—"conservators of . . . the public peace." They issued criminal warrants and were the first to examine suspects; with five-man juries, they tried all slaves brought to court for any but capital crimes; they decided all civil suits with less than $50 at stake. Justices' courts were meetings of neighbors who ruled on one another's debts and tried one another's slaves before a judge they had helped choose.[71]

County-level affairs seem to have had little direct connection with political parties. Party nominating meetings scarcely mention county offices. Elections to these local posts most likely depended on a man's general reputation, connections, and limited local campaigning; almost no records of elections survive. Disputes, no doubt, were frequent; the siting of a road or the levying of a tax to support a railroad were important issues to owners of farms or stores. Disputes occasionally surfaced in newspapers, as when "Vox Populi" of Burke County attacked "bogus" road commissioners; the commissioners had, it was charged, ordered people to travel unreasonable distances to fulfill their obligations to work on the roads, and "virtually exempted . . . several of the wealthiest citizens" whose heavy wagons most damaged the roads. "Vox Populi" went on to urge a vote for Bob Gray, the "people's candidate" for commissioner (by law, the road commissioners were appointed by the inferior court, so the Burke court on its own initiative seems to have allowed local elections for commissioners).[72] Local grand juries issued many complaints when they met (three times a year) during superior court sessions. These complaints ranged from almost universal condemnation of road conditions to specific charges of malfeasance against local officials. Such local disputes apparently did not involve party differences.[73]

Local leaders were by no means an exclusive economic elite. Many officials possessed small means. Since at least 1840, voters in Georgia's counties had elected to local offices men of widely varying circumstances, including men without slaves and with little or no property. In Taliaferro county, for example, nonslaveowners had served in the legislature, on the inferior court, and as sheriff. And while the average size of slaveholdings among all household heads had gradually increased during the two decades before the Civil War, the average slaveholding of county officers was lower in 1860 than it had been twenty years before (see Table 22, p. 208). In the early 1850s, voters in Warren county elected William H. Edwards, a nonslaveowner, to the inferior court, and Calvin Logue, owner of only one slave, as sheriff. In Glascock county, five of eight justices of the peace in 1860 were nonslaveholders. That year in Hart county, the number of non-slaveholding justices was seven of fifteen; in Taliaferro county, two of thirteen; in wealthy Hancock county, four of seventeen. The proportion of nonslaveowners among justices of the peace was, therefore, only a little smaller than that among each county's total voting population. Among Taliaferro's justices was a blacksmith; among Hancock's were a carpenter and a wheelwright.

Members of the inferior courts were usually, but not always, wealthier than justices of the peace. In 1861, voters in Hancock county elected John Little, a merchant with one slave and a total of $2,000 in property, to the inferior court, along with four planters who held, on average, thirty-one slaves each. In both Glascock and Hart counties, nonslaveholders were elected to the inferior courts that same year.[74] A comparison of officeholder wealth with average county wealth illustrates the same point. Rich men were more likely to hold office, but officeholders were not vastly richer than the men who elected them (see Table 16, p. 114).

As in South Carolina, turnouts for elections in Georgia were phenomenally high. Among counties in Augusta's hinterlands in 1859, the turnout in most was more than 90 percent, and in sev-

Table 16. Wealth of Officeholders in Augusta's Hinterlands, 1859–1861

Office and County	Mean Wealth ($)	Median Wealth ($)	(N)
Justice of the Peace			
Glascock	5,393	3,028	(8)
Hancock	15,082	6,000	(17)
Hart	7,501	6,522	(15)
Taliaferro	8,466	5,000	(13)
Inferior Court justice			
Glascock	8,953	8,990	(7)
Hancock	19,750	24,500	(5)
Hart	6,120	7,500	(5)
Taliaferro	14,825	15,000	(5)
All household heads (1860)			
Glascock	2,733	700	(325)
Hancock†	9,336	*	(954)
Hart	2,515	800	(346)
Taliaferro	7,334	2,900	(337)

SOURCES: Executive Officers Books, GDAH; the manuscript returns of the United States Bureau of the Census, 1860.
NOTE: Excludes officers not located in census.
*Data not available.
† Estimated from James C. Bonner, "Profile of a Late Ante-Bellum Community," *American Historical Review* 49 (1944): 671. Bonner's method is slightly different; the figures here exclude laborers living with parents, which he included.

eral approached 100 percent.[75] The "plain farmer" had power in running his community, as both elector and officer.

State politics in Georgia meant party politics. Like most states (and again unlike South Carolina), Georgia had, by 1840, two well-organized and highly competitive parties. In each county, Whigs and Democrats nominated candidates for the legislature, and sent representatives to district and state conventions. In a rough way, Georgia's parties divided along familiar national lines. The Whig party attracted merchants and commercially oriented planters, and its members were more likely to favor government intervention to spur economic development. Democrats found their greatest support in areas dominated by small farmers. Hence the Georgia side of Augusta's hinterlands was strong Whig territory until the mid-1850s, when the national Whig party disintegrated because of quarrels over slavery.[76] Still, this distinction is at best approximate. In the Augusta area, leaders of both parties (and of their successors) were typically drawn from the slaveowning elite (see Table 23, p. 209). Neither party followed a consistent ideological line, and both supported slavery without qualification.[77]

In form, local-party practices were democratic. All nominations were made, as in Oglethorpe county, in open meetings, usually on court day at the courthouse. If accounts of these meetings can be taken at face value, local parties were rare models of the community's general will in action. A chairman called the meeting to order and appointed a nominating committee. The committee retired for a short time, then emerged with a nomination and a set of resolutions. Both were approved—almost always "unanimously."[78] But as in David C. Barrow's campaign, this public ceremony often symbolically closed a bitter contest for support. As William McKinley aptly put it, there was "much wire-pulling" everywhere.

Obvious political maneuvering sometimes brought open complaint. A caustic letter to the Augusta *Constitutionalist* described a Columbia county nomination in 1853: "the caucus clique . . . [met] and appointed three gentlemen to the next Legislature. . . . The men appointed, are very clever young men, as much so, as inexperienced men of immature years could be. . . . There is evidently much dissatisfaction in Columbia, at the dictatorial spirit of a few in the county, who try to rile the people by their selfish appointments. . . . The system as practised here, is at war with the spirit of Republicanism; and strikes a death blow to one of our dearest privileges—the *freedom of action*."[79]

In 1860, another writer, this time from Oglethorpe, bitterly criticized a local-party faction for reneging on an agreement to divide the county's delegation to the state-party convention. Sometimes even the fixers felt things were too fixed.[80]

Yet party politics in Georgia cannot be dismissed as nothing more than manipulation of the many by the wealthy few. In the first place, party leaders, like local officials, included many men of little wealth. In Warren county from 1840 to 1855 (as long as two strong parties competed in that county), every organized party included nonslaveowners among its leaders (see Table 20, p. 204). Hancock county delegates to party conventions included such men as Democrat Alpheus Buckney, in 1853 a propertyless son of an overseer, and Thomas Powell, a young physician and nonslaveowner active in both the Constitutional Union party in 1851 and the American party in 1855.

In the second place, the parties had to compete for votes, and most men voted. Furthermore, parties faced competition among their own members for place and honor, which Barrow's campaigns again illustrate. Despite his brother-in-law's advice, Barrow lost to his rival, Willis Willingham, in 1857. Two years later, he again challenged his old opponent. His correspondence shows how party leaders cultivated popular support. One Barrow supporter in April wrote that "Willingham's friends are doing their best . . . let me enforce [on you] the propriety of a good friend of yours going over to the other side of the county."[81] Another was more explicit: "The contest is to be won or lost in 2 or 3 weeks— Just so soon as the evident inclination of the majority is manifest the weight of the party will settle accordingly. Willingham is very active . . . you must send out some of your best & influential Wolfskin friends into *the districts* for it is expected that Willingham will visit them in person & forestall them."[82]

This time, Barrow was successful, although the intensity of the campaigning led Willingham himself to speak publicly at the nominating meeting. Acknowledging that the "scramble between Mr. Barrow and myself for the candidacy for the Senate, and the incidents connected therewith, have produced all this disturbance—an antagonism between his friends and my friends," Willingham withdrew from the contest in the name of party harmony.[83] The resulting "unanimous" nomination of Barrow was not simply a false cover for undemocratic decision making; it was symbolic recognition that the party had, in an essentially democratic way, chosen its man and now must unite behind him.

The nomination did not end Barrow's campaign, for he still faced an opponent from the "Opposition," as the remnants of the Whig party called themselves. In August, Barrow was still receiving detailed advice, for example, to "spend the night with Wm. Colquitt he is a Democrat but a little careless about voting, or if you like you might go to Mr Griffiths & take a round through the district in the evening."[84] Barrow's overseer, who seems to have been familiar with such things, passed along to Barrow a complaint from one voter "that you had never was seen in a Grocery [grogshop] and some in the Glad destrick and in the Goosepond Destrick they Would knot vote for you if you did knot Gow in them too Destricks and treat them."[85]

Popular choice gave politics in Augusta's hinterlands a democratic cast. At the same time, the power of a relatively small elite guided and limited local democracy. As much as people voted, as much as their opinions mattered, political leadership was indispensable in rallying public opinion. Some men could sway fifty votes; some, hundreds. Wealthy planters with many slaves had resources in labor and capital to help build support among neighbors: they could afford the clothing, fine horses, and summer barbecues to display liberality suitable in a leader; they could attend expensive academies and colleges to polish their oratory; they had the time to stump for votes and the money to treat the patrons of local "groceries." Local leaders were, typically, wealthier than most of their constituents.

The ranks of the political elite were not closed. As it was possible for a poor man to get rich, it was also possible for him to get power. Young men, too, had their chances; recall the complaint that the Columbia county "clique" had chosen candidates who were too young and inexperienced for the job.

Political mobility, however, did not necessarily lessen elite influence. As in Columbia county, mobility was often "sponsored"; the existing elite deliberately infused itself with new blood. For a young man without money or influence, the right connections could substitute. Thus the very process of political mobility served to keep dissent within limits and to channel newcomers onto acceptable paths. In political networks of reciprocal obligations, a big planter usually could command more of those obligations than could a small farmer.[86]

The career of Alexander H. Stephens exemplifies this process superbly. Few politicians in the area could rival his power by the

1850s. As one man wrote to his brother Linton in 1855, Alexander could sway voters "by the hundreds. . . . You have no idea of the weight . . . [of] his influence with the masses."[87]

Stephens had been orphaned at the age of thirteen. A succession of relatives and well-to-do planters—including his uncle Aaron Grier and Adam Alexander of Wilkes county—had taken him in and educated him first in local academies and later at Franklin College (the future University of Georgia). After abandoning plans to become a minister, Stephens taught school and studied for the bar. The diary he kept while a young man is a record of his intense ambition, as well as an early expression of themes that would dominate his future political discourse: effusive praise of liberty, gloomy assessments of the corruptibility of human nature, celebrations of material progress. Sentiments not entirely in accord with acceptable political stances in the deep South are recorded. He recalled, for example, his feeling of bitter humiliation when he graduated from college and realized for the first time "the *use* and *importance* of *money*." He watched with envy his classmates as they were "released from all restraints into the luxuries of large patrimonies, rolling in fine carriages with splendid equipage, from the spring to the *falls* and from the *falls* to the mountains . . . with no care upon the mind but to search for the tastiest pleasures and the readiest enjoyment." Stephens, meanwhile, found himself "doomed to the dungeonary confinement of a school room."[88] A meeting with two slave traders in a stagecoach prompted a comment on "that abominable inhuman traffic which is now so common in this misnamed land of Liberty."[89] Here, one might expect, were the makings of a future antislavery politician.

Yet there was never much chance for that, quite aside from the repression of internal dissent on slavery in the deep South. Stephens's political career was guided from the beginning by the same kinds of connections that had guided his academic career. Dr. Stephen Foster, a member of one of the two major factions in Taliaferro county politics, became his patron. Foster invited Stephens to give the annual Fourth of July oration in Crawfordville in 1834, and Stephens's ambition was thereafter safely folded within the boundaries of conventional local politics.[90] His rise to wealth and power did not threaten, but rather, as he liked to point out, legitimated southern society. He seemed to demonstrate the claim of a local orator in 1850 that "we . . . acknowledge no pre-eminence, socially or personally, save that arising from superior merit, based upon virtue, intelligence, and morality."[91]

As neighbors, as Christians, and as citizens, white men met and talked, lent and borrowed, worshiped, campaigned and voted. This face-to-face interaction in small-scale communities helped give substance to white solidarity and forge "social and political ligaments" among southern classes, although white solidarity was imperfect—neighbors at times traded bullets instead of services and debts. Churches brought together rich and poor as well as black and white to seek a common salvation, but dissension sometimes wracked even these godly communities. Factionalism in and out of party politics could bitterly divide citizens. Counties and districts split over taxes, roads, or the location of the courthouse. But they did not fight over slavery.

In part, this was because slaveowners succeeded, most of the time, in getting poorer men to see themselves as part of a single white community, whose geographic and symbolic center was the courthouse. As one contemporary put it, the courthouse was the center for the South's "Oral System" of public education, where rich and poor learned more about the law through observation and conversation than any college could teach.[92] The almost universal response to a threat, a disaster, an opportunity, or a celebration was a public meeting at the courthouse. When some Oglethorpe county cotton growers thought that city merchants had cheated them, they called a meeting at the courthouse to protest.[93] When citizens of Edgefield district or of Hart or Hancock counties wanted to promote a railroad through their district or town, they called public meetings. When Warrenton almost burned to the ground in a sudden fire, leading planters immediately held a public meeting and formed a large committee including wealthy men from every part of Warren county to raise money for relief of the town's homeless citizens.[94]

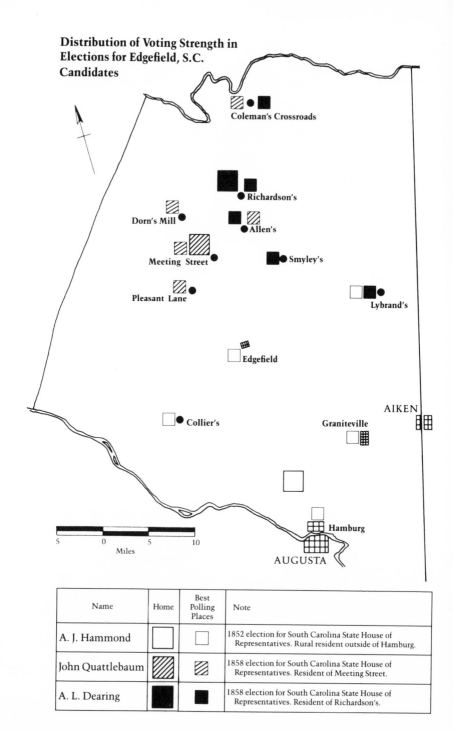

Distribution of Voting Strength in Elections for Edgefield, S.C. Candidates

Coleman's Crossroads

Richardson's

Dorn's Mill

Allen's

Meeting Street

Smyley's

Pleasant Lane

Lybrand's

Edgefield

AIKEN

Collier's

Graniteville

Hamburg

AUGUSTA

5   0   5   10
Miles

Name	Home	Best Polling Places	Note
A. J. Hammond			1852 election for South Carolina State House of Representatives. Rural resident outside of Hamburg.
John Quattlebaum			1858 election for South Carolina State House of Representatives. Resident of Meeting Street.
A. L. Dearing			1858 election for South Carolina State House of Representatives. Resident of Richardson's.

Community leaders responded the same way when they perceived threats. In Lincoln county in 1858, a public meeting considered "the outrages recently committed" by the Jeter family. Buck Jeter and his son Oliver had spent time in prison for shooting Dr. John Wightman, who had had the temerity to sue them. Another son, Ezekial, had shot at Wightman, killed a slave, and escaped from jail; he was finally shot dead by a sheriff and posse. Now Buck Jeter, out of prison, was threatening revenge. The meeting's resolutions (supposedly drawn up on the spot by a committee of twenty-four) justified the action of the sheriff, and while considering it "best, that we should not at this time take the execution of the laws into our own hands," pledged support to any who might choose to prosecute a Jeter.[95]

In Warren county, a public meeting in July 1851 gathered to consider another kind of threat. It resolved to expel from the county "one Nathan Bird Watson, who hails from New Haven, Connecticut, and who has been promulgating abolition sentiments, publicly and privately among our people, sentiments at war with our Institutions and intolerable in a slave community, and also been detected in visiting suspicious negro houses, as we suppose, for the purpose of inciting our slave and free negro population to insurrection and insubordination." The meeting appointed a committee of eleven men, most of them young and active in Whig or Democratic party affairs, to escort Watson to the railroad depot and send him on his way.[96] In both cases, prominent men acted to protect what they claimed were not class, but community interests. The form of action they took—the fully public open meeting—reflected confidence that while they might be acting technically outside the law, they were guided only by accepted rules of morality and common sense.

For the local elite, expelling abolitionists was part of exercising county leadership. On the Warren county expulsion committee were Edward Pottle, who would run for the state legislature two years later; William H. Pilcher, who would be among those in charge of the county's Fourth of July celebration in 1853; and J. M. Roberts, who would help raise money for the relief of Warrenton in 1858. That men such as Pottle and Pilcher could expel Watson shows how powerful they were.

Yet it also shows how vulnerable they felt. If slaves were contented, if nonslaveowners were united with slaveowners in their opinions about slavery, how could a Yankee mechanic possibly be a threat? The nervousness of the slaveholding elite makes apparent the ambiguity of their political position. True, slaveholders were, on the whole, *of* their communities; indeed, they were leaders of their communities. But equally true, the community was their master. They could rule only by consent; politically, they depended, simply and unequivocally, on the support of all white men. If the mass of small farmers—their community—turned against them *as slaveholders*, then slavery would be finished.

The public display of expelling Watson was thus as important, if not more so, as any practical effect it might have. The expulsion was one more dramatic statement that the South was, after all, a slave society and that every man must know it and act as though he knew it. Because men like Pottle, Pilcher, and Roberts belonged wholly to their community, they could define Watson out of it. Because they could belong nowhere else, they *had* to define him out of it.

Part II
A War for Liberty and Slavery

[Our new government's] foundations are laid, its corner-stone rests upon the great truth, that the negro is not equal to the white man; that slavery—subordination to the superior race—is his natural and normal condition.

ALEXANDER H. STEPHENS
1861

The sudden and unexpected development of the negro in his intellectual, moral, industrious capacity is the astounding fact of this war.

"MENTOR"
1865

₭ Prologue: **In The Midst of A Revolution**

In 1850, Colonel R. H. Ward addressed the Greene County Agricultural Society.[1] His subject was the place of farmers and farming in Georgia. He began with a brief review of American history, and a lament. "A system of culture has been persisted in," he told the crowd, "so destructive in its character, as to leave a large inheritance of exhausted fields." The remedy was not flight to the West, but reform and improvement of the soil. In the long run, he predicted, Georgia would prove best for cotton. Meanwhile, cotton planters should learn to act in concert, to prevent control of the market by Liverpool merchants. Too, planters should compete directly with England by investing in cotton manufacturing.

Turning to politics, Ward echoed Thomas Jefferson's praise of farmers. "Freer from the temptations that surround most other pursuits," they were "peculiarly prepared for the promotion of virtue." Still, farmers must educate themselves. All should cultivate the intellect; all should be "conversant with the various measures of State and National policy." Ward denounced those who spurned the poor with "*aristocratic condescension.*" We are "Democrats" who "acknowledge no pre-eminence, socially or personally, save that arising from superior merit, based upon virtue, intelligence, and morality." But to ensure that the farmer would be truly equal to all in "intelligence and virtuous refinement," farmers must educate their sons, and educate them as farmers. Ward concluded with a peroration in praise of women, who supported their men and made good homes possible.

Ward's address combined congratulation and anxious warning. It points up the dual role of republican thought in a slaveholding society. Republicanism described, but it also prescribed. It allowed southerners to point with pride to their institutions, but also served as a source of self-criticism. Republican thought by

125

its nature invited alternative emphases and interpretations. It required balance: democracy, but not too much democracy; stability, but not too much stability. Since the precise line of balance was impossible to identify, different men could see their society as facing different threats. The republican defense of slavery heightened this tension. Slavery made republics more stable, according to this defense. Therefore, slavery's defenders were naturally led to emphasize the dangers of change, which might easily lead to anarchy. At the same time, many citizens were nonslaveholders. Slaveowners could not afford to alienate them; therefore, republicanism must also be, for white men, a highly democratic ideal. Democracy, of course, threatened to bring on change and anarchy.

Political controversy brought this potential contradiction into the open. Political spokesmen of all kinds, whether editors, politicians, or influential private citizens, turned to familiar republican arguments in their debates. Often, both sides in political debate tried to make use of republican ideals.

In Georgia, with long-established party organizations, much of the logic of political argument between Democrats, on the one hand, and Whigs and their successors, on the other, was cast in republican forms. Typically, Democrats feared encroachments on popular power, and Whigs were more likely to express distrust for excessive democracy.[2] In 1853, for example, a major issue in the election for governor was the support that Whig Charles J. Jenkins had given to the so-called Algernine Law, which had tried to restrict voting in the city of Augusta to property owners.[3]

Whigs kept up a constant lament about the decline in virtue, which they not surprisingly blamed chiefly on the Democrats. The editors and correspondents of the Augusta *Chronicle* sounded this theme time and again under such headlines as "The Causes of the Crisis" (the causes being executive patronage, and the crisis being the diseased state of the body politic), "Congressional Venality" ("our representatives [are] . . . a collection of dishonest harpies"), and "Corruption Rules the Hour" (which concluded that "we are travelling that road, so often trod by nations before us, the road that leads through luxury, corruption, and effeminacy, to final destruction").[4]

The Georgia Democrats, in turn, tried to associate Whigs with "every aristocratic sentiment which is jealous of popular power." In 1851, the Constitutional Union party (in this area, made up mainly of former Whigs) was said to be composed of "every worshipper of station [who] disdain[s] the humble fortunes of a Republican State, to bask in the sunshine of Imperial Splendors."[5] In 1858, Governor Joseph E. Brown's popular denunciation of banks in Georgia following the panic of 1857 was in the tradition not only of Andrew Jackson, but also of English republican thinkers as far back as the founding of the Bank of England.[6]

Perhaps the clearest example of how both parties saw the political world with republican eyes and explained it with republican words was the debate over the nativist American party, which rose from the ashes of the Whigs in 1855. Alexander H. Stephens refused to accompany most of his supporters into the new party on the grounds that it was antirepublican. The secrecy of the Know-Nothings, who formed the backbone of the new party, was counter to the fundamental need in republics for "free discussion and full investigation by a virtuous and intelligent people."[7] The party's proscription of foreigners would create within the body politic a degraded and dangerous class of white men with no attachment to the public good. Like the Helots of Sparta, these immigrants would be a constant threat to the nation because, unlike the South's black slaves, they were not fitted by God and nature for any such subordination.[8]

The adherents of the new party replied with their own republican arguments. A writer who called himself "Sydney," after one of the early English heroes of republican liberty, argued that immigrants in the North already were a degraded and corrupt class, "mere tools in the hands of demagogues." Secrecy was justified to defeat these office-hungry demagogues and "restore our government to its pristine purity."[9] A public meeting in Hancock county resolved that "conventions and cliques have conspired to rule or ruin the country." The American party—"pure in its principles, patriotic in its designs"—had risen to cleanse the country of the "corrupt demagogues" whose power was based on the "ignorant and vicious hordes of Europe" flooding the North.[10]

In many ways, political debate in the South Carolina hinterlands of Augusta resounded even more strongly in eighteenth-century terms. South Carolina's government and political ethos, more than those of any other state, were strongly influenced by a constricted version of republican ideas. As an eighteenth-century ideology of opposition to established power, republicanism had been a radical creed. Antebellum South Carolinians were, by the 1850s, embracing a profoundly conservative interpretation of republican thought, in which change was virtually synonymous with error.

The state's all-powerful legislature would seem to violate basic republican principles because it concentrated so much power in a body elected by all adult white men. However, the absence of organized parties and the system of representation, which gave equal weight—balance—to property and numbers, enhanced the power of South Carolina's wealthy planters at the expense of poorer whites. South Carolina's republicanism was, to adapt an apt phrase of William W. Freehling, a democracy with the brakes on, and its political elite had managed to apply the brakes sooner and more strongly than had their Georgia neighbors.[11]

This made South Carolinians simultaneously more open than Georgians to charges of aristocratic leanings and more likely to see the dangers of anarchy in every move toward democratization. James Henry Hammond articulated the case against democracy in an unpublished "meditation" on "Democratick Republics." He conceded that democracies developed the energy and stimulated the capacities of the "underclasses," but was convinced that they were still "the worst of all forms of government." Since the great body of mankind was capable of only "sensual enjoyment," universal suffrage was simply the rule of "the low bred ignorant instead of the high-bred & enlightened, or passion instead of policy, of rulers ruled themselves by the basest appetites." Democracies required their leaders "to stoop, to cringe, to flatter the lowest of the people"; the rich "are carped at, annoyed & thwarted by the affectation of 'sturdy independence' among the poor & vulgar." Hammond, in the midst of a period of banishment from state politics, yearned for a government like Britain's, led by a "rich, hereditary, permanent aristocracy."[12]

Hammond was not alone in his detestation of democracy. In 1849, for example, a long series of letters in the Edgefield *Advertiser* from "One of the People" denounced the majority principles of democratic rule, identifying them with faction, licentiousness, and anarchy.[13] A decade later, "Hamburg" similarly denounced an attempt to sponsor a popular referendum in Edgefield district on using tax money to support a railroad project. This was, he wrote, an instance of "folly, demagoguism, and stupidity"; South Carolina, he haughtily proclaimed, is, in contrast to northern states, a *"representative* not a *mobocratic* government."[14]

This conservative, almost aristocratic republican vision was strongly challenged in Edgefield district in the 1850s by local leaders who attacked what they called the "aristocratic" features of South Carolina's government. These leaders played important roles in campaigns to increase the representation of the upcountry, to give election of the governor and presidential electors to the voters, and to make more local offices elective.[15] Their case was brilliantly, if caustically, argued in the state legislature by George D. Tillman.[16] In 1856, during debate on the presidential-elector bill, Tillman claimed that legislative choice of the electors was an open invitation to corruption of the legislature by federal patronage and money. But Tillman had a lot more to say about the legislature. It had far too much power, and "by its peculiar organization, an oligarchy of five hundred men are permitted to rule the State with iron will." Low-country representatives merely manipulated the state for local and selfish purposes. South Carolina may have no political parties, Tillman said, but its thirty or forty factions were worse than any parties. He declared that state politics were nothing more than a series of cabals, intrigues, and cliques united to monopolize the spoils of office and that an "odious, cunning, tyrannical, intriguing oligarchy" distracted the people by picking fights with Uncle Sam and branding the true friends of the people as demagogues and anarchists, all the while running the state with "deceit, hypocrasy, intrigue and diplomacy."[17]

William C. Moragne, Edgefield's state senator, rose to the defense of South Carolina's political traditions. "We live," he told a public meeting at the courthouse, "in a REPUBLIC, where the people are the legitimate source of all power—in which only one class is known to the law—where all are politically free and equal, enjoying the same rights and privileges." The people have all the power they need because they control the ballot box. They challenge comparison with those in any other state in "those enobling virtues upon which rest the stability and success of our republican institutions." A popular election for president would merely promote first party warfare, and then the "morbid diseased state" of "factious excitement" inimical to the unbiased feeling "so necessary to form the patriotic and enlightened republican." A change would create a "*Federal Government* party," with its corrupting tendencies and "wretched system of electioneering," and this change would beget more change—leading ultimately to the degradation now evident in other states. Once models of virtue and intelligence, most states, according to Moragne, were now "little better than the shackling democracies of old Greece and Rome." After New York had changed its constitution, a "wild spirit of mobocracy" had seized its people and dragged them down to Fourierism, socialism, and abolitionism. Rather than bring on these dangers, Moragne concluded, let us preserve the "balance of power— . . . the beautiful harmony in the body politic" brought about by our present constitution; South Carolinians should follow the wise advice of Bacon and Machiavelli that true reform consists always in bringing states back to their ancient customs.[18]

To conservatives like Moragne, Tillman's violent rhetoric must have seemed all too similar to that of the infamous "Brutus."[19] Tillman was not at all opposed to slavery; a large slaveholder himself, why would he be? But any change could be a threat to a society already in perfect balance. Was there not, after all, a contagion to liberty?

As Moragne's comments about New York show, the North

seemed to prove just that; it was a living lesson of the threat to every republic from excessive democracy and subsequent decay. As Hammond had pointed out, the inevitable "mud-sill" class in the North was made up of white men, and in their degradation, they were an immense threat to liberty. In 1845, Hammond had argued that the North's unenlightened voters would soon threaten "a fearful crisis in republican institutions."[20] To Reverend Iveson L. Brookes in 1849, the North was full of "sinks of sin and corruption"; as soon as the nonslaveholding states gained numerical majority in the Union, demagogues would "usurp control of the government and the days of this great Republic will be speedily numbered."[21] In 1860, the Augusta *Chronicle*'s editor wrote that northern society was "rotten and corrupt, and based on *wrong*. It cannot endure . . . its downfall [will] be speedy, and its destruction complete."[22]

The corruption of society, the degradation of politics, and the centralizing consolidation of power were all seen as part of an overall trend. To a correspondent of Stephens, the government was surely "becoming very corrupt, & I fear in truth the 'handwriting is upon the wall' and it is becoming too corrupt to last."[23] The editor of the Edgefield *Advertiser* thought that "perhaps more white men and voters at this day subsist upon our federal loaves and fishes than by any other single pursuit in the Union." As a small consolation, he added that the resulting "consolidated interest" might serve to delay the arrival of the violence, anarchy, and revolution "so strongly indicated by the general appearances of our political world."[24] The degraded condition of the North—filled as it was with "worthless and vicious" voters, overrun by mobs, and plagued with deism, Mormonism, Millerism, and other vile "isms"[25]—only confirmed the opinion of the *Chronicle*'s editor that "*no pure Republic can exist without the slavery of an inferior race as the basis of society.*"[26] Criticism of the North helped deflect the self-criticism that republicanism invited. At the same time, it held up for view an awful example of everything the South supposedly did not want to become.

During the presidential campaign of 1860, men and women throughout Augusta's hinterlands foresaw that if Abraham Lincoln should win, secession might well follow. Some delighted in the prospect; some fiercely opposed it; and many in both camps saw the election as a crisis in republican government. To them, the election was the climax of the fears and anxieties of a generation.

The Augusta *Constitutionalist*'s editor, who strongly backed Stephen A. Douglas, blamed the split in the Democratic party on those who sought a "consolidated government" controlled by "that aristocracy of wealth and intellect, the eldest born of monarchy."[27] As the election approached, he wrote a series of brooding editorials on world history, "seeking," he said, "in vain to find a parallel in reality to our dream of a perpetual republic." He could only conclude that "it is contrary to human experience to suppose [our government] eternal."[28]

The editor of the *Chronicle*, a supporter of Constitutional Union party candidate John Bell, agreed that party politics was utterly corrupt, but he placed even greater blame for the crisis on the "gradual demoralization of the people," which was now more of a threat to the Union "than all the abstract questions hatched from the scheming and seething brains of demagogues." This demoralization must end in "loss of liberty," he argued, for once a republic falls from its "original purity," it "sinks through successive stages of lawlessness, corruption, unbridled license and civil war, until from the depths of blood and degradation it rebounds to seek a fettered peace and an ignominious security in a military despotism. Such has been the history of all republics, cursed by ambitious and unscrupulous demagogues as is ours."[29]

Thomas G. Bacon, an Edgefield politician, drew a secessionist conclusion from a similar diagnosis. Speaking to the Edgefield militia on July 4, he lamented how the national government had lost the trust of the people. It had followed the course of other republics despite the efforts of the founding fathers to learn from history. It, like "all governments, . . . tend[s] to consolidation." The growing power of the central government had broken down republicanism by causing conflict between those with power and those without. "We cannot guard too strongly the gates leading to this almost impregnable fortress Power," he told his audience. If "this Republic shall crumble into ruins," though, the South could build a new confederacy with stronger safeguards that would last a century, if not forever.[30]

Lincoln's election focused these fears and hopes on the issue of secession. Would South Carolina and Georgia accept the result or withdraw from the Union? In South Carolina, the longstanding, if partly eroded, tradition of antiparty feeling helped produce a debate with only one side. Even before the election, a public meeting at the Edgefield district courthouse had appointed a committee of fifty to draw up resolutions and report to a second meeting the next week, after the election. The first meeting also had encouraged each neighborhood to form "Minuteman" associations to protect South Carolina from invasion, slave unrest, and, by implication, internal dissent. The force of public opinion and the potential intimidation by the associations, which formed throughout the district, served to silence almost all opposition.[31] The "committee of fifty," composed of some of the richest and most prominent men in the district, drew up resolutions urging immediate secession. On November 13, several hundred people endorsed the resolutions and listened to a series of secessionist speakers. Lincoln, they were told, represented a fanatical sectional party. He would use the purse and patronage of the national government to subdue the South quietly, by seduction, rather than by violence. The Black Republicans engendered only "pestilence and corruption in our body politic." South Carolina should follow the great example of its forbears; the state must have a new revolution analogous to the American Revolution.[32]

If anyone doubted Lincoln's power to interfere with slavery now, Francis W. Pickens told a third meeting, remember that the subversion of liberty under republican forms "has ever been the course and policy of usurpation in Republican Governments." As in Rome, he warned his audience, despotism might arise under the guise of law and order. He exhorted Edgefield's voters to separate from northern fanaticism. With a united South, he concluded, "we present at once the strongest Republican system on earth."[33] Edgefield's secessionist candidates to the state convention called to consider South Carolina's response won without opposition. The Committee of Fifty successfully symbolized the Edgefield elite's determination to enforce an image, and if possible a reality, of harmony in this republican crisis. Even James Henry Hammond, United States senator and in 1860 opposed to separate secession by South Carolina, was unwilling to speak out in public.

In Georgia, by contrast, the campaign for secession was a bitter and public one. The debate was also carried on in the language of republicanism. As in South Carolina, secessionists pointed to Lincoln's election as a sure sign of irretrievable corruption in the North. Miserable demagogues there had cynically manipulated the unreasoning masses. According to Robert Toombs, Lincoln had openly declared it his purpose *"to war against slavery until there shall not be a slave in America, and until the African is elevated to a social and political equality with the white man."*[34] Governor Joseph E. Brown linked the Black Republican external threat to fears of internal dissent and slave revolt. Lincoln now had control of federal money and patronage. As a result, Brown told the legislature, "a portion of our citizens, must if possible, be bribed into treachery to their own section, by the allurements of office; or a hungry swarm of abolition emissaries must be imported among us as officeholders, to eat out our substance, insult us with their arrogance, corrupt our slaves, and engender discontent among them." The South would be flooded with inflammatory abolitionist documents, and the result would be "a war of extermination between the white and black races."[35]

In Georgia, the opponents of secession were both important and outspoken. Georgia's tradition of party conflict ensured that they would organize, speak, and be heard. Unionists and cooperationists (those who would secede only in cooperation with other southern states) agreed with much of the secessionist diagnosis. Benjamin H. Hill argued that the northern people might still draw back from fanaticism. Hill blamed the crisis on the politicians of both North and South, who had stirred up the slavery question merely to achieve "party success and self-promotion." Echoing others—Unionists and secessionists—he placed ultimate blame on an English conspiracy to destroy the South's control of the world supply of cotton and promote cotton production in India.[36] Alexander H. Stephens was the most famous Georgian to oppose secession. He emphasized that Lincoln had no real power to disturb slavery and that northern fanaticism ultimately would spend its strength and die away.[37]

Some of those opposed to secession were more afraid of southern than of northern passions. If the old government were destroyed, what would prevent "wildest anarchy and confusion?"[38] In the analysis of the editor of the Augusta *Chronicle*, "unrestrained popular passion, personal ambition and party excesses have produced disunion. . . . And, unless these be checked, our fears are that they will finally result in civil war, loss of liberty, and the establishment of a military despotism."[39]

Private citizens echoed these dark views. H. C. Massengale of Columbia county asked Stephens, "What is this country coming to? Have not the people too much power, and what is the exact line of demarcation between Republican and Mobocratic institutions? It reminds me of France in '98."[40] The fears of secessionists and of Unionists were curiously alike, underneath their bitterly opposing opinions about the proper course of the South. Both saw the crisis as one of republican government and social stability threatened by power, greed, fanaticism, and the excesses of democracy. They could not, however, agree on which threats were greater: northern Black Republicans, or corrupt politicians throughout the country? A slave revolt instigated by abolition emissaries, or war and defeat followed by emancipation? Thousands of potential abolitionists among southern nonslaveholders, or thousands of deluded southern voters led by foolish radical leaders? In both cases, republican ideology served to highlight and exaggerate genuine social and political conflicts, to identify a threat and to suggest a solution.

Georgia's legislature called a convention to meet in January 1861 to consider secession; the election for delegates was held on January 2. The contest split local elites and the electorate. In Hancock county, a public meeting in Sparta, the county seat, nominated Linton Stephens on a cooperationist platform. Even though Stephens and other leaders had worked out compromise language on the resolutions, the key plank opposing secession was adopted only after "heated discussion." Even the secretary of the meeting registered his dissent when he reported the results to newspapers.[41]

Among the dissenters were a Dr. Jordan, who had borrowed money from Linton Stephens for his medical education, and Bill Lewis, who had been elected to the state legislature with Stephens's backing. Jordan and other secessionists organized another meeting, which nominated Lewis as a candidate for the convention, opposing Stephens. Linton Stephens was almost too disgusted to comment on their lack of gratitude when he wrote to his brother about the turn of events. He simply reported the facts, and added "so goes the world."[42] The crisis had pulled taut many lines of deference and reciprocal obligation, and some of them had snapped.

Georgia's contest went down to the last moment. Most radicals had supported John C. Breckenridge in the presidential election. Stephens had campaigned for Stephen A. Douglas, and many former Whigs had voted for John Bell. In November, in the Augusta area, Douglas and Bell combined had swamped Breckenridge by three to one; the results reflect in part the immense personal prestige of Stephens in this area. On January 2, though, secessionist candidates carried the election in the area, with 60 percent of the total vote.[43] In the crucial convention vote on January 19, nineteen of thirty-five delegates from the Augusta area voted for immediate secession. Augusta was strongly secessionist, and the small-farm counties of Glascock and Hart also voted for secession candidates. The big-plantation counties were split.[44] In many, perhaps most, counties, voters simply chose the most prominent leaders, conceding to them the decision. In Taliaferro county, Alexander Stephens, strongly opposed to secession, was elected without opposition. In neighboring Wilkes county, fire-eater Robert Toombs was elected, also without significant opposition. Despite the significance of the choice, most voters continued their patterns of deference. The vote in the Augusta area in January was less than two-thirds that cast in November for president. This was a sign, not of apathy, but of confusion, indecision, and resignation.

Contemporaries disagreed, and historians have continued to disagree, on the fundamental impulse behind secession. Secessionists claimed to be striking for independence to preserve white liberty and black slavery. Then and later, some saw the conflict with the North as largely a straightforward matter of economic interest; others, as more broadly a clash of different cultures. Then and later, still others argued that secession and war were really colossal blunders, in which fundamentally similar sections of the country were dragged into disaster by fanatical ideologues and foolish politicians.[45]

One recent study of South Carolina's secession found the cause in a "crisis of fear." The primary fear, shared by the great majority of whites, was of slave insurrection. According to this interpretation, fear was endemic in this society based on racial slavery, but had been brought to a pitch of near-hysteria by John Brown's raid in 1859 and the excitements of the presidential campaign, which had soon followed.[46] The most recent comprehensive study of Georgia's secession has argued, by contrast, that divisions among whites were the key to secession. Secession, in this interpretation, was essentially a conservative counterrevolution, designed to stave off challenges to slavery by nonslaveholding whites by erecting an independent, "patriarchal republic" on southern soil.[47]

It would be easy to cite evidence from the Augusta area for both these interpretations. Whites did, for good reason, fear that slaves might someday revolt; slaveowners did, for good reason, doubt the political loyalty of poor whites and yeomen. Yet both these interpretations are too simple. It was, first, the *combination* of slave resistance and white class conflict, together with the outside threat posed by a hostile, antislavery party in Washington, that fueled the fears of most secessionists. Any one of these threats, or even any two, would have seemed, and been, much less dangerous than all three.

Second, and most important, secessionists analyzed and interpreted their predicament with the help of a theory of politics and history that told them they ought to fear both internal conflict and outside power as threats to liberty, and that also told them what to do about their fears. Few secessionists thought Lincoln or his party would be able to harm slavery immediately. But their time frame was long, and they believed and argued that the ultimate result of that hostile power must be attack from without, division within, and, finally, the end of slavery—an end that this profoundly racist society would imagine only with horror. Too, secessionists struck for independence out of hope as well as fear. Secession, they thought, would guarantee both black slavery and white liberty. National independence promised to white southerners that sense of personal independence that was the highest of their civic values. Black slavery and white liberty, they had learned to argue, were inseparably bound together. Together they would be saved, or lost.

When South Carolina and Georgia seceded, many exulted. During the campaign for the secession convention, the editor of the Augusta *Constitutionalist* had predicted great things for a new southern republic. Perhaps slavery would, after all, help the South fulfill his dream of a "perpetual republic." He predicted that the North would soon be wracked with revolution. The safety valve of excess territory would soon be shut; "teeming millions" would be confined in the manufacturing districts until the rise of poverty produced an irrepressible conflict between capital and labor. "Thankful may they be," he concluded, "that when thinned by carnage and want, the people there submit to monarchy and a standing army." But from this fate, a southern republic would be exempt, for "a slave population, composed of an inferior race, kept ignorant of letters and of arms, had the effect of keeping out the vast population now swarming the North, and, strange but true, SLAVERY IS THE KEY TO THE SOLUTION OF THE PROBLEM, OF [PRESERVING] LIBERTY ON EARTH."[48]

Others were not so sure. Susan Cornwall, wife of a Burke county slaveowner, rejoiced to think of the new Confederacy, but her anxiety is evident in the question she asked in her diary: "We are in the midst of revolution. Who can prophecy its result?"[49] William McKinley, a Georgia planter and longtime member of the Democratic party, looked forward frankly, if privately, to the establishment of a monarchy in the new southern Confederacy. "Empires may last a thousand years and more," he wrote, "but Republics go down into democracy; and quietly end their brief race in radicalism and ruin. All Hail the Empire!"[50]

James Henry Hammond, brooding in his study, described demonstrations in Augusta in November 1860 as "quite French Revolutionary." Drunken mobs there would soon begin a reign of terror, he wrote to William Gilmore Simms, but the brutal "San Culotte" would be surprised to find his place at the pinnacle of power ultimately overturned by "the black & savage negro."[51] In Washington, Georgia, Judge Garnett Andrews paced back and forth in his darkened house, listening to a wild celebration outside. "Poor fools!" he exclaimed to his daughter. "They may ring their bells now, but they will wring their hands—yea, and their hearts, too—before they are done with it."[52]

A humbler correspondent of Alexander H. Stephens, neither planter nor senator nor judge, made his own prophecy. Joseph Campbell, of Fair Play in Morgan county, Georgia, wrote in April 1861, already condemning local politicians who, he claimed, had been elected to the state convention as Unionists, then basely voted for secession. He was worried about the new Confederate government. The people had as yet no voice in it; and would it not soon place duties on agricultural products, and waste money in extravagant public expenditures? In Morgan county, he said, there was already a serious division caused by ambitious politicians. "My convictions now are," he concluded, "that by a division in the people the very thing designed to be secured by cesesion will by the same be destroied [namely,] African Slavery[;] & if much evil comes upon the South, we are to blame for it."[53]

🍊 Chapter 5

Strains of War

The forebodings of a few were drowned out after the outbreak of hostilities at Fort Sumter in April 1861. By then, most dissidents, including Alexander H. Stephens, had pledged full support for their states and section, even if they had opposed secession. Indeed, Stephens had, in February 1861, been chosen vice president of the new Confederacy, as southern political leaders sought to demonstrate that they were now fully united and determined to establish the South's independence.[1]

This new-found unity seemed to be reflected in every local community near Augusta. The attack on Sumter and Abraham Lincoln's call for troops to suppress the Confederacy created an outburst of enthusiasm among the vast majority of whites in Augusta's hinterlands. Divisions over the wisdom of secession were apparently forgotten, as men everywhere rushed to volunteer. Wealthy men and ambitious men of lesser means competed to form their own companies, battalions, and regiments. Indeed, one Hart county correspondent of Governor Joseph E. Brown of Georgia complained of the "derangement" of men who were so anxious to join the army that they threatened to leave no one behind to take care of the women and children and get in the crops.[2]

No doubt, part of the enthusiasm was based on a conviction that the war would be glorious, short, and, of course, successful. In January 1861, the editor of the Augusta *Constitutionalist* predicted that if the northern armies were foolish enough to invade, southern volunteers would drive them out "as easily as the whirlwind sweeps the chaff before it."[3] The *Chronicle*'s editor echoed a standard argument that the North was "filled with festering corruption, the venality, the luxurious effeminacy" that presaged total decay and made that section obviously unfit to prevail in war with the South.[4] James Henry Hammond confidently predicted that southern men would "mow down" Lincoln's "foreign" troops "like sheep. Our trouble will be the fatigue of slaughtering."[5] Many volunteers feared the war might end before they got a chance to fight in it.

In every county and district near Augusta, companies were quickly organized with the support of all segments of the white population. Some companies, especially in South Carolina, were prepared to volunteer at the outset of hostilities. Typically, a large community ceremony, heavy with symbols of unity, sent each company off to battle. In Hamburg, for example, on April 24, the "ladies of Hamburg" presented Captain Spires's company with a flag, and Spires replied with an elaborate speech of acceptance, repeating the rhetoric of southern rights. The Stars and Stripes, Spires said, had been dishonored by the North, which had tried so hard to deprive southerners of their "rights and equality in the Union" and had aimed "a death blow to our institutions." To submit would have cost the South its wealth and honor and would have reduced "our mothers, our sisters, our wives, and our daughters to shame" and our progeny to equality with creatures fit by the Almighty only as "slaves for man."[6]

Public meetings in Georgia counties spurred volunteering and contributions to equip local companies.[7] In May, "the ladies of Hancock" presented a banner to Captain Arnold and his company; in July, two more companies left Hancock after speeches by Alexander H. Stephens and by a Methodist bishop. At this ceremony, a reporter assured the *Chronicle*'s readers, the soldiers vowed to abandon "the sin of profanity"; the spirit of self-sacrifice must have seemed boundless that day.[8] On July 11 in Gibson, the Glascock Independent Guards received their flag, the presentation preceded by a joint march with companies from neighboring Jefferson and Warren counties, which went through "some elegant evolutions." A Miss Cheeley, daughter of one of Glascock's richest planters, presented the flag, with an address that "evinced high female acquirements in rhetoric, logic and grace, bidding the soldiers to go forward, . . . [and] demonstrating very clearly that the ladies fully understand and appreciate the government of the Confederate States." After long and "deafening" applause, the crowd of 2,500 listened to a sermon, and concluded the day with a public barbecue.[9]

These ceremonies dramatized and cemented community support for the fight. It seemed that slaveowners and poor men would stand shoulder to shoulder in defense of their homes and their new nation. In an 1861 sample of Confederate volunteers from the area, forty-two were heads of or sons from slaveowning families, and forty-eight were from nonslaveowning families.[10]

Those who could not be soldiers volunteered in other ways. Women formed aid societies to make uniforms and blankets.[11] George W. Ray, of Warrenton, wrote to Stephens to volunteer as a nurse, since he was too old to serve as a soldier.[12] Older and also wealthier men contributed thousands of dollars to buy arms and uniforms. Hammond gave $100 to a company in Greenville, in the South Carolina upcountry.[13] Tillman Watson of Edgefield promised to equip the company raised by Martin W. Gary.[14] Public meetings in Taliaferro, Hancock, and other counties brought in contributions. By the summer of 1862, almost 200 people in Hancock had contributed to outfit volunteers.[15] In some areas, meetings resulted in plans to levy "voluntary" contributions on everyone in certain neighborhoods. In the Mt. Willing neighborhood of Edgefield district, a public meeting voted to assess an extra "tax" to furnish volunteers, and formed a committee to collect the assessments.[16] Other meetings urged county governments to borrow money immediately to equip local volunteers and to support the families of poor soldiers.[17] In August, one of Stephens's correspondents assured him that "the people in this section grow in their patriotism. Surely such a people cannot be subjugated."[18] Another wrote him that there had never "been a time when the People has more confidence in the Government, both civil and military—never was a time, when the officers of government were more beloved, by the people."[19]

Even in the midst of this enthusiasm, however, were portents of troubles to come. Many opponents of secession had been converted into strong Confederates, but others had simply fallen silent. In July, D. F. Bardon wrote to Stephens to urge a negotiated peace to avoid an invasion, and he worried that "a spirit of insubordination is rife all over this land."[20]

More significantly, problems that would come to plague the Confederate war effort appeared almost as soon as the army began to form. Secession was justified in terms of the ideals of the white community—centered on liberty, autonomy, and independence—but free, autonomous, and independent men and communities were not necessarily the best material for a long and massive war. Class strains that had been carefully contained by means both subtle and overt began to break out into the open almost at once. On May 1 in Hancock county, a fight erupted between members of the local infantry company and Eppes Sykes of the cavalry company. Sykes and most of the other men in the cavalry company were relatively wealthy and could afford fine horses; for them, the cavalry was a symbol of social prestige. On the contrary, according to Linton Stephens, in the infantry company, "a good many of the men" were poor. The company had accepted donations from local planters to buy uniforms and equipment. The fight began when Sykes made "some jeering remark" about these donations, and Sykes and two others were wounded. Poor men would accept support from the community's elite, but not at the expense of condescension from those whose right to own slaves they were going off to defend.[21]

The touchy individualism of southern white men permeated every level of the army and was exacerbated by the popular democracy that characterized the army as much as it did the local community. At the beginning of the war, most officers up to and including colonels were elected by their men. One obvious way to become an officer was to recruit a company or a regiment, and the skills of recruiting were much the same as those required for electioneering in general, from courting neighbors to building coalitions. So, not surprisingly, officers tended to be wealthier, and more often owned slaves, than the privates who formed most of the army. Privates in a sample of soldiers from three counties came from families that owned an average of two slaves and $2,809 in property; families of those who were elected officers (from corporal to captain) averaged twice those figures. And altogether, those from slaveowning families were twice as likely as those from nonslaveowning families to enter service at a rank above private.[22]

The competition in recruiting perhaps helped to swell the army's rolls at early stages, but it also created conflicts. David C. Barrow helped recruit five companies for the service, but G. B. Harben, a prospective colonel, complained that Barrow had enticed two Elbert county companies away from his own regiment and into Barrow's battalion.[23]

The Confederate army, in short, reflected the southern political community, with its strengths and weaknesses. The rather brief military career of Thomas W. Thomas, of Elbert county, epitomizes much of both. Thomas, a politician and a man of considerable wealth, was a friend of Alexander and Linton Stephens. During late spring and early summer of 1861, he exercised his political skills to form his new regiment. He began with men from his own county, and sought alliances with companies in other counties. He had the ear of Governor Brown, and was thus in a strong position to bargain with companies already formed and eager to get accepted into the service. His letters to Brown reveal local politics at work. On July 1, he wrote of his concern that "outside influence hostile to" its captain might break up one Lincoln county company. He asked Brown to accept one Hancock company that was not quite filled because that company was crucial to keeping a second Hancock company "so connected" to it that if the first were left out, the second might fall apart.[24] As in civilian politics, connections sometimes competed with one another. Thomas, for example, refused to appoint a Hancock man as quartermaster of the regiment because he had already chosen his own brother for the job; he would, he assured Linton Stephens, "gratify the Hancock men" in almost any other request, "reasonable or unreasonable."[25]

Thomas succeeded in becoming Colonel Thomas. By August, he was in Virginia. The life of an army camp, however, proved most uncongenial to this high-spirited political soldier. He was bored with inactivity, chafed under discipline, and, by October, was writing letters critical of Jefferson Davis and the administration of the army. "Matters are managed very badly here, without sense, system, or policy," he wrote to Alexander Stephens, and "there also exist partiality and corruption in high quarters. . . . The troops widely feel the unjust oppression and partial hand that is laid upon them, and in my opinion the spirit of the army is dying. I have seen some things that made my blood boil; and that makes one unconsciously begin to debate with himself whether the assassin's knife be justifiable."[26]

Shortly afterward, Thomas wrote that "we have to bear things here that no freeman ought to bear, and perhaps outraged nature may speak out in me and bring me into trouble"; indeed, he predicted, only half in jest, that he might be court-martialed within sixty days.[27] At the end of the year, he visited his family back in Elberton, and wrote that the people were "dispirited, uneasy, and apprehensive." He blamed it all on Jefferson Davis and the "peculiar people he trusts," who had given "sufficient cause to every gentleman in the army to mutiny." People in Elbert county "are whining and complaining and probably thinking of a compromise by going back."[28] Thomas himself was full of "an indignation" verging "on hate," and we may doubt his claim that he was covering this up to avoid damaging public opinion any further. By the spring of 1862, Thomas was trying to resign his commission and was bitterly protesting the treatment he received from his commanding officer; when his health deteriorated, his resignation was accepted.[29]

Many shared Thomas's reaction to army discipline. Robert Toombs, a former United States senator from Georgia, went through a similar trial of pride and independence. Toombs, from Wilkes county, was made Secretary of State in the Confederacy, but resigned in July 1861 to become a brigadier general in one of Georgia's new brigades then serving in Virginia. His letters, like those of Thomas, were filled with complaints about the army. General Joseph E. Johnston, in command, was a "poor devil, small, arbitrary and inefficient," who undertook everything merely out of a fondness for power; he "harasses and obstructs but cannot govern the army." The army, he predicted, would have as its epitaph, *"died of West Point."*[30] Toombs ultimately was court-martialed, although charges were dropped; he, too, finally resigned his commission and returned home to complain about the conduct of the war.[31]

Intense localism as well as individualism confronted the Confederate high command. In June 1861, Governor Brown was engaged in several disputes with companies that had received arms from the state. He claimed that these arms were to be used to defend Georgia from invasion, and forbade their export to Virginia without his express permission. He ordered one Newton county company to surrender its arms or to pledge in writing that it would not leave the state with them.[32] In commenting on these disputes, the Augusta *Constitutionalist*'s editor confidently remarked that "the old vexed question, as to the relative claims of the State and Federal Government upon the allegiance of the citizen, can never again arise at the South," that the first allegiance of citizens must be to the state.[33] This dispute was only a hint of many more to come, and attachments to states, rather than to the central government in Richmond, were only one aspect of a pervasive localism in Augusta's hinterlands that also characterized other regions of the South.

In May 1861, for example, an Edgefield, South Carolina, company was split when some of its members were recruited to enter a regiment being sent to Richmond from the South Carolina coast. Defending those who had not gone to Virginia, one officer explained that they wanted to defend South Carolina first.[34] That fall, the Edgefield *Advertiser*'s editor recommended that the state not call more upcountry men to defend Charleston, now threatened by the Union army at Port Royal, because Edgefield already had contributed more volunteers to the cause than had Charleston itself.[35] In April 1862, one South Carolina regiment was accused of mass desertion, and a defender explained that many members had joined on the assumption that they were liable for duty only in South Carolina; they had stopped off to visit their families when called out of the state.[36]

Similar disputes cropped up among Georgia's troops. An Augusta artillery company complained bitterly in a letter published in May 1862 that General Braxton Bragg had disallowed their election of a new captain and had given the captaincy to a man from Alabama. "We enlisted in this war as representatives from Georgia," the letter claimed, and now other states might get praise for the successes of Georgia troops. The editor of the

Augusta *Constitutionalist*, in which the letter appeared, agreed that the appointment of the Alabama captain was an "injustice which should not be tolerated" and that the members of the company were quite naturally "jealous of the rights of our citizens, and of the honor of our city and state."[37]

As the war stretched on, the Confederate government had to interfere in the lives of its citizens in countless ways, and that interference provoked resistance from many who regarded it as an unjustified assault on the independence and autonomy of states, local communities, and individuals.

In the spring of 1861, almost all southerners assumed that the war could be fought much as had others in the past, that the South would rely essentially on the voluntary efforts of public-spirited citizens and the cooperative efforts of local communities and state governments. Most obviously, volunteers would man the ranks. By the spring of 1862, it had become clear that volunteering would not suffice to supply the army. Many volunteers were sure to return home when their twelve-month terms expired.

In April 1862, the Confederate congress, at Jefferson Davis's behest, responded to the shortage of manpower by establishing the first national conscription system in U.S. history.[38] From the beginning, public leaders in the Augusta area were divided on the wisdom and justice of conscription. The editors of both the Augusta *Constitutionalist* and the Edgefield *Advertiser* supported a draft. As early as February 1862, the *Advertiser* argued that one salutary effect of a draft would be to force into the army some of those who wanted only to see "how much money they can make out of the war."[39] The *Constitutionalist* agreed that expediency required a draft, since volunteering had almost "run its course."[40] Others, however, denounced the draft as a violation of individual liberty and states' rights. "J. W. J.," a correspondent of the Augusta *Chronicle*, argued that conscription would turn the South into a military despotism.[41] Another correspondent raised a crucial issue when he argued that a draft would discriminate against the poor, who could not afford to hire substitutes, as allowed by the new law.[42]

Governor Joseph E. Brown of Georgia was one of the South's best known and most consistent opponents of conscription. His primary objection, he claimed, turned on the obscure point that the Confederate constitution, he maintained, allowed the central government to choose officers only for volunteer forces. Drafts had to depend on state militias and had to be called through the states, and therefore only the states (meaning, in Georgia, Brown himself) should have charge of appointing officers for conscripted troops.[43] This precious reasoning was shared by many influential leaders, including Alexander and Linton Stephens and the editor of the *Chronicle*, who called the conscription act a "most deadly" blow to the rights of states. Historians have attributed the opposition of the Stephens brothers and of Brown to selfish political motives or to sheer spite, and perhaps these were significant.[44] There can be no doubt, however, that they were sincere in their strenuous objections to conscription. Their private correspondence is filled with their denunciations of conscription and other "unconstitutional" acts of the Confederate congress. In August 1862, for example, Linton Stephens was lamenting the apparent acquiescence to conscription in the population at large. "Our public mind is unfit for the boon of constitutional liberty," he declared. "It is surprising and painful to see how utterly indifferent our people are to the observance of constitutional limitations upon the power of our rulers."[45] In December, he wrote a private, twenty-two-page letter to his brother outlining his objections to the draft. Not only was it patently unconstitutional to prevent soldiers from electing their own officers, but also the effect of the act would be "to mould the army into a fit instrument for despotism, and to *unfit* them for a return to the duties of citizens." An army in war is "essentially a despotism, and a *school* where despotism is learned"; the tendency of Davis's policies was "to destroy liberty."[46] Stephens was turning the old devotion to republican liberty against the Confederacy itself.

Defenders of the draft were content to point to its practical consequences and to the decisions of state courts, including the

Georgia Supreme Court, which confirmed the constitutionality of the conscription act. Despite briefly wavering on the question of constitutionality, the Augusta *Constitutionalist* by the end of 1862 was giving strong editorial support to the draft. In November, the editor deplored Brown's attack on conscription, arguing that publicizing his dissent might "greatly embarrass" the Confederate government. If the draft "fills up our armies . . . with good and reliable soldiers," he continued, "why should any patriot refuse to acquiesce in its enforcement?"[47] It was necessary, its editor later claimed, to satisfy those already in the army that the people at home supported their fight.[48]

Enforcement of conscription compounded the Confederacy's problems. It required the imposition of a new centralized bureaucracy on a population with hardly any experience in dealing with such an institution. No doubt, the bureaucrats were not always very good at their jobs; accusations of favoritism, interference with necessary work, and plain meddling abounded. More important, because more damaging to the Confederacy's cause, the draft inevitably bore more heavily on the poor than on the wealthy, and hence seriously widened class divisions among whites.

Poor men and women, for obvious reasons, saw the issue of conscription in a different light from that of the rich. While one argument for a draft was that it would spread the sacrifices of war more equally among all citizens, it was bound to affect the families of slaveless farmers much more than those who still had someone to plow and harvest. Letters of woe poured into the governor's offices and also to Alexander Stephens, who presumably had special influence as vice president of the Confederacy. From Hart county came a request for a discharge for Milton Grubbs, "son of a destitute widow";[49] from Sandersville, a plea for a discharge for a youngest son, for "i am left in a dredful Condision i am lo in health and unable to help myself. . . . i have no protection for all my boys wear gon in service but William . . . an he now gon too an lef me alone to shift for my self."[50] From Martha Denny, place unidentified, came this appeal: "I pray you may favour me as the pour all lays in your hans." Two of her sons had been killed; another had been drafted and had left her with his

three small motherless children. Now "they" wanted her youngest son; "I think I have done a nof for they army for you to let me
have my younges child. . . . pleas let me have my baby."[51] From
Taliaferro county came a request to have a son discharged; "he
left home without my knowledge or consent he was not 16 years
old when he left he is verry much distressed he rote to me for
God sake to get him home. . . . you know I am verry poor hardly
able at this to walk about."[52] From Warrenton was a petition to
be detailed to home to provide support for a family, including a
daughter and two daughters-in-law whose husbands were already
in the army, and all indigent, supported only by "the scanty al-
lowance made by the State, their own exertions, and the efforts I
can make by my own labor."[53]

The poor petitioned also to exclude their doctors and the teachers of their children from service. Greene county parents asked
for an exemption for a teacher of thirty-six children, whose parents could not afford to send them elsewhere. In the same county,
the petition noted, Penfield University had four exempted professors, even though "their parents are able to send them [the
students] anywhere to school."[54] From Lincoln county came a
petition to exempt Dr. B. F. Bently, who had given his word "to
many of the volunteers" that he would "attend to their families," without charge if necessary.[55]

Such people complained bitterly when wealthy men were exempted for no obvious reasons. Particularly galling was the policy of exempting one man, owner or overseer, on plantations of
twenty or more slaves. As a poor Mississippi woman explained
to Alexander Stephens, "our Army is making a great to do at the
Exemption Law It does look hard to exempt a man because he
has 20 Negroes they say it is a Rich mans war and a poor mans
fight."[56] When Governor Brown called up the Georgia militia to
aid the defense of Atlanta in the summer of 1864, one Crawfordville man wrote to Alexander Stephens that many of the local
men would refuse to go. "A great deal of dissatisfaction exists
among some at the course of others. I have heard some men
argue & complain that they being poor must go but that Ben
Reid and George Whitehall who have money are & will be permitted to remain."[57] At about the same time, a Wilkes county

man wrote to Brown that one miller who had been exempted from service not only "does not see his mill once a month," but also bragged that "you nor any other man could put him in service . . . and brags that he has made a fortune by the war."[58]

Wealthy planters did try to bend the rules of conscription to their favor, whether out of selfish or of patriotic motives. Connections, money, and the sophistication to deal with new bureaucracies all helped give the wealthy considerable advantage, quite aside from the "twenty Negro" law. Linton Stephens, for example, wrote his brother that he would be stuck at home "till I get my overseer [who had a bad leg] through the conscription gin."[59] David C. Barrow expended considerable energy attempting to keep his overseers out of the draft, arguing that they were needed to police the slaves and raise corn. At one point, Barrow convinced some of his neighbors to give an affidavit that his overseer Baker Daniel "does a great deal for the poor soldiers families in his neighborhood, and there are a good many of them around him."[60]

James Henry Hammond wanted, quite simply, to keep his sons out of danger. When they insisted on volunteering, he managed to have them assigned to staff positions, away from the front lines.[61] He rejoiced when his son Paul finally agreed to hire a substitute.[62] And he was incensed when the Davis administration planned to do away with substitutes, partly because of complaints that the substitute policy discriminated against the poor. Hammond agreed about the discrimination, but denounced the change. "The poor hate the rich," he wrote to James L. Orr, "& make war on them every where & here especially with universal suffrage & therefore they demand that rich men shall not put in substitutes. The war is based on the principle and *fact* of the inequality of mankind—for policy we say *races*, in reality, as all history shows it as the *truth* is *classes*."[63] More circumspectly, he wrote to Orr that substitutes were necessary to protect the planting interest so that the army could be supplied with provisions.[64] The editor of the Augusta *Constitutionalist*, who supported the draft, agreed with Hammond on exemptions. He noted that exemptions of overseers from the draft produced dissatisfaction about "an unjust and injurious distinction between rich and

Table 17. Wealth and Confederate Service, Soldiers from
Augusta's Hinterlands

WEALTH AND SLAVEHOLDINGS OF SOLDIERS AND NON-SOLDIERS

	Soldiers			Non-Soldiers		
Status and Age, 1860	Slaves	Mean Wealth ($)	(N)	Slaves	Mean Wealth ($)	(N)
Household heads						
20–25	.7	1,194	(39)	.2	350	(30)
26–35	1.1	1,835	(60)	2.0	2,448	(70)
36–45	2.1	3,771	(19)	5.4	5,136	(81)
All ages*	1.3	1,874	(146)	3.9	3,834	(309)
Living with parent						
Under 20	3.6	4,650	(87)	4.8	5,763	(155)
20–25	4.3	4,866	(25)	6.2	8,240	(21)
26–35	4.9	3,878	(10)	15.0	18,650	(3)
All ages*	3.8	4,638	(122)	5.2	6,269	(179)

WEALTH AND SLAVEHOLDINGS BY YEAR OF ENTRY INTO SERVICE

Status, 1860	Year	Slaves	Mean Wealth ($)	(N)
Living with parent	1861	5.6	5,768	(41)
	1862	3.3	4,507	(62)
	1863	2.0	2,658	(10)
	1864	.5	2,317	(6)
Household heads	1861	1.3	2,510	(49)
	1862	2.4	1,659	(83)
	1863	.9	1,094	(8)
	1864	1.0	525	(4)

SOURCE: Samples of men from Glascock, Hart, and Taliaferro counties from the manuscript returns of the United States Bureau of the Census, 1860, whose records were located in service records.
NOTE: See Appendix A for detailed description.
*Includes some ages not otherwise tabulated.

poor." Overseers, he thought, performed a vital police service, and "we have no patience with the miserable cant about rich and poor. The inequality of mankind, as regards wealth, can not be remedied by human laws."[65] When exemption of overseers was severely limited in the spring of 1863, the *Constitutionalist*'s editor complained that the new law discriminated against the rich because it did not specifically exempt owners of slaves as well as some overseers.[66]

For whatever reasons, the rich in Augusta's hinterlands did manage to avoid Confederate service more often than did the poor. When men of the same age and family status (such as household head, son, or boarder) are compared, those who did not serve in the army were wealthier, and owned more slaves, than those who did serve (see Table 17). And as the war continued, the disparity increased. Each year's new soldiers came from poorer families than did those who had joined the year before.

The discontent of the poor was, therefore, based on reality. And Governor Brown undoubtedly sharpened this discontent with his polemical attacks on the draft. The operation of the Conscription Act, he told the Georgia General Assembly, "has been grossly unjust and unequal between the two classes." While thousands of nonslaveholders were on the battlefield, "a large proportion of the wealthy class of people have avoided the fevers of the camp and the dangers of the battlefield, and have remained at home in comparative ease and comfort."[67]

Conscription filled the armies at the cost of alienating both rich and poor southerners. Simultaneously, the central government was failing disastrously to cope with financing the war. Richmond, capital of the Confederacy, at first refused to authorize significant direct taxation and hoped to rely on state support and borrowing. In fact, the war effort was financed primarily by printing money. When that was combined with the shortages inevitable during any large war, but especially in a country blockaded by a superior naval power, the result was first a steady and then an explosive inflation.[68] Burgeoning prices made it difficult either to supply the army or to care for the poor, including the families of poor soldiers. To supply the army, the Confederate government turned to impressment, and thus further alienated farmers and planters, who also were expected to carry the burden of supporting the poor with voluntary contributions or state and local taxes. This expectation, too, fell victim to the size of the war. Impressment and poverty, no less than conscription, raised vexing questions about liberty and equality in the Confederacy, questions that split white society many ways.[69]

From the beginning of the war, southerners had realized that special provision would have to be made for the families of poor soldiers if they were to be successfully recruited. In October 1861, for example, Elisha Cain of Hancock county had raised a new company of volunteers, but he wanted to wait until November 20 for the company to be accepted into the service, since "many of my men are farmers and poor men. . . . By that time my men can all make their arrangements gather their crops etc and be ready to leave home for the winter . . . otherwise my company will be disbanded."[70] By the beginning of 1862, little Glascock county was supporting the families of at least eight soldiers; by the end of that year, Edgefield, South Carolina, was supporting 500 families, or almost one-sixth of all families in the district.[71] Ultimately, Georgia and South Carolina together raised millions of dollars to provide relief for the poor during the war. Georgia's 1864 property-tax rates, for example, were fifteen times the 1860 rate, and the state also enacted a progressive income tax. More than half these taxes, by far the highest in Georgia's history, went directly to civilian welfare spending.[72]

These efforts were supplemented by a large expansion of the traditional support of neighbors by wealthier slaveowners. James Henry Hammond sold salt (to preserve meat) at bargain prices to needy neighbors and sold corn at below-market prices to several families.[73] In 1862, John Hollingsworth of Edgefield donated 500 bushels of corn to indigent soldiers' families.[74] In 1863, Dr. Thomas Janes of Greene county gave away or sold at low prices more than 3,000 bushels of wheat.[75] In 1862, Turner Clanton of Columbia county offered corn for sale to poor families of Augusta (in neighboring Richmond county) at half the prevailing market price.[76] David C. Barrow supplied corn to people who lived near all his plantations during the war.[77]

Yet these efforts could not prevent privation and destitution, especially as the war went on and prices soared. A Washington county woman complained to Governor Joseph E. Brown that women with two children "onley got 40 dollars for tha year and this year we hant got but 40 dollais and we cant get nothing but what we have to give government price." Local planters and farmers, she added, "has got so hardhearted tha wont let us have it without tha ful price."[78] An Oglethorpe county war widow wrote to Alexander H. Stephens that the county inferior court "gives me nothing from some cause I [know] not. . . . I am in greatt need I have no money."[79] The Edgefield "Vigilant Association," which pledged to support the poor in their neighborhood, was breaking down by the end of 1861, and little money was being contributed. A notice in the *Advertiser* asked nonattending members, "Will you leave it for a few to bear the burthens in which all are interested?"[80] In the spring of 1862, the *Advertiser's* editor noted that the $16,000 tax raised in Edgefield for the year to support the poor would fall far short of the need; as it turned out, the tax provided only $16 per person during the year, about enough to buy ten bushels of corn at Augusta wholesale prices.[81] In November 1862, the relief board, in charge of spending Edgefield's relief funds, received a petition signed by "ten suffering women of Edgefield" who alluded to "their privations in the pitiable terms of unaffected distress." All their husbands were in the army. (The editor of the *Advertiser* decided not to print the letter, although he did mention it in his columns.)[82] By August 1862, Hammond was not sure he could "keep up my poor neighbors another year."[83]

Inflation itself gave rise to almost universal complaints of "speculation" and "extortion." At first, in the autumn of 1861, these complaints were directed mainly against merchants and other middlemen. As early as September in a Charleston newspaper, "Phyllis" denounced merchants for raising their prices, and her letter was reprinted in Edgefield.[84] Cotton planters began to realize that their 1861 crop would have no market, and anxiously wondered "what is the prospect of getting money for our cotton"; people began to worry that their property would be "sacrificed to the advantage of a few whom the War makes fat."[85] Merchants replied, with some justice, that they simply passed on high prices for goods they bought.[86] In any case, attachment to free-market principles created a strong prejudice against any attempt to control prices directly. For example, when the price of salt rose precipitously in late 1861, Governor Brown ordered his agents to seize all salt being sold for more than $5 a sack, paying that amount in compensation. The Augusta *Chronicle* editorialized that his action showed a danger that the South would lose its liberty to an internal tyranny.[87] James Thomas, who had written the summer before about the great patriotism evident everywhere in Hancock county, thought by February 1862 that "we are wanting in patriotism, we hate the Yankees, but I fear we have no love of country. . . . I fear and believe we have started on our new government with all the corrupting influences we had." High prices were his chief evidence of corruption. If he were in power, he wrote, he would "hang without law ½ Doz. speculators & extortioners in this County."[88]

One response to the rise in prices and the prospects of a long war was the movement to replace cotton with corn in the fields. Even in 1861, some had seen the war as an opportunity to put into practice the old dream of a diversified agriculture, to get southern farmers off "the same old beaten track, planting each year all the cotton they can cultivate, and just enough corn and small grain to make out with."[89] Early in 1862, the necessity for a large grain crop was obvious; as the *Southern Cultivator* of Augusta put it, farmers must make an "OVERWHELMING AND SUPER-ABUNDANT CROP OF PROVISIONS."[90] The Edgefield *Advertiser* argued that "the poor soldier has a right . . . to expect that in pitching their crops, the aim should not be to keep corn and meat at extortionate prices, but to make them abundant and cheap. . . . He has a right to expect that the fortunate owners of lands and negroes will patriotically bend all their energies and resources to fill the land with plenty, and make its defence a cheap and cheerful task."[91] Planters in every neighborhood met to vow they would restrict the cotton crop. Warren county planters resolved that "no true and enlightened patriot will plant a full crop of cotton."[92] Hancock county planters resolved to "devote their whole resources to the production of provisions."[93] Greene county planters resolved to plant cotton for home production only, and that anyone who planted more would "give aid and comfort to the enemy, and make war upon his neighbors, his country, and his own prosperity."[94]

Even this common-sense plan was resisted by many farmers who wanted no direction from any quarter, including public opinion. The reporter of the Hancock meeting mentioned that "a

very few, have refused to PLEDGE, not, however, because of opposition to the policy, but because they are opposed to SIGNING
written pledges."[95] Many planters and farmers found it difficult
to give up the king of crops. Dolly Burge, in March 1862, noted
in her diary that "everybody says we must plant little or no cotton. I hardly know what to do about it." In May, she was planting
corn, but "dislike[d] doing it, however."[96] In a notorious incident, Robert Toombs himself defied local sentiment in the southwest Georgia county where he owned an absentee plantation.
Apparently just to assert his prerogatives and demonstrate his
personal independence, he ordered his overseer to plant a cotton
crop even larger than usual. The local "Committee of Safety" denounced his "avarice" with "unqualified indignation" and resolved that Toombs should destroy his crop in the field and turn
over his slaves to the committee to labor on river fortifications.[97]
Such attitudes led to state laws restricting cotton production in
both Georgia and South Carolina.[98] In Georgia, for example, cotton planting was restricted to a maximum of three acres per
hand. Governor Brown, indeed, urged a further restriction to a
maximum of one-quarter acre per hand. Slaveholders, Brown argued, "are dependent upon our white laborers in the field of
battle, for the protection of their property, and in turn this army
of white laborers and their families are dependent upon the
slaveowner for a support." The cotton restriction, Brown argued,
would help keep food prices within reach of the poor.[99] The legislature, however, left the three-acre restriction in place. In any
case, the restriction was one policy that was helped by the market, at least at first; as Dolly Burge noted, the cotton market was
too uncertain during the war.[100] Most planters finally turned almost wholly to grain crops. The tax assessments of Stephens and
of Barrow, for example, show that they were planting almost no
cotton by 1864.[101]

Still, the vast increase in the availability of grain crops did not
ease prices, nor make life much easier for the poor. As the war
continued, it became obvious that what critics called the "spirit
of extortion" had invaded almost every household. Farmers, like
everybody else, waited until the price was right. In September
1862, the Edgefield *Advertiser* mentioned in its weekly letter to

soldiers that wheat "is said to have stampeded and left the premises, *en masse*, to the tune of four, five and latterly, even *six dollars* per bushel. The temptation was irresistible, and the wheat
market is closed."[102] In October, the Hancock county grand jury
condemned the "spirit of extortion manifested by a considerable
portion of the citizens of these states and spreading with greatest
rapidity, to every branch of trade."[103] "Front Face," in a letter to
the Augusta *Chronicle*, declared that "landholders and slaveholders" were often as guilty of extortion as were merchants. He
argued that large slaveholders should sell "superfluous" land and
slaves to "their less fortunate neighbors for moderate prices," a
policy not likely to be of help to truly poor families.[104] In November 1862, Reverend John H. Cornish of Aiken, South Carolina,
spent an entire day "in quest of food," but was only partially successful, since "the country people" were bringing in little produce. "They seem to have caught the spirit of extortion." Four
months later, Cornish seems to have caught some of it himself.
He traded some tea, which had cost him $48, for 200 yards of
cloth and $75 in cash. He then sold the cloth in Augusta for an-
other $218, thus realizing, in the space of ten days, a profit of
some 500 percent.[105]

Inflation led to various official attempts to control or regulate
markets and prices. In addition to restrictions on cotton production, South Carolina and Georgia sharply limited distilling.[106]
Both states passed laws against extortion, and there were at least
some convictions under the laws.[107] Governor Bonham of South
Carolina forbade the export of corn into Augusta, presumably
the home of the worst speculators.[108] Hart county even forbade
corn to be taken beyond county lines, and set a maximum price
(in May 1863) of $2 a bushel.[109] "Justice," in a letter to the Edge-
field *Advertiser* in early 1863, urged the state legislature to regulate prices more generally.[110] These efforts came largely to nothing, partly because such economic regulation was anathema in
this free-market economy. The Augusta *Chronicle*'s editor denounced vigilance committees that tried to regulate corn markets, on the grounds that the interference would destroy the
markets altogether.[111] The *Constitutionalist* made the reasonable argument that financial policies and shortages, rather than

speculation and extortion, were at the bottom of price rises; it also made the less reasonable argument that seizing salt or other goods to distribute among the poor was a sign of "despotism."[112] When Kate Rowland of Augusta paid $30 for a pair of shoes, she wrote in her diary that she was "sure we shall never have peace so long as this spirit of extortion pervades the country." Yet in the same diary entry, she branded the government's seizure of salt for less than market prices as "a perfect species of *swindling* . . . I think a person perfectly justified in hiding it from the government."[113] Hammond was helpful to his poor neighbors when he could be, but he also casually assumed that "Negroes & poor people . . . must learn to do without bacon & the rich eat it sparingly, & all meat pretty much the same." Meanwhile, Hammond's brother and son were "involved in speculations—against my protest."[114]

So people were left with laments and jeremiads. "Peter the Hermit," in the Edgefield *Advertiser*, exhorted "The Farmers of South Carolina" to "*arise from the worship of your golden calves*" and save the country from the "*despotism—slavery*" brought on by speculators.[115] The Augusta *Constitutionalist* printed a "Sermon Suited to the Times" on the text "He that withholdeth corn, the people shall curse him; but blessings shall be upon the head of him that selleth it."[116] The *Chronicle*'s editor noted with regret "the spirit of selfishness and sordidness which has long prevailed among certain classes of our people."[117] The Morgan county grand jury denounced extortion, but did not single out any individuals because the practice was so extensive that "we know not where to begin, and if we begin where to end. . . . It is beyond human power to suppress it."[118]

Owners of slaves and land were, naturally, hurt less by inflation than were the poor who had to buy their food. Thus inflation was bound to create class resentments in the South. But another consequence of explosive inflation struck at the "liberties" of producers, especially landowners and slaveowners. The Confederate government had so much trouble buying provisions and the labor of slaves for war service that it was eventually impressing both provisions and slave labor on a large scale. Even patriotic planters tended to see this action as an intolerable invasion of treasured individual liberties.[119]

The practice was most widespread where the Confederate armies were actually operating, so Georgia and South Carolina farmers and planters did not at first feel the impact of impressment policies. One of the earliest calls for slaves in Georgia came for labor to build fortifications on the Savannah river south of Augusta in March 1862 (the Union army had taken Port Royal on the South Carolina coast in the previous autumn). James Henry Hammond refused to send any of his slaves, arguing that the plan to fortify nearby Shell Bluff was untenable.[120] In April, Hammond and other local planters were ordered to send slaves to work on fortifications at Charleston. Hammond remonstrated with General J. C. Pemberton, who was in charge of the Charleston project, that the slaves were needed to grow crops and that they would be more useful in fortifying the upper Savannah river (apparently the value of this plan had increased in his estimation since March). He also complained that "our upcountry negroes will be demoralized by going to the coast & bring up information & excite dispositions that may do serious hurt to the state."[121] He managed to hire six free black men to take the place of the fourteen slaves he was called on to contribute and promised to donate money to hire more; he refused, however, to send his own slaves.

In August 1862, upcountry Georgia planters' slaves were impressed, this time to help build fortifications at Savannah. Richmond county planters met to consider the requisitions, made by General Hugh W. Mercer, and decided that since Mercer did not have the express permission of the Secretary of War, slaveowners should not feel obliged to obey his orders.[122] Linton Stephens wrote to his brother that he had "made up my mind not to submit to this impressment at *present*—I shall acquiesce when it appears to be endorsed by the Government."[123] In September, Linton Stephens and other Hancock county planters held a "patriotic meeting" to denounce "all usurpations of authority, and General Mercer's impressment of negroes in particular." Since by this time, the secretary of war had countermanded Mercer's orders, the Hancock planters resolved to offer their slaves' labor voluntarily. "All this was excellent if it had only been carried out," Stephens wrote to his brother. "But when we came to subscribing the negroes there was a miserable failure." The meeting melted away, and "literally nothing was done."[124] As the Hancock episode had shown, the voluntarism congenial to traditional ideas of republican liberty was proving utterly inadequate to the task of carrying on a great war.

Impressment of food, cattle, and horses also provoked fierce resistance. The fundamental problem was that impressment almost always resulted in payments to farmers (and occasionally to merchants) at below-market prices. In August 1863, the editor of the Augusta *Constitutionalist* acknowledged this as an unfortunate evil, but one necessary to feed the armies. The next month, the editor was critical of the operation of the impressment law, but still urged support.[125] The newspapers also regularly lambasted the alleged partiality and incompetence of impressment officers. "Justice" wrote in the Edgefield *Advertiser* that impressment agents were very active in keeping prices down to government levels when the estates of deceased people were auctioned off, but allowed the "very honorable gentry" who held flour in villages to sell it at high prices in Augusta and Graniteville.[126]

Howell Cobb, Georgia politician and Confederate general, touring the Augusta area in February 1864, urged farmers and planters to lay aside their objections to government prices. They might have a legal right to market prices, but "when the country needs them, a patriot will not demand" those prices. Compare yourselves with soldiers and widows, he told them. By comparison, planters were well off, and their legal nitpickings were "a reproach to men seeking to be free. . . . The farmers have ever been regarded as the purest classes of society. Extortion, it must be admitted, had penetrated their ranks," but Cobb "was proud to believe that the infection was not deep-seated or general."[127]

Such appeals did little to abate farmers' and planters' resistance to Confederate policy. In May 1864, a man was killed by an impressment agent in Newton County over the seizure of cattle for the army.[128] Hammond himself was embroiled with impressment agents during the summer of that year. In January, he had written to his overseer, "You will not drive up my cattle to be Impressed, & you will forbid any person from entering on my premises for any such purposes, on penalty of being arrested as trespassers." Hammond insisted that if any of his property were impressed, he would get full market price.[129] In July, he received a notice impressing all his "surplus" corn for $5 a bushel. He had just signed contracts with the Graniteville Company and others to sell thousands of bushels at $10 each. As Hammond described the incident in his journal, when the agent showed up with the orders, Hammond "tore up & threw [them] out of the window in his presence, saying I paid no respect to the order . . . & simply defied him"; he concluded somewhat lamely that he had "not meant to offend."[130] Two weeks later, the agents returned with papers showing that several of Hammond's customers had canceled their contracts; the agents promised to seize the corn by force if Hammond did not surrender it, "thus branding upon my forehead 'slave,'" Hammond wrote in words that surely would have brought a smile to the faces of several hundred people on his plantations.[131] The impressors paid only the $5 they had originally offered. "Good God!" Hammond exclaimed in a letter to his friend William Gilmore Simms, "could I ever have conceived that I should be subjected to such humiliation & degredation at the hands of southern people; much less from my brother citizens native like myself to the State of South Carolina."[132]

The sacrifices of war created burdens far too heavy to be borne by a society determined to keep alive ideas of pristine liberty, for the liberty of white southerners was tied far too strongly to the right to pursue individual wealth; the South now had to choose between republican liberty and republican equality. The confusion that resulted is well illustrated in the editorial columns of the Augusta *Constitutionalist* in October 1863. The whole country, the editor wrote, should become an armed camp. The South should put 300,000 more men into the army. We might easily win the war in six months, he thought, if "we would have equality and brotherhood, . . . disarm the bitter prejudice of the veterans and soften the lot of their families, . . . put down speculation and extortion, . . . take possession of all the property of the country and all its provisions, give rations to soldiers and farmers and merchants, and all alike." Two days later, he was arguing that prices could not be regulated by law. The South, he thought, must simply endure and cultivate "a cheerful and hopeful frame of mind."[133]

Hammond was one of many planters and political leaders in the Augusta area who interpreted the policies of the Jefferson Davis government as egregious violations of individual, community, and states' rights. These opponents of Davis tended to interpret his actions in the only political language they knew: the republican values of liberty and the corresponding fears of corruption, tyranny, and conspiracy in the seats of power. Hammond, Governor Joseph Brown, Linton and Alexander Stephens, and Robert Toombs, among others, were among Davis's most powerful and, therefore, dangerous opponents in the South. They tended to concentrate on somewhat different issues: Brown was most critical of conscription; Toombs, of impressment and Confederate financial policies; the Stephens brothers, of the laws giving Davis the right to suspend habeas corpus in cases involving resistance to conscription. At various times, however, all agreed on most of the issues; all agreed that the Confederate government was violating people's liberties in unacceptable and unconstitutional ways. In every case, Davis had a reasonable constitutional argument to back up his own interpretation, and, indeed, even the Georgia Supreme Court consistently upheld him against the protests of its governor. Such arguments and decisions did not, however, silence the critics.[134]

As early as May 1861, Hammond wrote to his friend Simms that Lincoln was establishing a military despotism and that "Davis I fear is quite disposed to do the same."[135] The next year, he wrote to his brother that Davis's policies seemed designed to make a dictator necessary to win the war.[136] By the end of 1863, he was identifying resistance to impressment with defense of the Magna Carta.[137] The next spring, he thought that "our executive is entirely too strong now for our liberties;" the constitution should be amended to make the president a figurehead only, limited to two years in office.[138] In June 1864, he wrote to Simms that Davis was, by his legal powers alone, already the strongest dictator in history.[139]

The Stephens brothers interpreted Davis's policies in similar fashion. Shortly after the conscription act was passed in 1862, Alexander Stephens wrote to Thomas W. Thomas that "if the General Government has the power to conscript and control every fighting man in the States . . . it is a mockery to talk of States Rights and will soon be not much short of mockery to talk of Constitutional liberty."[140] Not surprisingly, Thomas, the same Thomas who had resigned his colonelcy and was now a superior court judge, ruled the act unconstitutional.[141]

Linton Stephens, the next year, thought that if Davis were given the right to suspend habeas corpus, "free government will be irretrievably gone." Davis, he added, has "pursued a *system* of policy which seems to me to look to absolutism; and therefore I am compelled to believe he aims at it." The people had committed a fatal error by submitting to conscription; they seemed "*never* to be able to appropriate the teachings of history. . . . These rapidly accumulating and gigantic usurpations, with a *connecting thread* running through the whole of them and binding them together as links in a chain, fill me with alarm."[142] By the end of 1863, Linton was brooding constantly on Davis's usurpations, and even told Alexander that "the knife of a Brutus would be a solution of the trouble *perhaps*."[143] Two months later, Alexander predicted that if the current version of a suspension of habeas corpus were to become law and if the people were to submit to it, constitutional liberty would "go down, never to rise again on this continent, I fear. This is the worst that can befall us. Far better that our country should be overrun by the enemy, our cities sacked and burned, and our land laid desolate, than that the people should thus suffer the citadel of their liberties to be entered and taken by professed friends."[144] He would, of course, see this preference satisfied.

Brown, meanwhile, had been denouncing Davis's policies regularly in messages to the General Assembly. Like Stephens, he based his arguments on narrow constructions of the Confederate constitution.[145] By 1864, Brown, both Stephenses, and Toombs had become outspoken in their opposition to Davis, although their public pronouncements were less inflammatory than were some of their private letters. Linton Stephens introduced resolutions in the General Assembly to denounce the suspension of habeas corpus, and Alexander appeared there to support the sentiments in the resolutions. In a long address, he rehearsed the arguments from policy, from his interpretation of the constitution, and from English liberty on the subject. He closed with an appeal to the legislature to reject any proffered choice between liberty and independence. "Liberty is the animating spirit, the soul of our system of government, and like the soul of man, when once lost it is lost forever." Liberty and independence must stand together, "and if such be our fate, let them and us all go down together in a common ruin. Without liberty, I would not turn upon my heel for independence." [146] Behind Stephens's fears of Davis and of loss of liberty were his old fears of corruption: "Power is corrupting," he wrote to one friend in 1864. "It fascinates, intoxicates, turns the brain and changes the nature of man. It transforms those who touch and handle it. Such is its unvarying tendency." [147]

These critics of Davis were by no means without their own opponents within Georgia and South Carolina. Many men were impatient with constitutional arguments about liberty; they wanted to win the war by any means and worry about liberty later.[148] The result of the anti-Davis movement was, in fact, to create a deep split within the planter elite. Linton Stephens complained that many legislators opposed his resolutions because they thought "the chances for enjoying all that they prize; that is life, and some master's permission to hold their substance and exercise locomotion, are better under a despot than in a fuss." [149] One Warren county resident wrote to Alexander Stephens that many people could not support Toombs's possible candidacy for Congress because they considered his opposition to Davis "morbid." The writer admired Toombs, but thought that if Toombs had really said, as reported, that "he would rather live under the dominion of Lincoln than the arbitrary rule of Jeff Davis," it was a sign of suicidal factionalism. Indeed, the writer believed that "any man taking issue with the Administration at this particular time, will find it an uphill business." [150]

As the war dragged on, however, those who disagreed with Confederate policies found it easy to adopt attacks on Davis as an antirepublican. Toward the end of the war, the Augusta *Chronicle*'s editor became bitterly hostile to Davis's "unconstitutional graspings for power" and his attempt to establish "military despotism."[151] Davis's defenders, in turn, attacked his opponents as factious, ambitious men, who would rule or ruin.[152] Some men had decided that there must be a choice between liberty and independence, and they chose liberty over a "despotism" at home. To others, independence was more important, even if a dictator were necessary. Many found it impossible to choose or even to conceive of such a choice. The history of republics also taught, after all, that states have most to fear from "internal discords and commotions"; if serious divisions "shall occur among us, no desperation of courage . . . can save us."[153] By 1864, the South's precious façade of social unity had broken, and southerners in Augusta's hinterlands seemed determined to test whether their new republic could survive in the face of fierce "discords and commotions."

Chapter 6

The Captives Set Free

O n October 3, 1863, Linton Stephens was in Atlanta with his company of state-militia troops from Hancock County. That day, he wrote to his brother, he had learned that his plantation smokehouse had been broken into by a band of slaves and that all his meat had been taken; many of the slaves "had been taken up and even in jail on account of it." Stephens claimed not to be surprised. "I feel very uneasy about the state of things at home and in the country similarly situated. This war can not be carried on successfully upon the present basis." If the South could not win the war without stripping the countryside of all its men, "we might as well abandon the contest." The problem was slavery: "Our negro population are going to give us great trouble. They are becoming extensively corrupted. The necessary pains to keep them on our side, and in order have been unwisely and sadly neglected. . . . I believe that the institution of slavery is already so undermined and demoralized as never to be of much use to us, even if we had peace and independence to day. The institution has received a terrible shock which is tending to its disintegration and ruin."[1]

Stephens's broodings were surely only strengthened when he learned more about the "negro affair in Hancock." A number of slaves had organized a conspiracy to arm themselves and, when Union troops reached within striking distance, make their way to freedom. The slaves included those owned by some of Hancock's wealthiest and most prominent slaveholders, including Linton Stephens himself and his father-in-law, James Thomas. William McKinley, of Baldwin county, when told of the conspiracy, wrote to David C. Barrow that the plot apparently had encompassed "all the country to Augusta, Athens & Eatonton."[2] Thirty-four of the slaves were charged, either formally in court or informally by a vigilance committee of slaveholders, with "attempt to excite an insurrection."[3] The ringleaders were a small group of artisans. Because most of them were highly mobile, they could communicate with slaves over a wide area. John Cain, a painter, had spent seven years in Savannah as a waiter. He was, apparently, the leading conspirator; other slaves told Hancock's white men that Cain was for shedding blood. Dick Shaw also was a painter, almost white in appearance. He apparently had tried to draw in slaves in Athens and Augusta. Mac Simmons, a blacksmith, and Spencer Beasley, a Crawfordville shoemaker, were deeply implicated. According to McKinley, the conspiracy was largely confined to those very slaves closest to their masters: artisans, carriage drivers, and body servants.[4]

At the trial at the end of November, Cain "refused to plead but stood mute." He and three others were sentenced to hang. The rest were sentenced to hundreds of lashes. Linton Stephens's own body servant, Cary, was among the group. He confessed his involvement, and Stephens promised to help save him from hanging.[5] As a result, Cary had to endure only the painful whippings, carried out daily over a week.

Alexander Stephens witnessed the whippings. They almost sickened him: "They stretch them upon a log make them fast— take off their britches—turn their shirts over their heads and strap them with a piece of buggy [leather]." The effect was designed to create maximum pain, and several slaves screamed loudly; some emptied their bowels involuntarily. Yet Cary preferred to "take all his whipping terrible as it is than to be a witness in the case."[6] Cary and the others had refused to testify against any fellow slaves even to lighten their own punishment. Linton Stephens had urged Cary to make a full confession in court, but although he "seem[ed] very much alarmed" by his fate, he was "yet resolved not to criminate any of his associates. . . . Poor Cary! The whole negro population is innoculated," Linton added. Slavery was "doomed, and I fear that it is doomed to go out in blood and horror."[7]

Soon after his sentence, Cain managed to escape from Hancock's jail, along with Beasley, another of those who had been sentenced to hang.[8] The Hancock inferior court appropriated $1,000 as a reward, and advertised for Cain's capture in the Augusta newspapers: a "dark mulatto" with "black sparkling eyes, long eye lashes, mustache and whiskers, bad countenance."[9] Cain was caught in Jefferson county near the plantation of a former owner; in January 1864, his sentence was carried out.[10] Beasley was caught in Augusta. With the support of both Stephens brothers, a petition—signed by more than "120 odd of the best citizens in the county"[11]—was circulated to have Beasley's punishment commuted to whipping. No doubt this was prompted in part by a genuine sympathy for Beasley and his fellow slaves, but there were other considerations as well. As Alexander Stephens argued, a commutation would "have a good effect upon the negroe population and we dont know how much we may stand in need of the encouragement of such feelings amongst them as he manifested" in the counsels of the conspirators, since Beasley had urged them to avoid violence and simply strike for freedom.[12] Governor Joseph E. Brown did commute the sentence, to 400 lashes.[13]

No one knows how many such plans were laid by slaves, how many plots were hatched or failed to be hatched. The Hancock episode was reported in the Milledgeville newspapers, and then picked up by the Augusta *Constitutionalist*; yet the editor of the *Constitutionalist* noted that he would have preferred not to have mentioned such an event.[14] However, another paper already had. Outsiders praised the discretion of the vigilance committee of slaveholders, which apparently had gone to great lengths to try to hide the affair even from local whites. McKinley thought that Hancock's poor white men had been kept "in total ignorance of the matter."[15] It is hard to believe the effort succeeded. Thomas W. Thomas, a prominent Democratic politician, praised Hancock's committee for having prevented a total breakdown of law; he feared an outbreak of "hanging, burning and torturing without delay and without discrimination."[16] Even the relatively protected enclave of Augusta's hinterlands had reached such a point of crisis after two years of war. The resistance of slaves was only one indication of the tremendous problems that war had brought.

Society in Augusta's hinterlands was slowly cracking apart under the strains of war. The ideological and social underpinnings of a slaveholding republic were proving unequal to the supreme test.

The social unity of the South had always been founded, southerners claimed, on black slavery. And while the unity itself was breaking, the foundation, too, was crumbling. When the war began, slaves knew that it involved slavery. As the fighting continued, slaves made it their war, too.

At the outset of secession, public spokesmen professed to be sanguine about slavery in a nation perhaps soon to be at war. Secession would demonstrate, one writer said, that perpetual democracy was possible in a society based on "democratic aristocracy—an aristocracy of race, with a democracy of power."[17] Another confessed to be "perfectly assured . . . that slavery is the great conservative element of this country, and the best foundation for a *permanent* Republican government."[18] When war broke out at Fort Sumter, people continued to insist that slavery would not be a handicap to the South. On the contrary, the South was especially suited for war abroad and peace at home because it had young men fit for war, slaves suited solely and peculiarly for tilling the earth, and family heads available for a home guard and supervision of farming.[19] The Augusta *Constitutionalist*'s editor agreed: "Our negroes will remain quietly and faithfully at home, and cultivate our lands, to feed our armies, while our entire adult white population, if need be, will be under arms." He even thought the war might be a good thing in part because it would demonstrate that slavery was a source of social strength, not weakness. "Vague apprehensions" of insurrection had been entertained "by some of the nervous and timid of the weaker sex among us," he admitted, but "our slaves will prove the most efficient laborer[s] a people at war ever left at home."[20] James Henry Hammond agreed with this argument. He earlier had written that it was a "great mistake to suppose, as is generally done abroad, that in case of war slavery would be a source of weakness." On the contrary, in case of war, slaves would remain "peaceful on our plantations," and so the South could "put forth more strength in such an emergency, at less sacrifice, than any other people of the same numbers."[21] In June 1861, he asserted that the South's mission was now "to come out of this with Negro slavery established [and] *recognized* as the true basis of Society & Govt. in all staple growing countries."[22] The Reverend J. R. Pickett, in a sermon preached in Edgefield, South Carolina, about the same time, noted that the North predicted that the slaves would rise, but he smugly predicted that "it will only be in price that they will rise. The pure negro never did rebel—he never will—and men know this who know the negro best. He will not give up one of his first rights—the right of a master."[23]

Yet it was obvious that "vague apprehensions" of insurrection were shared by many people, not all of them among the "nervous and timid of the weaker sex." In May, the Edgefield *Advertiser* warned that slaves should not be left in their quarters without white supervision and that patrols must be kept up constantly.[24] Local "vigilance committees" and "home guards" were organized to keep up patrols and keep watch over all "suspicious persons."[25] In July 1861, two white men known to have traded with blacks in Columbia county were ordered to leave the area.[26] "A Word to the Women," from "Lucy Lavender," urged women to learn to use firearms and to keep servants away from places where firearms were stored—"for fear of an accident."[27] But an address by a Miss Hammond to the Edgefield Rangers used no such coy language when she told them that "we know not at what moment a John Brown may spring up in our very midst."[28]

White nervousness, in fact, appeared almost immediately in the form of fears of arson and insurrection. A Hancock county vigilance committee hanged a slave in July 1861 for allegedly having burned his master's house.[29] In Greene county in June, a patrol caught David C. Barrow's slave Israel off the plantation; they soon had convinced themselves that, as Barrow's overseer told him, "there is an Insurrectionary movement among the negroes and Several of your boys are strongly implicated."[30] Five days later, Barrow heard a similar tale from the overseer of his southwest Georgia plantation: "The country Has Been in great excitement for the Last two weeks on account of an insurrection plot that Had gotten up among the Negroes. Nearly all of yours were implicated. . . . I was the first man they were going to kill. Evry Negro for 20 miles told the same tale."[31] Information about these scares is sketchy, and they may have been largely a product of white anxieties.[32] The anxieties show, however, that slaveowners were more than a little nervous about the ultimate loyalty of their slaves.

As the war continued and more and more white men left for the army, these anxieties increased. In November 1861, the Edgefield *Advertiser*'s editor called for heightened discipline by vigilance groups to control, as he discreetly put it, the "loose conduct in a certain class of our population."[33] The next week, he was more explicit: "Our peculiar domestic establishment is undergoing trial by fire." While it was the best social system known, the "weak and susceptible" among the "cheerful . . . class of our population" might be led to harbor "absurd visions . . . destructive of the order and well-being of the South."[34] In late 1861, E. R. Carswell of Burke County wrote to Governor Joseph E. Brown to suggest that an executive proclamation to ban the traditional Christmas holiday for slaves would prevent "the corrupting influence of association and interviews" with unnamed persons.[35] By May 1862, Hammond was confiding in his journal that "these are terrible times. All our young in the armies, not [enough] men left to suppress a negro insurrection." He added that as yet, there were no symptoms of one.[36]

Most masters must have realized that slaves somehow understood the stakes of the war. Before the attack on Fort Sumter, Hammond told a northern acquaintance that "our black people know all about" abolition. "Why there are thousands of slaves in the South who can read as well as you or me. I have at least a dozen on my plantation. They teach each other and I never interfere with it." Usually, he insisted, these were the most intelligent, loyal, and faithful slaves. In any case, "at every public meeting to discuss the topics of the day about ten per cent of the audience are negroes who know everything."[37]

Jacob Stroyer, a former South Carolina slave, remembered that he and his family had been well aware of the import of the war. They had prayed regularly for a Union victory.[38] Former slaves interviewed in the 1930s remembered having heard talk of freedom during the war. Marshall Butler said he had seen "a red cloud in de West in 1860. I knew war was brewing."[39] Elisha Gary remembered thinking "joy was on de way when us heared 'bout freedom, if us did have to whisper."[40] Adeline Willis told her interviewer about "a little old black sassy woman in the Quarters that was a talkin' all the time about 'freedom.' She give our white folks lots of trouble—she was so sassy to them."[41] Minnie Davis's mother stole newspapers and read about the war; she passed on the information to other slaves in church. Her mother used to pray, "Oh, Lord, please send the Yankees on and let them set us free."[42]

The evidence is scattered and impossible to quantify, but it seems certain that there was a steady and perceptible increase in slave resistance, violence, and general discontent during the war. Linton Stephens had trouble on his Jefferson County plantation with slaves who complained that the overseer was driving them too hard. One slave told him that they were "all very much dissatisfied." Later he heard that "all my negroes there intend to run away unless I go to see them soon."[43] One formerly favorite servant of Alexander H. Stephens, named Pierce, became a chronic troublemaker. He was jailed for damaging someone's property, and finally was shot and killed during an alleged robbery.[44] Barrow's overseers suffered with several seemingly incorrigible runaways and shirkers. Peter ran away from the Greene county plantation, and when he returned, he refused to let the overseer whip him.[45] Sam repeatedly ran away from Barrow's Camilla plantation, even though the overseer "whiped Hime time & again but all to no purpos."[46] Barrow's Oglethorpe overseer discovered, in January 1864, secret tunnels into the smokehouse and the chicken house.[47] In October 1864, after General William Sherman had taken Atlanta, Barrow's Greene county overseer wrote, "I can tell you that most any of the negroes will go to the yankee if they can get half a chance. I can see a wide difference in them what they were three months ago it is time for every man to keep his eyes open."[48]

Hammond experienced a similar loss of confidence in his power over his slaves. In November 1861, he noted that his slaves "look as they have for sometime *anxious*. Cant tell which side."[49] In the spring of 1863, he complained in his journal of a general failure of discipline at his river landing, and ordered that two of his slaves there be "well thrashed."[50] That June, he noticed a "heavy gloom which seems settled on all the negro faces. I have seen this gradually thickening ever since the Richmond battles of last year & more especially since the late repulse at Charleston. They seem utterly subdued as if by blasted hopes. . . . I have no doubt they have all along been well aprised with the abolition version of what is going on & *may* thus shut up their faces & cease their cheerful greetings in view of the future, not the past. They would wish to be passive & take what comes. But the roar of a single cannon of the Federals would make them frantic— savage cutthroats & incendiaries."[51] In August 1863, he described the slaves as "demoralized greatly—Stealing right & left. Corn and salt now. Found a closed hole apparently old standing in Bluff Barn through which any quantity of corn had doubtless passed."[52]

More slaves ran away, and many sought permanent freedom. Bill Austin, a Greene county slave, helped run his master's Greensboro store while the master was in the army. Many of the slaves in the neighborhood gathered at the store and told him stories "of how this or that slave ran away, and with the white man-power of the section engaged in war, remained at large for long periods or escaped altogether."[53]

After Sherman's army forced its way into Georgia in early 1864, Yankee lines proved to be an irresistible magnet for many slaves. In March, George Spencer of Augusta offered $500 for the return of Peter, who possibly was "making his way to the enemy."[54] Alfred Baker of Warren county advertised in May 1864 for five runaway slaves who "no doubt . . . are endeavoring to reach East Tennessee."[55] Lampkin, who was "quite intelligent, [and] can read and write," ran away in August. His owner thought that he was "undoubtedly making his way to the enemy's lines."[56] Peter ran away from his Edgefield, South Carolina, master, Josiah Sibley, that same month. Sibley noted that he had "reasons for believing that he is trying to make his way to Georgia to the Yankee lines."[57]

Blacks, shown in 1870 photograph, working much as slaves
twenty years earlier in the cotton fields, the heart of Augusta's
economy. (*Robert Williams Collection, University of Georgia
Libraries Special Collections*)

Storage jar made at Lewis Miles' plantation, Edgefield, South Carolina, by a literate slave artisan Dave, who also set type for the *Edgefield Hive*. (*Permanent Collections, McKissick Museum, University of South Carolina*)

Black family and their cabin, Augusta area. (*Robert Williams Collection, University of Georgia Libraries Special Collections*)

Cabin and adjacent buildings, slave quarters, Georgia. (*Robert Williams Collection, University of Georgia Libraries Special Collections*)

Black family and cabin, Georgia. (*Robert Williams Collection, University of Georgia Libraries Special Collections*)

The Jordan Cabin, cabin of poor Georgian whites, Washington county. (*Historic American Buildings Survey, Library of Congress*)

Simple four-room frame home of Parker Calloway, Wilkes county, Georgia, typical of most affluent slave owners. (*Terry Kay Rockefeller*)

Plantation home, Glen Mary, stately Hancock county mansion built in 1853 by slave owner-politician Theophilus Smith, similar to some homes of affluent whites. (*Georgia Department of Natural Resources, Historic Preservation Section. National Register of Historic Places, photograph by Van Jones Martin*)

Alexander H. Stephens, vice-president of the Confederacy, one of the most prominent Augusta-area men. (*National Archives and Records Service, photograph by Mathew Brady*)

Stephens's home, Liberty Hall, in Taliaferro county, Georgia. Like his portrait, it is dignified but unpretentious in style, much like Georgia politics. (*Alexander H. Stephens*, Constitutional View of The War Between the States States (*1868*))

James Henry Hammond, U.S. senator from South
Carolina, leading figure in the Augusta area. (*South
Caroliniana Library, photograph by Mathew Brady*)

Hammond's home, Redcliffe, in Edgefield district, South Carolina, reserved, almost haughty in style, much like South Carolina politics. (*Terry Kay Rockefeller*)

Courthouse, Wilkes county, Georgia, and Hancock Methodist church, Hancock county, Georgia, symbols of the white community's primary institutions and meeting places, the church of the slaves, as well. (*Georgia Department of Archives and History*)

William and Henry Bailey, sons of a Hart county day laborer, one a farmhand, one a mechanic, two of thousands of nonslaveholders who volunteered for the Confederate army. (*Georgia Department of Archives and History*)

Edward Porter Alexander, son of planter Adam Alexander of Washington, Georgia, after graduation from West Point; he commanded Confederate artillery at Gettysburg. (*Marian Alexander Boggs, ed.*, The Alexander Letters. *By permission of the Houghton Library, Harvard University*)

Advertisement for escaped slaves, John Cain and Spencer Beasley, after slave scheme to flee from Hancock county to Yankee lines; Cain was hung, Beasley whipped. (Augusta Daily Chronicle and Sentinel, *December 5, 1863*)

"Treasure hunters," *Harper's* illustration, slaves showing General Sherman's men where slaveholders' valuables are buried. (Harper's New Monthly Magazine, *October 1865*)

Many owners tried to blame other whites for problems with runaways. Iveson L. Brookes's overseer reported that Cole had run off after getting a pass "from some white man."[58] Thomas Chapman promised a $200 reward for the recovery of Henry, a slave carpenter—$100 of it for the conviction of a white harborer.[59] A Waynesboro owner offered $550 for the return of Solomon—$500 of it "for the person who decoyed him, if such be the case." Yet the description of Solomon suggested no need for decoys: he was "quite intelligent, knows the alphabet, can read words of two or three syllables, and is well posted in current events."[60]

Meanwhile, slave arrogance in public seemed to reach new proportions. The Edgefield *Advertiser*'s editor complained about rude slaves who crowded white customers at the local post office. "A Citizen" was upset at the many "negro parties" in and near the village of Edgefield; they must be stealing, he thought, since they seemed to have more to eat and drink than many poor whites.[61] The editor of the Augusta *Constitutionalist* complained of the "excessive indulgences" allowed local blacks, who somehow managed to ride around in "fine carriages" to their "balls" and parties; this "epidemic" should be curbed to prevent thefts.[62]

The Hancock conspiracy of 1863 had grown naturally from these circumstances: it involved slaves who knew not only about the general import of the war, but also about its specific progress; slaves who were emboldened both by growing hopes and by increasingly weaker supervision; slaves who never had accepted the masters' definition of their situation. Most slaves did not react violently; personal ties and fear of violent repression kept their protests and their expressions of hope largely within safer channels: prayer, running away, shirking work. Whites, though, had good reason to fear outbreaks of violence or conspiratorial behavior. In the apt words of historian Armstead Robinson, "the shadow of old John Brown" hampered the full mobilization of white manpower and left many soldiers with divided hearts.[63] William C. Wright wrote to Stephens from Atlanta that he had left his family in "the most awful condition," surrounded by "larger Negro Quarters" and without "any Protection." He wanted to go home. "I have not flinched from any duty that has been imposed upon me since the war commenced, and am still willing to do all that I can" he informed Stephens, "but my mind is now in such a frame that I shall be unable to do anything that will benefit the cause while I think of the condition of my children."[64] Barrow warned his overseer in 1864 to "keep a *sharp* lookout all the time. There are so few men left in the country those who are left must use redoubled vigilance. . . . Patrol frequently and punish Eny unlawful assembly of negroes."[65]

In 1863 and 1864, petitions and letters poured into Governor Brown's office requesting exemptions and details from Brown's requisitions of militia to defend the state from invasion by Sherman's army. A Burke county man wanted an exemption because he had charge of "three places on which there is no white persons but females & children. And there are thirty field hands on the three places . . . it would not be safe."[66] An Elbert county petition asked Brown to exempt Dr. L. L. Clark, who not only was a physician, but also was "peculiarly gifted in the capacity for governing." His presence would have "a salutary effect upon any disposed to be insubordinate."[67] Fifty-one women signed a petition requesting Brown to exempt or assign Michael Wiggins to preserve good order among slaves. "We confess our inability to govern so large a number of negroes."[68] From Lincoln county came two petitions to exempt from service Walker Hawes, "one of the best men we ever saw to patroll, govern and keep order among black people, and his services in this respect is now greatly needed."[69] From Jefferson county, three women whose husbands were soldiers asked Brown to detail Augustus J. Pugsley, an overseer who kept "a wholesome police in the vicinity."[70] Twenty-one women asked Brown to exempt Eli A. Veazey, an overseer on a large plantation that had many slaves with "vicious habits."[71] "Twenty-three ladies, some of us widows," asked Brown to release from militia service John H. Boyd of Columbia county, "on the ground that many slaves in this county are becoming ungovernable by the women & children & old men, insubordinate & insolent, that many are now runaways & some speak of making their way to the enemy." Boyd, they told Brown, not only was an "active, energetic & vigilant man," but also had "a number of dogs well-trained to hunt negroes."[72]

Exemptions and details for slaveowners and overseers were the rawest sore for many poor whites. The conflicting implications for the South of this dilemma were obvious to all, and nervous editors and politicians, by the middle of the war, had begun again to rehearse all their arguments for the superiority of slavery and its special benefits for white nonslaveowners.

Governor Joseph E. Brown of Georgia made this a major theme in his public messages. The war was not, he wrote in November 1863, the "rich man's quarrel and the poor man's fight," although he admitted that "many of the rich" had fallen short in fulfilling their obligations. Upon abolition, Brown claimed, the rich would flee with their money, leaving the poor to share the ballot and the jury box with the Negro and to compete with former slaves in the market for labor. Worse, defeat would destroy republican government. Under this government, "wealth and honors . . . like the waves of an ocean . . . are constantly changing place, and are transferred as generations pass, from one family to another." Should the North conquer the South, a military despotism would destroy the "equal political rights" that formed the basis of economic opportunities for the poor.[73]

Yet it was obvious that the poor were suffering much more than the wealthy and that the wealthy were, indeed, falling short in their support of poor families. In 1863, the Augusta *Constitutionalist*'s editors felt it necessary to remind slaveholders that "the non-slaveholder has shouldered the musket" in the war, so they must be assured that "their women and children at home are also well provided for."[74] Food riots in Atlanta and Milledgeville, Georgia, as well as in North Carolina and Richmond, indicated that not all families were being cared for.[75] In June 1863, the Edgefield *Advertiser*'s editor urged the rich to do something to relieve the poor, or else not be surprised when poor soldiers deserted the army.[76] Late that summer, the *Constitutionalist* returned to the subject, trying to excuse slaveowners who had resisted impressment of their slaves. It was not lack of patriotism, the editor assured his readers; he was obviously worried about having heard "a good deal of talk" about the "supposed conflict of interests, of the rich and the poor."[77] In November 1863, the editor argued that the Confederacy's "real difficulties are at home," in the neglect of orphans and widows, the riotous living among the rich, the "refusal to give of our abundance or to sell at prices within the reach of the mass of poor customers."[78]

With the Confederacy reeling from the losses at Gettysburg and Vicksburg in 1863, and in the face of the widening ideological and class divisions in the white community, a long season of demoralization set in. Even before then, many people had lost their enthusiasm for the fight. Women stopped attending meetings to raise money and to make clothing for soldiers.[79] Merchants and farmers began to refuse to accept Confederate money altogether.[80] In June 1863, Governor Brown called for volunteers to join the state troops who would defend Georgia from invasion, but volunteers were few. On July 15, Linton Stephens reported that a concerted effort, including three public meetings, to raise two companies of home guards had resulted in only twenty-five recruits.[81] Thomas W. Thomas told Brown that his efforts to raise a company in Elbert county were a failure; despite having been "industriously engaged . . . we have not raised a company."[82] Linton Stephens informed his brother that "there is a *fearful* giving away among our people. The spirit of volunteering is dead, dead, *dead*."[83] A woman wrote to Alexander Stephens from Lexington, Georgia, that the Confederacy's reverses had "cast a gloom over our community, and a deep despondency in the minds of many of the citizens."[84] When volunteer troops did go to Atlanta, the spirit of localism championed by Brown and the Stephens brothers against the government in Richmond bore fruit in the decision of one company "by a vote to adhere to their bounds—that is to say in effect, that they will go with us to the extremity of Cobb county [still 100 miles from the Yankee lines] and wait for us till we get there."[85] The Augusta *Constitutionalist* drew attention to the "stragglers" who began to appear in ever greater numbers at home. The editor blamed their "want of discipline" on "the election of officers" and "the disgust and dissatisfaction the men in ranks feel regarding the conduct of men at home."[86]

That "disgust and dissatisfaction" festered all the more in the face of continued inflation at home. The Athens *Southern Banner* published a letter to a Hart county citizen from a soldier in Virginia. "What has become," asked the soldier, "of all those boasted deeds of charity . . . that were heard from every stump and cross-road in Georgia and upon the faith of which hundreds of poor men left their homes, their wives and children. . . . I leave the tales of destitution and distress that reach us by every mail from these poor families, to answer." It was well known, the writer continued, that the cause was speculation, not scarcity: farmers were selling provisions in Athens for high prices and were refusing to help poor women. "I warn such men," he concluded, "that they are slumbering on the crest of a volcano, which, if things don't change, will break through and envelope them in ruin."[87]

Few men replaced the thousands of dead and disabled as the war took its fearful toll. Of a sample of almost 300 soldiers from three area counties, more than 35 percent were killed in action or died of wounds or disease.[88] Another 25 percent were disabled or captured. The incidence of outright desertion noted in the records was not high—only 3 percent. But almost 20 percent of these soldiers simply disappeared from the muster rolls before the end of the war. Despite the conscription act, which required service for the duration of the war, only 17 percent of the soldiers formally surrendered in 1865. The men who did desert were typically poor. Only one of nine owned slaves. One deserter was Harmon Dawson of Glascock county, a tenant farmer whose family was receiving assistance from the county in 1862.[89] A list of Edgefield, South Carolina, residents reported as absent without leave in April 1865 included S. J. Brooks, an overseer in 1860; Josiah B. Smith, a tenant farmer; James B. Crouch, son of an overseer; and John Walton, a laborer.[90]

The decimation of the armies is most apparent when we compare the year of entry into military service with the year of last mention. Of 263 soldiers in the sample, 90 entered in 1861; 145

in 1862; 18 in 1863; and only 10 in 1864. By the beginning of 1865, only 105 of these men were still in the service.[91]

As 1864 began, Dolly Burge wrote in her diary, "A new year is ushered in but peace comes not with it. A bloody war is still decimating our nation & thousands of hearts are today bleeding over the loss of loved ones. Scarcely a family in the land but has given some of its members to their country. Terrible, terrible indeed is war . . ."[92] The year proved no savior to her or to the Confederacy, as the home front disintegrated with the armies. Desertion, "straggling," and crime steadily increased. James Henry Hammond complained that one of his plantation residences and one barn had been robbed by the "wild negroes, deserters & a white population in perfect association with them," who "infested" the local swamps.[93] A deserter in Augusta shot the sheriff who tried to arrest him.[94] A rumored Yankee raid turned out to be a sheriff's party in Edgefield that had been sent to seize slaves being withheld from the impressment agents.[95]

In the autumn of 1864 came Sherman's devastating and triumphant march from Atlanta to Savannah. Sherman feinted toward Augusta, but finally skirted the area, leaving a trail of destruction through parts of Newton, Hancock, Glascock, Jefferson, and other counties. The Edgefield *Advertiser* headlined Sherman's withdrawal from Atlanta, with superabundant optimism, "Sherman's Retreat Through Georgia."[96] Many slaves went off with the Yankees; many others remained behind; and some exhibited the loyalty that so gratified their masters then and later. Kate Rowland was at her parents' plantation when the Yankees arrived, and she wrote in her diary that "all of our negroes remained faithful. . . . Jacob & Frank have immortalized themselves & stood by us more like brothers than servants."[97] Many slaves, no doubt, were not enamored of the Union soldiers, whom many remembered chiefly for stealing everything they could carry away. Yet a week after Sherman had passed through, Mrs. Rowland mentioned that "the negroes are all very much frightened & so demoralized by the visit from the Yankees that they do nothing at all."[98] This was the kind of "demoralization" that the slaves recognized as freedom. And thousands of slaves greeted the Yankees joyfully and followed them to Savannah.

In Sherman's wake came the stragglers and deserters from Confederate armies whom many people, rightly, feared more than Sherman's own men. In Madison county, bands of cavalry were stealing all the horses and mules.[99] The counties north of Augusta, according to the Augusta *Chronicle*'s editor, were "being plundered by parties in Confederate uniforms. . . . No man is secure. Every one at any moment is liable to be robbed."[100] A letter from Warrenton claimed that the Yankees had been under strict discipline when compared with the "band of outlaws and plunderers who follow on the flank of the enemy, and steal horses and mules & under pretense of impressing them. . . . Our people are more in dread of them than they are now of the Yankees."[101]

The *Chronicle*, at the end of the year, lamented the "incipient anarchy" at home, which the editor blamed somehow on the impressment policies of the government.[102] According to a grand jury that met in Richmond County in January 1865, "The amount of crime existing in the county at the present time is appalling. . . . We shall ere long be in danger of falling into anarchy."[103] The *Southern Cultivator* predicted that bread riots would spring up all over the South if "the course of those who have corn to spare is still persisted in. Persons who are sending their corn off clandestinely to the distilleries of the country, to realize enormous profits on it, may be unconsciously paving the way to have their own families in the end brought to want a piece of bread."[104] Several Hancock county women apparently agreed with the *Cultivator*, as they smashed stills belonging to Leroy Gunn and Joseph Gonder that April.[105] And when Sherman turned north again to march on Columbia, he skirted the Augusta area on the South Carolina side, bringing with him the same train of plunder, slave losses, and stragglers. When his troops entered Aiken, a motley crew of slaves, children, and women ransacked the store belonging to the Graniteville company.[106]

As the war drew to a close, men and women grasped at any straws that seemed to promise an end without total "subjugation." Beginning in September 1864, the Augusta *Chronicle*

repeatedly called for negotiations to end the war, although the editor seemed to feel that the South could hope to remain independent if it only were led with proper "statesmanship."[107] People looked to Alexander H. Stephens as the man of the hour, partly because in 1860 and 1861, he had opposed secession. Several wrote to him, some of them anonymously, urging him to work for an end to the war on the basis of reunion, but retaining slavery.[108] In public, at least, most still resisted any overt move toward capitulation. When in early 1865 a group of Jackson county men met to call for a state convention, which might lead in turn to the secession of Georgia from the Confederacy, they were dispersed at bayonet point by Confederate troops.[109] Robert Toombs told a crowd in Augusta in February 1865 that the South could still win the war if the government would reverse the despotic policies that had destroyed the spirit of the people.[110] By April, the *Chronicle*'s editor, in what seems almost a flight of fantasy, claimed to think that the South might still end the war on the "fair terms" of uniting the North and South for foreign and commercial affairs, while each section would retain its own president, legislature, and judiciary.[111]

The final months of the war were marked by one of the most ironic debates in American history: whether the South should arm its slaves and promise them freedom in return for entering the army. Jefferson Davis proposed arming slaves in the autumn of 1864, and he was insistent that only freedom would be a proper and effective reward.[112]

Such a policy presented a truly awful dilemma. Even the Augusta *Constitutionalist*'s editor, by late 1864 an almost militant supporter of President Davis, drew back. He had, after all, regarded the North's decision to enlist escaped slaves in the army as "absolutely intolerable, and not to be submitted to," since the effect would be "that the Confederate soldier should be put on a footing with his own slave."[113] In July 1864, he had called slavery "our defence—our protection; it is our statute of Pallas." The "ultimate safety" of the South, he claimed, "lies in the preservation and slavery of the negro race on this continent—to its increase after this war shall have ended." He suggested that the South pass its own version of a "Homestead Law" by guaranteeing "universally throughout the land, . . . a family of slaves to each white family." Slavery ought to be, he concluded, "an inheritance of the people" as much as the right to trial by jury.[114]

The next month, the editor had endorsed views, attributed to Davis, that the South was fighting for its rights, not just for slavery. He went on to argue, though, that independence could not be more important than slavery, for "without slavery as the very foundation of Southern society, independence to the poorer class of laborers amongst us, . . . is not a boon worth an ounce of blood, or for which this war should be continued one hour longer." Since slavery was "the cap-stone of our liberty," which guaranteed freedom to poor whites, "future generations [would] write us down as asses, for entering into war, which has brought debt and anarchy to the continent, only to gain the independence of enslaving a portion of our own race and blood."[115] And in October 1864, the editor refused to accept communications in favor of arming slaves, and he urged others to "mark with the severest reprobation" any public man who "dares" to give such a policy "the slightest encouragement."[116]

As late as December 1864, the editor still predicted that North America would come to be divided into Southern, Atlantic, and Pacific republics, and that the Southern Republic would be the most stable because of African slavery. The South, especially, would never make the error of other great slave societies of freeing and arming its slaves.[117]

Such attitudes crumbled as the South's situation became more desperate. After Sherman swept through Georgia, local newspapers began to open their columns to arguments on the subject of arming slaves. The result was perhaps the first genuine public debate in the Augusta area on the wisdom and justice of slavery since the colony of Georgia had legalized the institution 100 years before.

Those who favored arming slaves had one incontrovertible fact on their side: former slaves already were fighting quite effectively in the Union armies. As "Mentor," a correspondent of the *Constitutionalist*, noted, "Despite of ourselves . . . the negro has become a military fact." Those who accepted the idea that emancipation must be a part of the overall policy of arming slaves went much further than arguing simply from necessity. "Mentor," for example, insisted that *the sudden and unexpected development of the negro* in his intellectual, moral, industrious capacity is the astounding fact of this war."[118] He went on to lay out an elaborate plan not only to free slaves, but also to bring the freedmen into factories and industrialize a future, independent South.[119]

The most far-reaching arguments to appear in public came from "W. W.", another correspondent. "The spirit of freedom," he claimed, "has been kindled in the breast of the slaves and under the influences by which he will be surrounded in the Union it will never die." Black Union soldiers were "a living, moving, armed admonition to the slave, stirring his soul to its deepest foundations and urging him to strike for freedom." The war had demonstrated that southerners, in an overreaction to abolitionism, had underestimated the Negro race; for black people, too, "love of freedom is an instinct."[120] To be sure, "W. W." was no egalitarian; he argued that emancipation should be gradual and that afterward, white men could regulate black labor to "retain him, where he would be content to remain, in a subordinate position and an efficient laborer." Yet he suggested powerfully that with emancipation, a "single impulse" of liberty, the "all pervading passion of the human heart," would unite white and black southerners, and that the South's "war worn veterans" would be newly inspired by "the loud glad shout of three millions of emancipated beings."[121] John C. Calhoun could not have made a more ringing endorsement of the charms of liberty.

These arguments were, for many, hard to bear. As the *Constitutionalist*'s editor noted in his dissent from one letter writer who favored arming and freeing slaves, "our proslavery argument is abandoned and branded" by the logic. "We confess at once, that freedom to the black race is preferable to servitude, thus yielding the field of controversy to the detestable Puritan forever."[122] Georgia's General (and former governor) Howell Cobb put the same argument more succinctly when he wrote that "if slaves will make good soldiers our whole theory of slavery is wrong."[123] Southerners were thus driven to a compromise position as they sought a way to profit from armed slaves without giving up slavery itself. One compromise was a logical extension of the pro-slavery argument.

Southerners had long argued that slavery was best for blacks. Why, then, should slaves not fight to defend their right to remain slaves? The *Constitutionalist*'s editor finally became willing to arm slaves, but insisted that "they will fight for the old plantation or city home much sooner than for a word which is, at best, an unsubstantial quibble."[124] The Edgefield *Advertiser*'s editor made a similar argument. Slaves, he thought, would fight "for the blessings of their present condition . . . for the food and raiment they now have without care and without forethought." He added, "Let us not blast them by making them free"; freedom would be nothing but "a great curse to them—a great danger to us."[125] A week later, the editor proposed a plan to reward slave soldiers by attaching them to the soil in feudal fashion; he admitted that it would be a "gross injustice to send them back into their *present condition* of slavery." In January 1865, he returned to this theme, still opposed to freeing slaves. Negroes would make much better soldiers under southern than northern officers; southerners would not commit the "blunders" of making the slave "demoralized by having false notions of equality instilled into his mind," including "the notion that he is as good as anybody."[126]

Others made similar arguments. "A Private Soldier" wrote from Warrenton urging the Confederacy to recruit 300,000 slave volunteers; they could be rewarded with a choice of new masters at the end of the war.[127] "W. L. M.," replying extensively to "W. W." and "Mentor," also opposed emancipation. "African Slavery," according to "W. L. M.," was "a Divinely appointed permanent institution." It was a "moral impossibility" to free black slaves. Yet they could still be good soldiers. Indeed, under the "combined influence of high bred officers and evangelical ministers of the gospel," slave soldiers would be converted and "return home after the war to exert a wholesome religious influence upon the entire negro population."[128]

Others would make no compromise, admit no faults in slavery. "S.," in the *Constitutionalist*, also aimed his fire at "W. W." He acknowledged that "W. W." was sincere, but his sincerity only made his views the more dangerous. Slavery, "S." wrote, is "a trust committed to the Christian people of the Southern states," and southerners must defend it "precisely as we would defend any other of our social relations, our life, our liberty, or our property." Neither peace nor independence nor the slaves' desires— and the slave was, in any case, a child incapable of knowing what was good for him—could justify the South's giving up its "religious obligations." "S." deplored the despondency that led some to believe that God was chastising the South for its "arrangement of society."[129] "Ninety-Six" made the same argument with greater vituperation in the *Advertiser*. If every able-bodied man were in the army, the South would need no slaves to defend itself; those favoring abolition of any kind were "wolves in sheep's clothing" and "traitors to their country."[130]

The most bitter attacks on emancipation, however, came from N. S. Morse, editor of the Augusta *Chronicle*. Morse had long been an outspoken critic of Jefferson Davis, but his denunciations of the plan to arm slaves reached new levels of invective. Abolition was a "monstrous" and "suicidal" idea.[131] Morse interpreted Sherman's reluctance to carry away slaves by force as a sign that the North was uncommitted to emancipation, and this was a key to his argument. By the spring of 1865, he clearly had decided that slavery without independence was far preferable to independence without slavery. Thus the "abolition doctrine" of "W. W." was "more dangerous" than were those of Massachusetts Senator Charles Sumner or other northern abolitionists.[132] He was outraged that a newspaper would dare to publish such "incendiary" ideas.[133] At the end of March, he offered his readers a full-blown proslavery essay, bringing in economics, Scripture, and especially race as defenses, and concluding in a slight twist of the old phrase that slavery was the "keystone" of southern society. If even a few slaves were freed, the "contagion" would spread: "The idea of liberty leavens the whole slave population— and presently they are transformed into a race of demons shrieking for freedom and howling for blood."[134]

To a "poor soldier" from "near Augusta," Morse's opposition to emancipating and arming slaves was one more sign that this was war for only the rich man's property. The rich had "cried secession because their slave property was endangered," and now that slavery was endangered by the war, the rich would sacrifice anything for their property. Morse and his kind were "traitors"; the South either could allow "slavery, cotton, tobacco, &c" to "buy our honor and enslave us" or could sell them for freedom. If the South lost the war, poor whites would lose their land through ruinous taxation and would be reduced to "*tenants*" of these "same traitors."[135]

To Morse, this letter and an approving comment from the editor of the *Constitutionalist* were a further sign that "traitors in power" would use the "ignorant" and "deluded" among the soldiers as tools for "enslaving the citizens" by setting the army against the rich.[136] Yet Morse's own columns made it clear that by 1865 he did see the South's poor whites as a greater danger than the Yankee armies. In April, he clung to his belief that "it is yet possible to save slavery."[137] Not defeat, but guerrilla warfare would be "the most crushing calamity that could befall us."[138] If the army were to break into guerrilla bands, "the property of the rich [would] be the spoil of the many who have lost all they had, or never had anything; and the irresponsible and unorganized bands of men in uniform, will plunder from all who have homes, or goods, or provisions."[139] So southerners had found it impossible, after all, to combine liberty and equality for some with slavery for others. And meanwhile, the slave markets in Augusta were flooded with masters eager to rid themselves of a property they knew probably would soon be no longer theirs.[140]

The debate was, in any case, only the last gasp of both the proslavery and the antislavery arguments; the editors and their supporters, in truth, had nothing to debate about. Four years of war, 500,000 deaths, and the big and small acts of hundreds of thousands of slaves already had decided that the South would be neither independent nor a slave society. It was a time for reflection rather than for debate, and reflection took over as one southerner after another realized that the end had finally come. For Dolly Burge, it came perhaps when she surveyed the remains of the little town of Covington, after Sherman passed through. "How very different is Covington from what it used to be & how little did they who tore down the old flag & raised the red white and blue realize the results that have ensued." [141] The next April, she decided that the defeat of the South could be attributed only to "the hand of Providence working out some problem which has not been revealed to us poor, erring mortals." [142] "Peter the Hermit," who had filled many columns of the Edgefield *Advertiser* with tirades against conscription and exemptions, cowards and extortioners and subenrolling officers, wrote a last letter, noting he had "single-handed, breasted the corruptions of the times," but "failing to be of service, now retires from the stage of public exhortation." [143] Eliza Francis Andrews, a spirited teen-age southern patriot, could only survey the results of the war from her Washington, Georgia, home and think that "the props that held society up are broken. . . . The suspense and anxiety in which we live are terrible." [144] James Henry Hammond had died even while Sherman marched through Georgia. Hammond had told his son to bury him in a spot with a view of Augusta, but had asked him to "run a plow over my grave" if the South were finally subjugated. [145] Linton Stephens, gloomy as usual, wrote to his now imprisoned brother that "anybody who rejoices in our calamity has surely had enough to gratify his vengeance." [146]

The majority of people in Augusta's hinterlands, who were black, had quite a different view of what had happened, and they thought they knew what Providence had intended as the result of the war. To them, freedom was the long-promised day of Jubilee. Seventy years after it happened, Eugene Smith remembered that magic moment when black Yankee troops had first entered Augusta, singing as they marched:

> Don't you see the lightning?
> Don't you hear the thunder?
> It isn't the lightning,
> It isn't the thunder,
> But it's the buttons on
> The Negro uniforms! [147]

The flash of that lightning and the peal of that thunder had helped ensure that a new age of republican liberty—with its own hopes, contradictions, and failures—would now begin.

In his study of the impact of the First World War, *The Great War and Modern Memory*, literary critic Paul Fussell remarked that "every war is ironic because every war is worse than expected. Every war constitutes an irony of situation because its means are so melodramatically disproportionate to its presumed ends."[148] From the point of view of white southerners, in the Civil War, like the First World War for a later generation, the ironies were not merely present, but overwhelming.

The social order of the Old South (for among other effects, the Civil War turned the pre-1865 South into the Old South) was an anomaly in the mid-nineteenth century. The white South was fully committed to republican liberty for white men, and to degrading slavery for black people. Southern whites shared with other Americans their commitment to liberty. Liberty meant that men must be free to elect their own leaders and to control their own communities. It also meant that men must themselves be independent, not under the power of any other man. Liberty, therefore, required a measure of equality among citizens. These two aspects of liberty were always to some extent in tension. Autonomous men had to be virtuous; they had to be willing to subordinate the pursuit of purely private gain in order to cooperate for the good of the community as a whole. If they did not, a republic would inevitably deteriorate into an anarchic pursuit of private interest. In particular, if the gap between the rich and the poor were too great, the poor would always be tempted to use their votes to control the state and seize the property of the rich. The resulting anarchy, as the lamentable history of republics had shown, would end only when a military despotism had restored order.

The tensions between public and private good, and between liberty and equality, were sharply exacerbated by slavery. In the first place, slavery seemed to mock the very idea of liberty. Slavery also divided whites into owners and nonowners of slaves, thus undermining the equality so necessary among republican citizens. At least some poor men in the Old South regarded slavery as the cause of their poverty; they formed a potential base of political opposition to slavery.

Southerners attempted to reconcile liberty and slavery by appealing to one important conservative strain of republican ideology. Slavery, they claimed, actually enhanced the sense of equality among white men, and confined to the most debased categories of society—menial labor—an inferior race. Every white man was at least one giant step above all slaves in status, and thus, relative to slaves, true republican equality existed in the ruling group of citizens. Meanwhile slaves, whose aspirations as well as whose capabilities were seen as inferior, were content in their subordination. Wanting neither equality nor liberty, they never would become the cause of social tumults.

The confidence with which many southern spokesmen made such arguments belied their anxieties about their truth. Slave masters knew that all slaves were not content in their slavery. Masters therefore depended on nonslaveowning whites to bolster their control over slaves. The gentry did have to accept the plain folk as equals, at least in most public situations, and especially at election time. Planters also helped out poor neighbors economically when times were hard. Such actions helped to reduce the perceived distance between white classes. But the rise of the powerful antislavery Republican party in the North threatened the South's delicate balance of white liberty and black slavery. Republicans might appeal to black slaves to strike directly for freedom, and Republicans certainly would try to build up among the plain folk an antislavery party within the South. To many slave masters, the party of Abraham Lincoln thus appeared to be a mortal threat to their entire society. They pulled the South into secession and war to preserve both the liberty and the slavery in that society.

The great irony was that the war itself produced within the South exactly those threats to liberty and slavery that slaveowners had most feared. The demands of modern war led the Confederate government to place unprecedented restrictions on individual liberties—conscripting men into the army, seizing property, suspending such ancient rights as habeus corpus, this alone enough to alienate thousands of planters, including even Alexander H. Stephens, vice president of the Confederacy. The war also markedly widened the gap between rich and poor. Wealthy planters suffered inconveniences, but their slaves continued to grow food and care for white families, while the families of poor soldiers might face enormous privations. The informal methods by which planters had carried poor neighbors through hard times were completely inadequate for wartime conditions, and neither state nor Confederate governments successfully coped with wartime inflation and poverty. The ranks of the armies were filled with the husbands and sons of the plain folk, and as the war continued, those ranks gradually but inexorably melted away.

The war also undermined slavery directly. Blacks had always known about liberty, and now they could see that the war might bring them liberty. Many slaves did all they could to hasten that result, whether by resisting overseers or fleeing to the Union lines or, ultimately, joining the Union army. And southern attempts to guarantee control of slaves by exempting overseers or owners of slaves simply widened class consciousness among whites. The war effort itself, therefore, produced the "military despotism," class divisions, and slave resistance that masters had gone to war to prevent. The resulting internal conflicts were a principal cause of the final collapse of the Confederacy.

The contradictions and irony of the war were epitomized in the decision, in 1865, to emancipate slaves and put them into the Confederate army. The disproportion between the means needed to win the war and one supposed purpose of the war hardly could have been stronger. Having gone to war to defend liberty and slavery, southerners were destroying both in order to win. Yet their commitment to slavery and to an archaic kind of liberty had made it impossible for them to win the war otherwise. Southerners were finally willing to ask their own slaves to defend the South's liberty. And some of them finally had to admit that the South's own commitment to liberty was, in the end, shared by the people whom they had so long held in bondage.

㊍ Appendixes

Notes

Essay on Sources

Index

☸ Appendix A
Definitions, Procedures, and Methods

Definition of Augusta's hinterlands

In this book, the word *hinterlands* has essentially an economic definition; it refers to the geographical area for which Augusta served as the
principal cotton and wholesale market. A preliminary list of counties
was drawn up based on the comments in United States Bureau of the
Census, "Report of Cotton Production," in *Tenth Census, 1880.* The report includes a county-by-county survey of all aspects of the cotton industry, and tells where each county's farmers sold their cotton. One or
two counties were later added to this list based on information from
antebellum sources, chiefly factors' records, planters' financial records,
and newspaper accounts.

Since statistical data are generally available for the county level only,
it is necessary to assume that an entire county was either inside or outside the Augusta hinterlands area. For borderline counties, the decision
was based on my judgment as to whether most of the county's cotton
was sent to Augusta. Although farmers in southern Burke and Jefferson
counties probably sent cotton directly to Savannah, those counties were
included in the hinterlands when calculating summary statistics. Northern Barnwell District was certainly in the hinterlands of Augusta, but
probably most farmers in this large district sent cotton directly to
Charleston. No county was included without specific evidence from contemporary sources that Augusta was the principal cotton market for its
farmers. The counties included for statistical summaries of the hinterland area (as in, for example, Table 2) were, in Georgia, Burke, Columbia, Elbert, Glascock, Greene, Hancock, Hart, Jefferson, Lincoln, Morgan, Oglethorpe, Richmond, Taliaferro, Warren, and Wilkes; in South
Carolina, Abbeville and Edgefield. These are all on Map 1, page xv.

United States census

Quantitative evidence presented in this study comes in large part
from samples drawn from the manuscript schedules of the United
States Bureau of the Census for 1840, 1850, and 1860. These schedules,

in large bound volumes, are stored in the National Archives and Records Service (NARS) vaults in Washington, D.C. I used microfilms of the volumes, which are available from NARS by either loan or purchase, as well as at various branches of NARS around the country.

The manuscript schedules contain the original entries made by census takers for each person, farm, factory, and so on and for each question asked. There is a schedule for free inhabitants, which contains an entry for every free person enumerated; a corresponding schedule for slaves; and a schedule for agriculture, which contains an entry for every farm of three or more improved acres, or that produced at least $100 worth of crops during 1849 or 1859. I also consulted the special schedules for manufacturing and social statistics.

In 1860, the census takers enumerated people by "dwelling," and within dwellings, by family. However, no explicit questions were asked about family relationships. For each person, the schedules record name, age, race, sex, place of birth, value of personal or real property owned, and a few other pieces of information. From the 1860 census schedules, four samples were derived: the household sample, farm sample, family sample, and soldier sample.

The household sample includes data on households, including all information about the head of household, for each of three Georgia counties—Glascock, Hart, and Taliaferro. (An additional sample for Richmond county, including Augusta, was drawn and used for a few limited purposes.) For Glascock and Taliaferro, all households in the county were included (see "Sample sizes and sampling procedures" in this appendix).

In the slave schedules, all the slaves of one owner are listed together, with information only about age and sex. For each county, household heads were linked, if possible, to the slave schedules, and the total number of slaves was coded along with household information. If a farmer with large personal-property holdings (over $1,500) or a non-farmer with very large personal-property holdings (over $5,000) was not located in the slave schedules, his or her slaveholdings were counted as missing data and were not included in analyses involving slaves.

The farm sample includes all farms operated by members of households—almost always a household head—in the household sample. The agricultural schedules were searched to locate information on farms; data on all farms (including farm characteristics, outputs in 1859, and slaveholdings) that were operated by people in the household sample were recorded. If "real property" in the population schedules was greater than or approximately equal to "farm value" in the agriculture schedules, the household head was counted as a farm owner; otherwise the household head was counted as a tenant. In most cases, "farm value" was left blank by the census takers when the farm operator owned no real property, which I interpret as an informal way of indicating the owner's status. Women who owned property and were included in the agricultural schedules were coded as farmers even if the population schedules listed their occupations as "at home" or "domestic." Thus for the Georgia counties, a data-set was created that consisted of all the household information plus the farm information for each farm operator, but not including households that were headed by those who did not own farms. For Glascock and Taliaferro counties, a few farms were included that could not be matched with households in the population schedules, so that the complete census of farms is included. Numbers are given in "Sample sizes and sampling procedures."

In order to increase the amount of data from areas with large plantations and with a majority of black inhabitants, the farm sample was supplemented with a sample of farms taken from the agricultural schedules for Edgefield District, South Carolina. Because I wanted to create a data-set that could be used for a future comparison with similar data for 1880, and because Edgefield was divided into two counties before 1880, I selected farms from only that part of Edgefield District in 1860 that fell within the boundaries of the future Edgefield county (after the Civil War, the districts were renamed counties). I used the post office listed at the top of each page of both agricultural and population schedules, together with contemporary maps and gazetteers, to identify these farms. While this procedure is by no means exact, since all of the forty farms listed on a census page may not have been very close to the post office listed for that page, I believe that this sampling method ensures that the farms analyzed here are repesentative of those within the future, smaller boundaries of the county.

Operators of the farms included in the 1860 sample for Edgefield District were then sought out in the population and slave schedules, and enough information coded to enable an analysis of farm production and operation analogous to that done for Geogia counties: wealth, slaveholdings, occupations, and household size. Thus the procedure for Edgefield reversed that for the Georgia counties, since it went from agricultural schedule to population schedule. It is thus representative of the farm population only. In sum, the farm sample is based on a subsample of the household sample, plus data from Edgefield District.

For the family sample, about one-half of the households from each county included in the household sample were randomly chosen for further analysis. Complete information on name, sex, occupation, and so on for each household member was recorded. Then the schedules for the 1850 census were searched for the 1860 household heads in the family sample. Taliaferro county was searched for Taliaferro heads. Glascock county was created in 1857 from part of Warren county, so the 1850 returns for Warren county were searched for Glascock heads. Hart county was created in 1854 from parts of Franklin and Elbert counties, so the 1850 returns for those two counties were searched for Hart heads. When the 1860 household head was located in an 1850 schedule, complete data for the 1850 household were recorded, whether or not the 1860 head had also been the household head in 1850. The family sample was the basis for the analyses of mobility in Chapter 3. The family sample is thus a subsample of the household sample.

The soldier sample consists of all males, ages eleven to sixty-five in 1860, living in the households included in the family sample. Each of these men and boys was then sought out in Lillian Henderson, comp., *Rosters of the Confederate Soldiers of Georgia, 1861–1865,* 6 vols. (1959–64; reprint, Spartanburg, S.C.: Reprint Company, 1982). A separate index, completed under the direction of Juanita S. Brightwell, was published in 1982. *Rosters* is an abstract of the Compiled Service Records—on microfilm at the National Archives and Records Service—of each man who served in a unit of regular infantry raised in Georgia during the Civil War. While the *Rosters* is accurate in what it contains, it excludes some categories of those who served: (1) those who entered the Confederate army directly, rather than through a state organization; (2) those Georgians who volunteered for service in another state; (3) those who served only in state units, which were never incorporated into the Confederate army; and (4) those who served only in artillery or cavalry units. Categories 1 and 2 include very few men, and can safely be ignored for an overall statistical analysis. Category 3 is much larger; but the large majority of these men did little or no serious fighting, and typically served for only a few months at most. Since service in these units did not compare in danger and sacrifice with service in the Confederate army, I decided to omit these men from the analysis. Category 4 is a serious omission from the standpoint of statistical analysis. While the number of men excluded is small, artillery and cavalry units probably included a disproportionate number of wealthy men (or sons of wealthy parents). Therefore, I searched for members of the soldier sample directly in the microfilmed Compiled Service Records of all Georgia cavalry and artillery units in the NARS in Washington, D.C., and identified about a dozen men who served in these units.

There almost certainly were a few men who served and were not identified as having served in the records I used; they may have been in categories I excluded, or may never have been included in the records. Therefore, the analysis will understate by an indeterminate but probably small amount the incidence of service. Since all major units were included, there is no reason to assume that this underestimation would be biased toward either rich or poor men.

Aside from the four major samples, additional census data were used for several specific purposes. Wealth and occupations of officeholders, political candidates, church members, and so on were located in the most appropriate census (1840, 1850, or 1860). Tables 7 and 19 (pp. 45,

203), which categorize slaveholdings by size, are based on a separate, 1 in 10 sample of slaveholding for all counties and districts in Augusta and its hinterlands, as listed in the 1840 population schedule and the 1850 and 1860 slave schedules. These schedules do not distinguish owners from slave hirers or overseers, and so overstate somewhat the number of true owners. In addition, slaves in the 1840 census are listed with the free households, so it is not possible to distinguish those owned or held by the household head from those held by other members of the household. A comparison of the complete schedule of slaveholdings and the complete schedule of free households for three counties in 1850 (Warren, Hancock, and Taliaferro) indicates that from 5 percent to 8 percent of slaveholdings were in the hands of non-household heads. The "adjusted" estimate of the number of household heads with slaveholdings, in Table 19, assumes that 5 percent of all holdings in 1860 and 1850 were in the hands of nonhousehold heads.

The 1840 census was also crucial for measuring mobility of slaveholdings between 1840 and 1850. For this measurement, a list of household heads in Taliaferro county and in the part of Warren county that later became Glascock county was made from the 1850 census; another list of household heads was made from the 1840 census. These lists were compared in order to trace changes in slaveholdings. Because the data do not allow us to distinguish ownership from other kinds of holdings, these comparisons and analyses should be considered as only approximate measures of the real situation.

There are many difficulties with the census data. Collection and analysis may introduce errors at any of several stages: coding, entering into a computer, programming, and calculating by hand or with hand calculator. For this book, almost all data were checked against the original microfilm data several months after the original coding. Data were also checked for internal consistency and for unusual or extraordinary values. Summary statistics were compared with published census data whenever possible.

The greatest single source of error is probably the original census reporting. Many people misstated their ages and, especially, their property holdings. Farm outputs are for the year before the census was taken, and most are estimates only. Most percentages are rounded off to whole numbers to avoid a false impression of exactness. Furthermore, census takers no doubt missed some people and families entirely, as they still do.

However, the census remains the most complete and comprehensive, and therefore the best, source of demographic and economic information for the nineteenth century. Where comparable data exists—for example, in tax records—census figures are usually identical to or very close to the alternative source. Furthermore, there is no reason to believe that errors were greater or smaller or biased in different directions in different counties. In general, I share the confidence of most other historians who have used the census records that they are accurate enough to be useful, and useful enough to be, for certain purposes, indispensable.

Procedures for food self-sufficiency, debt, and Edgefield elections

Calculations of self-sufficiency are based on a number of assumptions. First, for each potential food crop, a portion of the 1859 output was subtracted to allow for seed for the next year's crop. Percentages subtracted were corn, 2 percent; Irish and sweet potatoes, 3 percent; oats, 7 percent; peas, 8 percent; and wheat and rye, 9 percent. These values were taken from Roger Ransom and Richard Sutch, "Debt Peonage in the Cotton South After the Civil War," *Journal of Economic History* 32 (1972): 660, n. 44; their estimates are conservative.

Second, remaining food products were converted to calorie equivalents of corn in the following ratios: 1 bushel rye = 1.05 bushels corn; wheat = 1.104 bushels corn; peas = .946 bushels corn; Irish potatoes = .220 bushels corn; sweet potatoes = .362 bushels corn; and oats = .443 bushels corn. These values are listed and defended in Roger Ransom and Richard Sutch, *One Kind of Freedom: The Economic Consequences of Emancipation* (New York: Cambridge University Press, 1977), Appendix E, Table E.2.

Third, allowances for feed were deducted for each horse or ox, 35 bushels corn-equivalent; for each mule, 30 bushels; for each milch cow, 5 bushels; and for each sheep, .25 bushels. No corn was deducted for feed for swine or "other" cattle, on the assumption that any corn fed to these animals eventually was consumed by the household. The procedure followed was the same as that explained in Ransom and Sutch, *One Kind of Freedom*, Appendix E, Table E.4.

Finally, the net remaining food, expressed as bushels of corn, was divided by the number of people on the farm. Slaves under age fifteen and whites under age twenty were counted as two-thirds of an adult for purposes of calculation. The calculation was made only for farms operated by farm owners or tenants; those operated by overseers with absentee owners, by operators with less than $10 worth of produce in 1859, or by persons with a second occupation and thus outside income, were excluded.

The resulting analysis should not be taken as an exact indication of food supply or consumption. Possibilities for error are obviously large. However, the procedures probably overestimate food available for consumption, and probably are not biased by size of farm.

For three Georgia counties, twenty probate inventories were selected for analysis of debtor–creditor relationships. The twenty inventories were those closest in time to 1860, since the census for that year was the source for wealth data on debtors. Civil War inflation did not noticeably affect values as listed in inventories until late 1863, after the latest inventory used.

Map 2 on page xv, showing patterns of support for Edgefield candidates, is based on returns for elections for the South Carolina House of Representatives, as reported in the Edgefield *Advertiser*, 20 October 1852 and 20 October 1858. The four polling places shown for each candidate are those that could be located on contemporary maps, and at which the candidate received his highest percentages of votes cast. The three candidates shown illustrate a pattern that appears for all candidates whose residences could be located. If all polling places could be located, the pattern would almost certainly be stronger; for example, two of A. J. Hammond's best places are omitted. Residences and polling places were located with the help of the manuscript schedules of the 1860 census; John A. Chapman, *A History of Edgefield County from the Earliest Settlements to 1897* (Newberry, S.C., 1897); and a variety of maps, especially the one of Edgefield by Isaac Boles in the South Carolina Department of Archives and History.

Sample sizes and sampling procedures

The household and farm samples for Glascock and Taliaferro counties include every household and farm in the counties, as listed in the manuscript schedules of the 1860 census. The Hart county household sample includes the first three dwellings on each page of the census schedules; the farm sample includes all farms in Hart county that were operated by a head of household included in the household sample. The family sample for all counties consists of a random sample from the household sample. The soldier sample includes all eleven- to sixty-five-year-old males who are listed in the family sample. The farm sample for Edgefield district includes the last five farms listed on each page of the 1860 agricultural schedules, when the post office at the top of the page and the post office on the page of the population schedules were also

Table 18. Sizes of Samples

Area Sampled	Household Sample	Farm Sample	Family Sample	Soldier Sample
Glascock County	325	214	163	251
Hart County	346	253	154	261
Taliaferro County	337	244	166	262
Edgefield District	0	197	0	0

within the boundaries of Edgefield county in 1880, as listed in the *Rand-McNally Atlas* (1882).

It should be noted that because of missing data, not all persons or farms in each sample were used in tabulating data for each table in the text.

Additional Tables

Table 19. Distribution of Slave Ownership, 1840–1860

SLAVES OWNED BY DECILE OF OWNER

	Slaves Owned		
Decile	1840 (%)	1850 (%)	1860 (%)
1 (poorest tenth)	.8	.8	.7
2	1.3	1.2	1.2
3	2.2	2.2	2.2
4	3.4	3.2	3.3
5	5.0	4.7	4.8
6	6.8	6.5	6.8
7	9.6	8.8	9.2
8	12.8	12.2	12.5
9	15.5	18.4	18.7
10 (richest tenth)	42.6	42.0	40.5

ESTIMATED NONSLAVEOWNERS AMONG HOUSEHOLD HEADS

Category	1840	1850	1860
Number of households*	15,387	16,911	17,657
Number of slaveholdings	9,017	10,390	9,890
Correction for holdings by nonhousehold heads	0	(519)	(495)
Holdings by household heads	9,017	9,871	9,395
Nonslaveowners (%)	41.4	41.6	46.8

SOURCES: Slaveholdings from 10 percent sample of households from the manuscript returns of the United States Bureau of the Census, 1840; 10 percent sample of slaveholdings from the manuscript returns of the census of slaves, 1850 and 1860; households from U.S. Bureau of the Census, "Population," *Seventh Census, 1850* and "Population," in *Eighth Census, 1860.*

NOTE: See Appendix A for detailed description. Data for 1850 and 1840 include a small adjustment made by adding a portion of Franklin county households and slaveholdings to duplicate the part of Hart county taken from Franklin in 1854 and included as part of Augusta's hinterlands in 1860.

*The censuses of 1850 and 1860 enumerated both "dwellings" and "families," but in most counties, these numbers were identical.

Table 20. Social Mobility of Men* by County in Augusta's
Hinterlands, 1850–1860

| Occupation, 1860 | OCCUPATIONS Occupation, 1850 | | | | | |
	Farmer	Overseer	Artisan	Laborer	Nonmanual	Other
Glascock County						
Farmer	48	1	0	3	2	1
Overseer	0	0	0	0	0	0
Artisan	1	0	4	0	0	0
Laborer	1	0	0	5	0	1
Nonmanual	0	0	0	0	0	0
Other	0	0	0	0	0	0
Hart County						
Farmer	51	0	2	1	1	2
Overseer	0	0	0	0	0	0
Artisan	2	0	1	0	0	0
Laborer	4	0	0	0	0	0
Nonmanual	0	0	0	0	0	0
Other	0	0	0	0	0	0
Taliaferro County						
Farmer	52	0	1	0	2	0
Overseer	1	0	1	0	0	0
Artisan	0	0	4	0	0	0
Laborer	2	0	0	1	0	0
Nonmanual	1	0	1	0	6	0
Other	2	0	0	0	0	1

Table 20 (continued)

| | SLAVE OWNERSHIP | | |
| | | Slaves Owned, 1850 | |
Slaves Owned, 1860	0	1–10	11+
Glascock County			
0	40	2	0
1–10	7	11	0
11+	0	2	3
Hart County			
0	42	2	0
1–10	4	9	0
11+	0	3	5
Taliaferro County			
0	11	3	0
1–10	18	20	4
11+	0	5	14

| | REAL ESTATE | | |
| | | Real Property, 1850 ($) | |
Real Property, 1860 ($)	0	1–1,499	1,500+
Glascock County			
0	15	3	0
1–1,499	9	18	0
1,500+	2	11	9
Hart County			
0	14	3	1
1–1,499	7	16	2
1,500+	5	7	10
Taliaferro County			
0	11	3	0
1–1,499	10	15	2
1,500+	4	11	21

SOURCE: Family sample from the manuscript returns of the United States Bureau of the Census, 1850 and 1860.
  NOTE: See Appendix A for detailed description. Numbers may vary slightly due to missing data.
  *Household heads, but includes a few men who boarded in 1850 or 1860.

Table 21. Social Mobility of Parents and Sons in Augusta's Hinterlands, 1850–1860

| | OCCUPATIONS | | | | | |
| | Parent, 1850 | | | | | |
Son, 1860	Farmer	Overseer	Artisan	Laborer	Nonmanual	Other
Glascock County						
Farmer	23	0	2	0	0	4
Overseer	1	0	0	0	1	1
Artisan	3	0	0	0	0	0
Laborer	0	0	1	3	0	1
Nonmanual	0	0	1	0	0	0
Other	1	0	0	0	0	0
Hart County						
Farmer	11	0	0	0	1	0
Overseer	1	0	0	0	0	0
Artisan	1	0	0	0	0	0
Laborer	0	0	0	0	0	1
Nonmanual	2	0	0	0	0	0
Other	0	0	0	0	0	0
Taliaferro County						
Farmer	16	0	0	0	0	1
Overseer	1	0	0	0	0	1
Artisan	0	0	0	0	0	0
Laborer	1	0	0	0	0	0
Nonmanual	4	0	0	0	1	0
Other	0	0	0	0	0	0

Table 21 (continued)

| | SLAVE OWNERSHIP | | |
| | | Slaves Owned by Parent, 1850 | |
Slaves Owned by Son, 1860	0	1–10	11+
Glascock County			
0	25	7	0
1–10	2	5	3
11+	0	0	0
Hart County			
0	12	3	0
1–10	1	1	0
11+	0	0	0
Taliaferro County			
0	4	2	0
1–10	0	3	15
11+	0	0	1

| | REAL ESTATE | | |
| | | Real Property of Parent, 1850 ($) | |
Real Property of Son, 1860 ($)	0	1–1,499	1,500+
Glascock County			
0	8	7	4
1–1,499	4	7	6
1,500+	1	1	4
Hart County			
0	0	6	3
1–1,499	0	5	3
1,500+	0	0	0
Taliaferro County			
0	4	1	5
1–1,499	1	1	7
1,500+	0	0	6

SOURCE: Family sample from the manuscript returns of the United States Bureau of the Census, 1850 and 1860.

NOTE: See Appendix A for detailed description. Includes men who headed households in 1860 and who were living with parents in 1850. Numbers may vary slightly due to missing data.

Table 22. Slaveholdings of Officeholders in Augusta's
Hinterlands, 1840–1861

Years	Office and County	Nonslave-owners (%)	Mean slaves	(N)
1840–44	Justice of the Peace			
	Hancock	18	13	(22)
	Taliaferro	12	5	(17)
	Warren	25	8	(20)
	Inferior Court justice			
	Hancock	0	17	(5)
	Taliaferro	0	17	(10)
	Warren	17	20	(6)
	All officers*			
	Hancock	14	14	(37)
	Taliaferro	10	10	(39)
	Warren	36	9	(36)
1849–54	Justice of the Peace			
	Hancock	36	9	(36)
	Hart	55	4	(20)
	Taliaferro	28	7	(25)
	Warren	24	6	(33)
	Inferior Court justice			
	Hancock	18	22	(11)
	Hart †	20	5	(5)
	Taliaferro	10	17	(10)
	Warren	22	21	(9)
	All officers*			
	Hancock	33	12	(52)
	Hart	50	4	(30)
	Taliaferro	26	9	(39)
	Warren	24	10	(51)
1859–61	Justice of the Peace			
	Glascock	63	4	(8)
	Hancock	24	16	(17)
	Hart	47	5	(15)
	Taliaferro	15	8	(13)
	Inferior Court justice			
	Glascock	43	6	(7)
	Hancock	20	25	(5)
	Hart	40	5	(5)
	Taliaferro	0	15	(3)
	All officers*			
	Glascock	62	4	(21)
	Hancock	21	15	(29)
	Hart	45	4	(29)
	Taliaferro	18	4	(22)

SOURCES: Executive Officers Books, GDAH; slaveholdings from the manuscript returns of the United States Bureau of the Census, 1840, 1850, and 1860.
   NOTE: Excludes officers not located in the census.
   *Justice of the Peace; inferior court justice; representative; clerks of inferior court and superior court; ordinary, sheriff, tax collector and receiver, and coroner.
   † Hart created 1854; data for 1854–56.

Table 23. Slaveholdings of Party Elites in Augusta's
Hinterlands, 1840–1855

County	Year	Party	Mean Slaves Owned	No Slaves (%)	(N)
Warren	1840–44	Whig	11	24	(111)
		Democrat	8	22	(27)
	1850–55	Union	17	17	(36)
		American†	13	26	(19)
		Democrat	12	40	(5)
Taliaferro	1840–44	Whig	9	9	(113)
		Democrat	*	*	*
	1850–55	Union	17	22	(18)
		American†	13	8	(12)
		Democrat	10	9	(11)
Hancock	1840–44	Whig	*	*	*
		Democrat	32	8	(13)
	1850–55	Union	24	29	(42)
		Southern Rights	36	0	(9)
		American	18	14	(29)
		Democrat	30	22	(9)

SOURCES: Officers of public meetings and delegates to state or district conventions reported in Augusta *Chronicle* or Augusta *Constitutionalist*; slaveholdings from the manuscript returns of the United States Bureau of the Census, 1840 and 1850.

*Fewer than five members found in newspaper reports.

†Includes members of Whig and Conservative parties.

🏵 NOTES

Abbreviations

AHSLC	Alexander H. Stephens Papers, Library of Congress
AHSM	Alexander H. Stephens Papers, Manhattanville College of the Sacred Heart
Brown IC	Incoming Correspondence, Governor Joseph E. Brown Papers, Georgia Department of Archives and History
Brown Petitions	Petitions Received, Governor Joseph E. Brown Papers, Georgia Department of Archives and History
CR	Allen D. Candler, ed. *The Confederate Records of the State of Georgia.* 3 vols. Atlanta: Charles P. Byrd, 1909–11.
DCB	David C. Barrow Papers, University of Georgia Library
GDAH	Georgia Department of Archives and History
JHHLC	James Henry Hammond Papers, Library of Congress
JHHSCL	James Henry Hammond Papers, South Caroliniana Library
JSH	*Journal of Southern History*
Rawick	George Rawick, ed. *The American Slave: A Composite Autobiography*, 19 vols. Supplement series 1, 12 vols.; Supplement series 2, 10 vols. Westport, Conn.: Greenwood Press, 1972–79
SCL	South Caroliniana Library, University of South Carolina
SHC	Southern Historical Collection, University of North Carolina Library

Full Names of Newspapers Cited

Augusta *Chronicle*   Augusta *Daily Chronicle and Sentinel*

Augusta *Constitutionalist* Augusta *Daily Constitutionalist*

Introduction

1. Hinton Rowan Helper, *The Impending Crisis of the South. How to Meet It*, ed. George Fredrickson (1857; Cambridge, Mass.: Harvard University Press, 1968).

2. William B. Hesseltine, "Some New Aspects of the Proslavery Argument," *Journal of Negro History* 21 (1936): 9–10. This neglected essay covers far more than its title would suggest.

3. Genovese has pursued this interpretation in a number of significant books, beginning with the rather rigid *Political Economy of Slavery: Studies in the Economy and Society of the Slave South* (New York: Random House, Pantheon, 1965). The most recent restatement of his interpretation is Genovese and Elizabeth Fox-Genovese, *The Fruits of Merchant Capital: Slavery and Bourgeois Property in the Rise and Expansion of Capitalism* (New York: Oxford University Press, 1983), esp. chaps. 5, 6, 9.

4. Genovese and Fox-Genovese, *Merchant Capital*, chap. 9.

5. Ulrich B. Phillips, "The Central Theme of Southern History," *American Historical Review* 34 (1928): 31. In other writings, Phillips often placed less emphasis on race, at times arguing in terms that Genovese has found essentially similar to his own; see Genovese's "Foreword" to the reprint of Phillips, *American Negro Slavery: A Survey of the Supply, Employment, and Control of Negro Labor as Determined by the Plantation Regime* (New York, 1918; reprint, Baton Rouge: Louisiana State University Press, 1966). For a discussion of Phillips, see also Daniel Joseph Singal, *The War Within: From Victorian to Modernist Thought in the South, 1919–1945* (Chapel Hill: University of North Carolina Press, 1982), chap 2.

6. George Fredrickson, *The Black Image in the White Mind: The Debate on Afro-American Character and Destiny, 1817–1914* (New York: Harper & Row, 1971), chap. 2. Fredrickson argues that a second strain of proslavery thought stressed hierarchy and paternalism, but believes that the democratic version was more broadly based and important.

7. Avery Craven, *The Coming of the Civil War* (New York: Scribner, 1942), 33, 93. Craven adds that racism also played a part in creating white unity.

8. Frank Owsley, *Plain Folk of the Old South* (Baton Rouge: Louisiana State University Press, 1949; Chicago: Quadrangle Books, 1972).

9. Fletcher M. Green, "Democracy in the Old South," *JSH* 12 (1946): 177–92.

10. Charles G. Sellers, "The Travail of Slavery," in *The Southerner as American*, ed. Sellers (Chapel Hill: University of North Carolina

Press, 1960); Craven, *Coming of the Civil War.* A recent effort to combine the approaches of Owsley and Sellers to analyze slave-owners themselves is James Oakes, *The Ruling Race: A History of American Slaveowners* (New York: Knopf, 1982). Oakes, however, lays much heavier stress on simple economic self-interest than did either Owsley or Sellers.

11. Wilbur Cash, *The Mind of the South* (New York: Knopf, 1941).
12. Bertram Wyatt-Brown, *Southern Honor: Ethics and Behavior in the Old South* (New York: Oxford University Press, 1982). See also Wyatt-Brown, "W. J. Cash and Southern Culture," in *From the Old South to the New: Essays on the Transitional South*, ed. Walter Fraser, Jr., and Winfred B. Moore, Jr. (Westport, Conn.: Greenwood Press, 1981).

Prologue: The Land of Cotton

1. Mark Van Doren, ed., *The Travels of William Bartram* (1792; n.p., Macy-Masius, 1928), 50–54; Louis DeVorsey, Jr., *The Indian Boundary in the Southern Colonies, 1763–1775* (Chapel Hill: University of North Carolina Press, 1966), 170.
2. Kenneth Coleman, ed., *A History of Georgia* (Athens: University of Georgia Press, 1977), 40–42, 51; Coleman, *Colonial Georgia* (New York: Scribner, 1976), 50–51, 215–16.
3. DeVorsey, *Indian Boundary*, 151–61.
4. Ibid., 170. The old boundary touched the Savannah River about twenty-five miles north of Augusta.
5. Van Doren, *Travels*, 56.
6. Quoted in DeVorsey, *Indian Boundary*, 171.
7. Robert L. Meriwether, *The Expansion of South Carolina, 1729–1765* (Kingsport, Tenn.: Southern Press, 1940), 113–15; Arthur R. Hall, "Soil Erosion and Agriculture in the Southern Piedmont: A History" (Ph.D. diss., Duke University, 1948).
8. Meriwether, *Expansion*, chaps. 7, 15, 16; Carl Bridenbaugh, *Myths and Realities: Societies of the Colonial South* (Baton Rouge: Louisiana State University Press, 1952), chap. 3.
9. Otis Ashmore, "Wilkes County: Its Place in Georgia History," *Georgia Historical Quarterly* 1 (1917): 59–69; Lucien Roberts, "Sectional Problems in Georgia During the Formative Period, 1776–1798," *Georgia Historical Quarterly* 18 (1934): 207–10.
10. James C. Bonner, *A History of Georgia Agriculture, 1732–1860* (Athens: University of Georgia Press, 1964), 32–35, 49–50; E. Merton Coulter, *Old Petersburg and the Broad River Valley of Georgia: Their Rise and Decline* (Athens: University of Georgia Press, 1965).
11. Calculated from U.S. Bureau of the Census, *First Census, 1790.* See Appendix A for precise definition of Augusta's hinterlands.
12. Gavin Wright, *The Political Economy of the Cotton South: Households, Markets, and Wealth in the Nineteenth Century* (New York: Norton, 1978), 14–15.

13. Lewis Cecil Gray, *History of Agriculture in the Southern United States to 1860*, 2 vols. (Washington, D.C., 1933; reprint, Gloucester, Mass.: Peter Smith, 1958), 2:678–81.

14. Calculated from U.S. Bureau of the Census, *Second Census, 1800*.

15. J. Orin Oliphant, ed., *Through the South and West with Jeremiah Evarts in 1826* (Lewisburg, Pa.: Bucknell University Press, 1956), 96.

16. Ulrich B. Phillips, *History of Transportation in the Eastern Cotton Belt to 1860* (New York, 1908), chap. 4.

17. See Map 1, p. xv. Augusta's economic reach can be traced in the account books of a cotton factor in the Stephen D. Heard Papers, SHC. See also Phillips, *History of Transportation*, chap. 3. Hereafter, references to particular localities in South Carolina will be so identified; counties and towns not specifically identified by state are in Georgia. Until 1868, South Carolina's local units of government in the Piedmont were called districts, not counties; and in the low country, parishes.

18. Jonathon Evans, comp., *A Journal of the Life, Travels, and Religious Labors of William Savery* (London, 1844), 10.

19. Ralph G. Scott, "The Quaker Settlement of Wrightsboro, Georgia," *Georgia Historical Quarterly* 56 (1972): 210–23.

1. Slavery and Liberty

1. The speech is reprinted in Henry C. Cleveland, *Alexander H. Stephens in Public and Private, With Letters and Speeches, Before, During, and Since the War* (Philadelphia, 1867), 637–50.

2. Duncan MacLeod, *Slavery, Race, and the American Revolution* (New York: Cambridge University Press, 1974).

3. E. N. Elliot, ed., "Introduction," in *Cotton Is King; And Proslavery Arguments* (Augusta, Ga., 1860), viii–ix.

4. William W. Freehling, *Prelude to Civil War: The Nullification Crisis in South Carolina, 1816–1836* (New York: Harper & Row, 1864).

5. John Bauskett to Iveson L. Brookes, 19 April 1851, Iveson L. Brookes Papers, SHC; Iveson L. Brookes to Reverend William Heath, 20 March 1849, Iveson L. Brookes Papers, SHC. All quotes from this and other primary sources are reproduced as in the original.

6. Henry C. Cleveland to Alexander H. Stephens, 11 July 1859, AHSLC.

7. The basic study of eighteenth-century republicanism is Bernard Bailyn, *The Ideological Origins of the American Revolution* (Cambridge, Mass.: Harvard University Press, 1967). See also Gordon S. Wood, *The Creation of the American Republic, 1776–1787* (Chapel Hill: University of North Carolina Press, 1969); Robert Shalhope, "Toward a Republican Synthesis: The Emergence of an Understanding of Republicanism in American Historiography," *William and Mary Quarterly*, 3rd ser., 24 (1972): 49–80; Shalhope, "Republicanism and Early American Historiography," *William and Mary Quarterly* 34 (1982): 334–56.

8. Alexander H. Stephens to Linton Stephens, 19 April 1850, AHSM

(reprinted in James D. Waddell, ed., *Biographical Sketch of Linton Stephens, Containing a Selection of His Letters, Speeches, State Papers, Etc.* [Atlanta, 1877], 101−05).

9. J. G. A. Pocock, *The Machiavellian Moment: Florentine Political Thought and the Atlantic Republican Tradition* (Princeton, N.J.: Princeton University Press, 1975), esp. chap. 5.

10. Benton Miller Farm Journal, 15 April 1858, GDAH (manuscript on microfilm).

11. *Southern Cultivator* 7 (1849), quoted in James C. Bonner, "Profile of a Late Ante-Bellum Community," *American Historical Review* 49 (1944): 673.

12. Thomas Jefferson, *Notes on the State of Virginia,* "Query XIX" (1785; reprint, New York: Harper & Row, 1964); Leo Marx, *The Machine in the Garden: Technology and the Pastoral Ideal in America* (New York: Oxford University Press, 1964), 117−44; Pocock, *Machiavellian Moment,* chap. 15, esp. 532−33; Robert Shalhope, *John Taylor of Caroline: Pastoral Republican* (Columbia: University of South Carolina Press, 1980).

13. Arthur Simkins, *An Address before the State Agricultural Society of South Carolina* (Edgefield, S.C., 1855). Simkins was editor of the Edgefield *Advertiser.*

14. Colonel R. H. Ward, Address to the Greene County Agricultural Society, Augusta *Chronicle,* 12 February 1851 (delivered 15 November 1850).

15. Quoted in Frank L. Owsley, *Plain Folk of the Old South* (Baton Rouge: Louisiana State University Press, 1949; reprint, Chicago: Quadrangle Books, 1972), 4.

16. Ulrich B. Phillips, *American Negro Slavery: A Survey of the Supply, Employment, and Control of Negro Labor as Determined by the Plantation Regime* (New York, 1918; reprint, Baton Rouge: Louisiana State University Press, 1966), 215−18; Drew Gilpin Faust, *James Henry Hammond and the Old South: A Design for Mastery* (Baton Rouge: Louisiana State University Press, 1982).

17. Benton Miller Farm Journal, GDAH; David C. Barrow Plantation Diary, DCB.

18. *Southern Cultivator* 18 (1861): 10, quoted in Gavin Wright, *The Political Economy of the Cotton South: Households, Markets, and Wealth in the Nineteenth Century* (New York: Norton, 1978), 64.

19. Steven Hahn, *The Roots of Southern Populism: Yeoman Farmers and the Transformation of the Georgia Upcountry, 1850–1890* (New York: Oxford University Press, 1983), chap. 1.

20. Ibid., 33−40; Augusta *Chronicle,* 2 October 1858.

21. The fullest treatment is James C. Bonner, "Agricultural Reform in the Georgia Piedmont, 1820–1860" (Ph.D. diss., University of North Carolina, 1944). See also Bonner, "Genesis of Agricultural Reform in the Cotton Belt," *JSH* 9 (1943): 475−500; Drew Gilpin Faust, "The Rhetoric and Ritual of Agriculture in Antebellum South Carolina," *JSH* 45 (1979): 541−68. For a contemporary ex-

ample, see M. C. M. Hammond, *Anniversary Oration Delivered before the Burke County Central Agricultural Society* (Augusta, Ga., 1846).

22. Quoted in Bonner, "Genesis of Agricultural Reform," 475. It should be noted that complaints of soil depletion caused by poor agricultural practices were exaggerated. Cotton is one of the least soil-exhausting of all commercial crops. Dilapidated mansions and gullied fields usually appeared after farms were abandoned—not because soil was unproductive, but because western soil was even more productive, often fabulously so. See J. B. McBryde and W. H. Beal, "Chemistry of Cotton," pp. 83–84, and H. C. White, "The Manuring of Cotton," pp. 169–71, both in U.S. Office of Experiment Stations, *The Cotton Plant: Its History, Botany, Chemistry, Culture, Enemies, and Uses*, Bulletin no. 33 (Washington, D.C., Government Printing Office, 1896); Wright, *Political Economy of the Cotton South*, 15–17.

23. Minutes of the Beech Island Farmers Club, 5 April 1856, SCL (typescript).

24. Ibid; Edgefield *Advertiser*, 29 April 1852.

25. Sam B. Hilliard, *Hogmeat and Hoecake: Food Supply in the Old South, 1840–1860* (Carbondale: Southern Illinois University Press, 1972), 105–11, 158–61.

26. This view is expressed most sharply in Genovese's earliest major work, *The Political Economy of Slavery: Studies in the Economy and Society of the Slave South* (New York: Random House, Pantheon, 1965). A more recent argument is Eugene Genovese and Elizabeth Fox-Genovese, *The Fruits of Merchant Capital: Slavery and Bourgeois Property in the Rise and Expansion of Capitalism* (New York: Oxford University Press, 1983), chaps. 5, 6. See also Genovese, *The World the Slaveholders Made: Two Essays in Interpretation* (New York: Random House, Pantheon, 1969); *Roll, Jordan, Roll: The World the Slaves Made* (New York: Random House, Pantheon, 1974).

27. Chester Destler, "David Dickson's 'System of Farming' and the Agricultural Revolution in the Deep South," *Agricultural History* 31 (1957): 30–39; Faust, *James Henry Hammond*, chap. 6.

28. Robert E. Gallman and Ralph V. Anderson, "Slaves as Fixed Capital: Slave Labor and Southern Economic Development," *Journal of American History* 64 (1977): 24–46.

29. Self-sufficiency on large southern plantations was first demonstrated convincingly by Robert E. Gallman, "Self-Sufficiency in the Cotton Economy of the Antebellum South," *Agricultural History* 44 (1970): 5–24, and by Raymond C. Battalio and John Kagel, "The Structure of Antebellum Southern Agriculture: South Carolina, a Case Study," *Agricultural History* 44 (1970): 25–37. The information displayed in Table 4 would show the same trend if farms were classified by number of slaves.

30. Heywood Fleisig, "Slavery, the Supply of Agricultural Labor, and the Industrialization of the South," *Journal of Economic History* 36

(1976): 572−97; Wright, *Political Economy of the Cotton South*, 44−55.

31. Julius Rubin, "The Limits of Agricultural Progress in the Nineteenth-Century South," *Agricultural History* 49 (1975): 362−73. The argument in the following paragraph closely follows Rubin's. See also Arthur R. Hall, "Soil Erosion and Agriculture in the Southern Piedmont: A History" (Ph.D. diss., Duke University, 1948); comments on the difficulty of raising wheat in Minutes of the Beech Island Farmers Club, 2 August 1856, SCL; Hilliard, *Hogmeat and Hoecake*, 31. Farmers who turned to wheat in this area during the Civil War suffered severely from attacks of wheat rust.

32. On the connection between slavery and urban markets, see Genovese, *Political Economy of Slavery*, chap. 7; Julius Rubin, "Urban Growth and Regional Development," in *The Growth of Seaport Cities, 1790−1825*, ed. David T. Gilchrist (Charlottesville: University Press of Virginia, 1967), 3−21; Wright, *Political Economy of the Cotton South*, 121−25.

33. Such markets as local villages provided were apparently so unpredictable that their food needs were provided in large part by hogs driven in from the upper Piedmont and upper South. See Edgefield *Advertiser*, 15 December 1852 and 9 November 1853.

34. These figures are based on county data published in U.S. Bureau of the Census, *Agriculture in 1860*. See also Augusta *Chronicle*, 7 October 1858, on the "constantly increasing value of the lands in the immediate neighborhood of Augusta, for small farms, market gardens, and orchards."

35. Nathan B. Moore Farm Journal, Perkins Library, Duke University (manuscript); Herbert A. Kellar, ed., *Solon Robinson, Pioneer and Agriculturalist: Selected Writings*, 2 vols. (Indianapolis: Indiana Historical Bureau, 1936), 2:358.

36. Ralph B. Flanders, *Plantation Slavery in Georgia* (Chapel Hill: University of North Carolina Press, 1933), 158.

37. Kellar, *Solon Robinson*, 2:356−57.

38. James C. Bonner, *A History of Georgia Agriculture, 1732−1860* (Athens: University of Georgia Press, 1964), 172.

39. James H. Hammond Plantation Journal, 8 November 1853, JHHSCL; E. Spann Hammond Day Book, 8 April 1858, E. Spann Hammond Papers, SCL. See also Edgefield *Advertiser*, 22 June 1859. Beech Island's rich river bottom land made it in some ways more suitable for corn than for cotton. Cotton on such land tended to produce too many branches and not enough bolls. The William Eve plantation was on similar land.

40. Based on analysis of every Hancock County farm producing cotton or corn as listed in the manuscript schedules of the United States census of agriculture, 1860 (microfilm, National Archives and Records Service, Washington, D.C.). Georgia's upcountry small farmers also sharply increased cotton production during the decade; see Hahn, *Roots of Southern Populism*, Appendix, Tables v−vi.

41. Sarah Alexander to Lou, 10 January 1850, Alexander–Hillhouse Papers, SHC.
42. Augusta *Chronicle*, 12 February 1851.
43. James H. Hammond to William Gilmore Simms, 26 March 1850, JHHLC.
44. U.S. Bureau of the Census, *Manufactures in 1860*. See also articles by Richard W. Griffin: "The Textile Industry in Greene County, Georgia, Before 1860," *Georgia Historical Quarterly* 48 (1964): 81–84, which claims three mills for the county in 1860; "The Origins of the Industrial Revolution in Georgia: Cotton Textiles, 1810–65," *Georgia Historical Quarterly* 42 (1958): 355–75; "Poor White Laborers in Southern Cotton Factories, 1789–1865," *South Carolina Historical Magazine* 61 (1960): 26–40; "The Augusta (Ga.) Manufacturing Company in Peace, War and Reconstruction, 1847–1877," *Business History Review* 32 (1958): 60–73; and Ernest M. Lander, *The Textile Industry in Antebellum South Carolina* (Baton Rouge: Louisiana State University Press, 1969).
45. Broadus Mitchell, *William Gregg, Factory Master of the Old South* (Chapel Hill: University of North Carolina Press, 1928).
46. Edgefield *Advertiser*, 16 July 1856.
47. Ibid., 21 November 1850 (quotation slightly rearranged). The census property figures for mill workers confirm their poverty: in Hancock County, not one of the almost 100 mill workers in 1860 owned as much as $100 worth of personal property, and only one owned any real property; Bonner, "Profile," 671, 675. For a somewhat different analysis, see Tom E. Terrill, "Eager Hands: Labor for Southern Textiles, 1850–1860," *Journal of Economic History* 36 (1976): 84–99.
48. Volumes for Hancock and Morgan counties, R. G. Dun Ledgers, Dun & Bradstreet Collection, Baker Library, Harvard University. Occupations and property of stockholders were checked in manuscript returns of the United States Bureau of the Census, 1850 and 1860.
49. Private communication from David Carlton, who kindly shared with me some of the results of his own research on Graniteville.
50. R. G. Dun Co. Ledgers, Dun & Bradstreet Collection, Baker Library, Harvard University.
51. Fred Bateman and Thomas Weiss, *A Deplorable Scarcity: The Failure of Industrialization in the Slave Economy* (Chapel Hill: University of North Carolina Press, 1981).
52. Augusta *Chronicle*, 27 November 1860.
53. See p. 22; Simkins, *Address*.
54. Edgefield *Advertiser*, 7 May 1856.
55. Augusta *Chronicle*, 3 January 1855.
56. Minutes of the Beech Island Agricultural and Police Society, 28 June 1851, SCL (typescript).
57. Edgefield *Advertiser*, 16 February 1859; Augusta *Chronicle*, 7 October 1851.
58. Christopher C. Memminger to James H. Hammond, 28 April 1849,

reprinted in Thomas P. Marten, "The Advent of William Gregg and the Graniteville Company," *JSH* 11 (1945): 413–14.

59. Edmund S. Morgan, *American Slavery, American Freedom: The Ordeal of Colonial Virginia* (New York: Norton, 1975), esp. 363–87.

60. Freehling, *Prelude to Civil War*, 81–82.

61. George McDuffie, "Message to the South Carolina Legislature on the Slavery Question, 1835," in *American History Leaflets, Colonial and Constitutional*, no. 10, ed. Albert B. Hart and Edward Channing (New York: Lovell, 1893).

62. Iveson L. Brookes, *A Defense of Southern Slavery. Against the Attacks of Henry Clay and Alexander Campbell* (Hamburg, S.C., 1851), 44. This pamphlet reprinted articles that first appeared in 1849.

63. Edgefield *Advertiser*, 26 August 1857.

64. Simkins, *Address*.

65. Iveson L. Brookes, *A Defense of the South Against the Reproaches of the North: in which Slavery Is Shown to Be an Institution of God Intended to Form the Basis of the Best Social State and the Only Safeguard to the Permanence of a Republican Government* (Hamburg, S.C., 1850), 45.

66. Augusta *Chronicle*, 1 March 1860.

67. For a different argument, see Kenneth Greenberg, "Revolutionary Ideology and the Proslavery Argument: The Abolition of Slavery in South Carolina," *Journal of American History* 42 (1976): 365–84.

68. Brookes, *Defense of Southern Slavery*, 24, 43.

69. James H. Hammond, Speech in the United States Senate, *Congressional Globe*, 35th Cong., 1st sess., 6 March 1858.

70. Brookes, *Defense of the South*, 46.

71. James H. Hammond, "Slavery in the Light of Political Science," in Elliot, *Cotton Is King*, 638–39. This was first published in 1845 in the Columbia *South Carolinian*, and reprinted as *Two Letters on Slavery in the United States Addressed to Thomas Clarkson, Esq.*

72. Cleveland, *Alexander H. Stephens*, 723. By this time, the phrase was something of a cliché; see, for example, Hammond, "Slavery," in Elliot, *Cotton Is King*, 637; Augusta *Chronicle*, 1 March 1860.

73. Altogether in Augusta and its hinterlands, there were about 10,000 slaveowners and 10,000 farmers. The large majority of slaveowners were farmers, and vice versa. See U.S. Bureau of the Census, "Agriculture," in *Eighth Census, 1860* (Washington, D.C., 1865). In Hancock County in 1860, 81 percent of all farmers owned slaves; Bonner, "Profile," 671.

74. See pp. 91–2.

2. The Underlife of Slavery

1. This account is based on an undated broadside in the South Caroliniana Library. Most of the broadside consists of copies of letters

published in the Abbeville *Banner* in the summer of 1850. It was printed and distributed by Reverend Grier as a defense of his conduct some time after the controversy had died down.

2. Thomas R. R. Cobb, *An Historical Sketch of Slavery from the Earliest Periods* (Philadelphia and Savannah, 1858), ccxviii.

3. Clyde N. Wilson, ed., *The Papers of John C. Calhoun* (Columbia: University of South Carolina Press, 1958–), 14:85; J. William Harris, "Last of the Classical Republicans: An Interpretation of John C. Calhoun," *Civil War History* 30 (1984): 255−67.

4. Among important works contributing to this reinterpretation of slave society and culture are John Blassingame, *The Slave Community: Plantation Life in the Antebellum South*, rev. and enl. ed. (New York: Oxford University Press, 1979); Eugene Genovese, *Roll, Jordan, Roll: The World the Slaves Made* (New York: Random House, Pantheon, 1974); Herbert G. Gutman, *The Black Family in Slavery and Freedom, 1750–1925* (New York: Random House, Pantheon, 1976); Leslie Howard Owens, *This Species of Property: Slave Life and Culture in the Old South* (New York: Oxford University Press, 1976); Albert Raboteau, *Slave Religion: The Invisible Institution in the Antebellum South* (New York: Oxford University Press, 1978); Thomas Webber, *Deep Like the Rivers: Education in the Slave Community* (New York: Norton, 1978).

5. Benton Miller Farm Journal, 16 March 1858, GDAH.

6. Ibid., 26 and 27 February, 13 March, 12 April, 7, 8, and 11 June, 26 October, 6 and 8 November 1858, GDAH.

7. The high estimate is in Robert Fogel and Stanley Engerman, *Time on the Cross: The Economics of American Negro Slavery* (Boston: Little, Brown, 1974), 38−40; the low estimate is in Herbert G. Gutman, *Slavery and the Numbers Game: A Critique of Time on the Cross* (Urbana: University of Illinois Press, 1975), 51−77.

8. Roger Ransom and Richard Sutch, *One Kind of Freedom: The Economic Consequences of Emancipation* (New York: Cambridge University Press, 1977), 220−24.

9. The Edgefield data are in Vernon O. Burton, "Unfaithful Servants? Edgefield's Black Reconstruction: Part I of the Total History of Edgefield County, South Carolina" (Ph.D. diss., Princeton University, 1976), 217, 251. Georgia data is based on samples from the manuscript census returns for 1880 for Taliaferro, Hart, Glascock, and Richmond counties.

10. Rawick, *Florida Narratives*, 17:22−25. These volumes are a compilation of the original typescripts of interviews with thousands of former slaves, mostly in the 1930s and mostly under the auspices of the United States Works Progress Administration (WPA). In addition to the original compilation of nineteen volumes, two supplementary series—Supplement 1, with 14 volumes, and Supplement 2, with 10 volumes—have been published. I have used the narratives of about 130 men and women who lived under slavery in Augusta's hinterlands, or occasionally in adjacent counties. Most still lived in Georgia in the 1930s; others were as far away as Texas or Ohio.

Hereafter, citations to the interviews, commonly known as the WPA Narratives, will be: Rawick, *Ga. Narr.*, Sup. 1, 13(3):210, the numbers referring (in order) to volume, part, and page.

11. Ibid., *Ark. Narr.*, 10(6):240−41.
12. David C. Barrow Plantation Diary, 1856, DCB; J. M. Harrison to David C. Barrow, 13 February 1855, DCB; Ralph B. Flanders, *Plantation Slavery in Georgia* (Chapel Hill: University of North Carolina Press, 1933), 201−08.
13. Rawick, *Tex. Narr.*, Sup. 2, 5(4):1843.
14. Ibid., *Ga. Narr.*, 12(2):347. For similar descriptions, see 12(1): 99−100; 12(2):110; 13(4):19.
15. Edgefield *Advertiser*, 10 August 1854.
16. Linton Stephens to Alexander H. Stephens, 27 December 1854, AHSM.
17. Edward P. Alexander to "Dear Brother," 31 December 1850, Alexander–Hillhouse Papers, SHC.
18. Alexander H. Stephens to William M. Reese, 27 December 1860, AHSLC.
19. W. R. Wright to David C. Barrow, 4 December 1856, DCB.
20. J. A. Spratlin to David C. Barrow, 18 February 1864, DCB.
21. Rawick, *Ga. Narr.*, Sup. 1, 3:215.
22. Ibid., 4:468.
23. Ibid., *Ark. Narr.*, 10(5):155.
24. Of 130 former slaves from the Augusta area interviewed for the WPA Narratives, 20 mentioned parents who had lived on different plantations.
25. Rawick, *Ga. Narr.*, 12(1):161.
26. Robert Toombs, *An Oration delivered before the Few and Phi Gamma Societies of Emory College: Slavery in the United States; its consistency with republican institutions, and its effects upon the slave and society* (Augusta, Ga., 1853), extensively excerpted in Ulrich B. Phillips, *The Life of Robert Toombs* (New York: Macmillan, 1913), 156−65, quote on p. 161.
27. Rawick, *Ga. Narr.*, 12(2):15−16; *Fla. Narr.*, 17:70.
28. Edgefield *Advertiser*, 25 September 1851. South Carolina law forbade teaching slaves to read.
29. Minutes of Goshen Baptist Church, p. 72, and entry for 18 March 1854, Goshen Baptist Church [Lincoln County] Records, GDAH (typescript).
30. Ibid., 21 August 1853.
31. Ibid., 15 September 1850, 21 April and 17 May 1851, 20 May 1855.
32. Ella Gertrude (Clanton) Thomas Diary, 12 July 1855, Perkins Library, Duke University (manuscript).
33. One of many descriptions of funerals is in Rawick, *Ga. Narr.*, 13(3): 329−30. "Hark from de Tomb" was clearly the favorite spiritual; I have used the version in Genovese, *Roll, Jordan, Roll*, 199.
34. Linton Stephens to Alexander H. Stephens, 1 February 1861, AHSM.
35. Rawick, *Ark. Narr.*, 10(5):161.
36. Ibid., *Ga. Narr.*, 12(2):220−32.

37. Ibid., 13(3):171−77.
38. Ibid., 12(2):338−42.
39. Ibid., 12(1):195.
40. James H. Hammond, Instructions to Overseers, JHHSCL. A convenient published version is in Willie Lee Rose, ed., *A Documentary History of Slavery in North America* (New York: Oxford University Press, 1976), quote 352.
41. James H. Hammond Plantation Journal, 14 January 1851, JHHSCL. See also the study of the Hammond plantations by Drew Gilpin Faust, "Culture, Conflict, and Community: The Meaning of Power on an Antebellum Plantation," *Journal of Social History* 14 (1980): 83−97.
42. Rawick, *Ga. Narr.*, 12(1):168−71.
43. Ibid., *Tenn. Narr.*, 16(6):49.
44. Jacob Stroyer, "My Life in the South," in *Five Slave Narratives: A Compendium* (1898; reprint, New York: Arno Press and the New York Times, 1968).
45. Rawick, *Ga. Narr.*, 12(1):174.
46. Edgefield *Advertiser*, 27 January 1858.
47. Octavious T. Porcher Diary, 12 September 1852, Octavious T. Porcher Papers, SCL; Alexander H. Stephens to Linton Stephens, 11 March 1860, AHSM.
48. George W. Onie to Iveson L. Brookes, 1 April 1847, Iveson L. Brookes Papers, SHC.
49. Minutes of the Beech Island Agricultural and Police Society, 28 June 1851, SCL.
50. Minutes of the Beech Island Farmers Club, 3 December 1859, SCL.
51. Ibid., 7 March 1857.
52. The most complete discussion of the patrol system is in Howell M. Henry, *Police Control of the Slave in South Carolina* (Emory, Va., 1914; reprint, New York: Negro Universities Press, 1968).
53. Minutes of the Beech Island Farmers Club, 3 December 1859, SCL.
54. Rawick, *Md. Narr.*, 16(3):47.
55. Ibid., *Ark. Narr.*, 8(2):18.
56. Ibid., 10(5):160−61.
57. Ibid., *Ga. Narr.*, 12(1):163. Many of the WPA Narratives describe Saturday night "frolics."
58. Ibid., 13(4):224.
59. Edgefield *Advertiser*, 10 July 1850.
60. Rawick, *Ark. Narr.*, 10(5):160−61.
61. Ibid., *Ga. Narr.*, Sup. 1, 3:320−21.
62. Ibid., *N.C. Narr.*, 14(1):157. It is not certain where Burnett lived, but she probably was owned by William Joyner of Richmond County.
63. Ibid., *Fla. Narr.*, 17:14.
64. F. Nash Boney, ed., *Slave Life in Georgia: A Narrative of the Life, Sufferings and Escape of John Brown, A Fugitive Slave* (London, 1855; reprint, Savannah: Beehive Press, 1972). Brown lived on small farms in Baldwin and DeKalb counties, just outside Au-

gusta's hinterlands. In preparing his narrative, Brown had considerable assistance from a British antislavery writer. Boney has, however, used other sources to check details in Brown's story, and it appears to be very reliable.

65. Rawick, *Fla. Narr.*, 17 : 14.

66. Ibid., *Ga. Narr.*, 12(2) : 52.

67. Ibid., 13(4) : 224–25.

68. Stroyer, "My Life," 64–66. Other cases of assistance to runaways are mentioned in Rawick, *Ga. Narr.*, 12(2) : 14–15, 52; 13(4) : 224–25.

69. Stroyer, "My Life," 61–64.

70. Michael S. Hindus, "Black Justice Under White Law: Criminal Prosecutions of Blacks in Antebellum South Carolina," *Journal of American History* 63 (1976) : 587.

71. Minutes of Glascock County Superior Court, terms of June 1858 and November 1858, GDAH (microfilm).

72. Burton, "Unfaithful Servants?" 54–56.

73. John H. Cornish Diary, 22 February 1856, SHC (manuscript and typescript).

74. Augusta *Chronicle*, 2 January 1852.

75. Ibid., 13 January 1852.

76. Linton Stephens to Alexander H. Stephens, 7 February 1860, AHSM.

77. Letter from "K.," Augusta *Chronicle*, 28 August 1853.

78. George Ball, *Slavery in the United States; A Narrative of the Life and Adventures of George Ball* (1837; reprint, New York: Negro Universities Press, 1969), 220–34. The time and place (near Columbia) of these events fall somewhat outside the bounds of this study, but Ball's account is one of the most valuable by a South Carolina slave.

79. Boney, *Slave Life in Georgia*, 47.

80. Minutes of Long Creek Baptist Church, 21 June 1856, GDAH (microfilm).

81. Minutes of Hancock County Superior Court, 12 and 15 April 1859, GDAH (microfilm).

82. Ibid., 4 October 1858.

83. Minutes of Taliaferro County Superior Court, term of February 1861, GDAH (microfilm).

84. Minutes of Oglethorpe County Superior Court, 1842–1847, term of October 1842 (p. 407); 1847–1853, term of April 1848 (p. 83), undated (pp. 285–86), term of April 1850 (pp. 177–93), GDAH (microfilm).

85. Minutes of Greene County Superior Court, vol. 10, term of March 1845 (pp. 101–03); vol. 12, terms of March 1856 (pp. 61–62) and March 1858 (p. 226), GDAH.

86. Ibid., vol. 10, Grand Jury Presentments, September 1848 (pp. 341–42); vol. 12, Grand Jury Presentments, September 1858 (p. 303), GDAH.

87. Minutes of Columbia County Superior Court, 1850–1860, Grand Jury Presentments, September 1850 (p. 26), Grand Jury Presentments, September 1858 (p. 329), Grand Jury Presentments, March 1861 (p. 134), GDAH.

88. Minutes of Burke County Superior Court, 1835–1843, Grand Jury Presentments, May 1838 (pp. 88–90); 1850–1866, Grand Jury Presentments, May 1851 (p. 50), GDAH.

89. Augusta *Constitutionalist*, 1 September 1858.

90. Edgefield *Advertiser*, 30 April 1856.

91. *Preamble and Regulations of the Savannah River Anti-Slave Traffick Association* (1846), SCL (pamphlet).

92. Greensboro *Planter's Weekly*, 5 September 1860.

93. Boney, *Slave Life in Georgia*, 166–67.

94. Rawick, *Ga. Narr.*, 12(1):8.

95. Stroyer, "My Life," 29.

96. Boney, *Slave Life in Georgia*, 90.

97. Ella Gertrude Thomas Diary, 25 December 1858, Perkins Library, Duke University.

98. Minutes of the Beech Island Farmers Club, 3 December 1859, SCL.

99. Augusta *Chronicle*, 9 September 1860.

100. Ibid., 13 July 1851.

101. See p. 36; Christopher C. Hemminger to James H. Hammond, 28 April 1849, quoted in Thomas P. Marten, "The Advent of William Gregg and the Graniteville Company, *JSH* 11 (1945):413–14.

3. Portents of Class Division

1. The source for the incident described in this and the following paragraphs is a letter from Linton Stephens to Alexander H. Stephens, 3 February 1860, AHSM.

2. Linton Stephens did not give Pool's first name in his letter, but identifies him as a county native and a son of "old Pool the Shingle-getter." Neither the 1850 nor the 1860 census lists a Pool as a shingle cutter. The persons who fit the description most closely are John and Peter Pool, in 1850 listed as twin sons, age sixteen, of tenant farmer Henry Pool. In 1860, both were listed as married heads of households, twenty-four years old, and without property. I have no way of knowing whether the Pool in question was John or Peter, and use "John" in the text to avoid the repetitious use of "John or Peter."

3. Thomas R. R. Cobb, *An Historical Sketch of Slavery from the Earliest Periods* (Philadelphia and Savannah, 1858), ccxiii.

4. Ella Gertrude (Clanton) Thomas Diary, 12 February 1858, Perkins Library, Duke University. For an excellent essay on Mrs. Thomas and her dislike of slavery, see Mary Elizabeth Massey, "The Making of a Feminist," *JSH* 39 (1973):3–22.

5. William Thomson, *A Tradesman's Travels in the United States and Canada, in the Years 1840, 1841, and 1842* (Edinburgh, 1842), 16.

6. James H. Hammond, Letter to the *Spectator* (London), 14 July 1856,

JHHLC (copy). See also Hammond, "Slavery in the Light of Political Science," in *Cotton Is King; And Proslavery Arguments*, ed. E. N. Elliot (Augusta, Ga., 1860), 627–88.

7. James H. Hammond to Lewis Tappan, 6 September 1850, JHHLC (copy).
8. James H. Hammond to William Gilmore Simms, 19 November and 6 December 1854, JHHLC.
9. James H. Hammond to William Gilmore Simms, 19 November 1854, JHHLC.
10. Ada Sterling, ed., *A Belle of the Fifties, Memoirs of Mrs. Clay, of Alabama, covering Social and Political Life in Washington and the South, 1856–1866* (New York, 1905), 217.
11. Thomson, *Tradesman's Travels*, 117.
12. James M. Darnal [spelling uncertain] to Alexander H. Stephens, 9 July 1857, AHSLC.
13. Ella Gertrude Thomas Diary, 4 April 1856, Perkins Library, Duke University.
14. *Preamble and Regulations of the Savannah River Anti-Slave Traffick Association* (1846), SCL.
15. E. Spann Hammond Diary, 22 February 1857, E. Spann Hammond Papers, SCL.
16. Remarks of Mr. Mills, Minutes of the Beech Island Farmers Club, 3 December 1859, SCL.
17. Edgefield *Advertiser*, 16 July 1856.
18. Augusta *Chronicle*, 30 December 1857.
19. William McKinley to David C. Barrow, 14 April 1857, DCB.
20. Edgefield *Advertiser*, 17 July 1851.
21. Ibid., 5 January 1853.
22. Ibid., 23 July 1856.
23. Resolutions of a public meeting in Morgan county, reported in the Augusta *Chronicle*, 12 February 1853. See also, resolutions of a public meeting in Hancock County, ibid., 13 July 1853.
24. Ibid., 2 March 1853.
25. The largest and wealthiest planters usually lived on or near the Savannah river, both because the growing season was longer in that part of the county and because in the 1850s the river was the main artery for transporting cotton to Augusta and its markets.
26. Augusta *Constitutionalist*, 2 June 1854.
27. Ibid., 24 June and 4 July 1854. The latter quotes are taken from a report of a second meeting of the dissidents, which included quotes from their opponents.
28. John William Baker, *History of Hart County* (Atlanta: Foote & Davies, 1933), 25–26.
29. Respectively, 7.2 to 4.3, and $2,900 to $1,709. Leaders were identified from the reports in the Augusta *Constitutionalist*, 2 and 24 June, 4 July 1854. The manuscript returns of the United States Bureau of the Census, 1850, were the source for land and slave ownership.
30. Steven Hahn, *The Roots of Southern Populism: Yeoman Farmers*

and the Transformation of the Georgia Upcountry, 1850–1890
(New York: Oxford University Press, 1983), chap. 1.

31. Edgefield *Advertiser*, 20 May 1852.
32. Augusta *Chronicle*, 23 October 1851. The edition of the *Constitutionalist* has not survived; it is quoted in the *Chronicle*.
33. Hinton Rowan Helper, *The Impending Crisis of the South. How to Meet It*, ed. George Fredrickson (1857; Cambridge, Mass.: Harvard University Press, 1968).
34. Ibid., 42−44.
35. Ibid., 155−66.
36. Quoted in ibid., xviii.
37. A copy of the pamphlet by "Brutus," *An Address to the Citizens of South Carolina* (n.p., ca. 1849), is preserved among the James H. Hammond Papers in the SCL. See also Edgefield *Advertiser*, 6 and 27 June, 8 August 1849, for references to the pamphlet and quotes from the *Spartan*.
38. Quoted in Augusta *Constitutionalist*, 2 February 1850.
39. Augusta *Chronicle*, 23 October 1851.
40. Francis W. Pickens, *Speech of Hon. F. W. Pickens, Delivered before a Public Meeting of the People of the District, Held at Edgefield, S.C., July 7, 1851* (Edgefield, S.C., 1851), 17.
41. Augusta *Constitutionalist*, 7 March 1851; Ralph B. Flanders, *Plantation Slavery in Georgia* (Chapel Hill: University of North Carolina Press, 1933), 205−07.
42. B. C. Warner to Alexander H. Stephens, 1 August 1861, AHSLC.
43. Edgefield *Advertiser*, 12 December 1850, quoting the Columbus (Ga.) *Times*.
44. Ibid.
45. Pickens, *Speech of F. W. Pickens*, 17−18 (order of quotation reversed).
46. William Schley, Jr., to Alexander H. Stephens, 12 September 1854, AHSLC. For other examples of interracial violence, see Edgefield *Advertiser*, 4 March 1857 and 10 October 1860; Augusta *Chronicle*, 19 October 1852.
47. Quoted in James C. Bonner, "Genesis of Agricultural Reform in the Cotton Belt," *JSH* 9 (1943): 481.
48. James C. Bonner, "Profile of a Late Ante-Bellum Community," *American Historical Review* 49 (1944): 671, 676.
49. Benton Miller Farm Journal, 5 May 1859, GDAH. By the end of the year, Renfrow had left Miller's farm; but regular diary entries stop in midsummer, so the reason he left remains unknown.
50. For a recent exception, see Hahn, *Roots of Southern Populism*, chaps. 1 and 2.

51. **Table 24.** Status of Farm Operators in Augusta's Hinterlands, 1860

Type of Operator	Glascock County (N = 211) (%)	Hart County (N = 253) (%)	Taliaferro County (N = 229) (%)	Edgefield District (N = 185) (%)
Owners	80	76	86	89
Tenants*	20	24	14	11

SOURCE: Farm Sample from the manuscript returns of the Bureau of the Census, 1860.
NOTE: See Appendix A for detailed description.
*Tenants are farm operators listed in the census of agriculture and the census of population as owning no real property.

52. Wilie D. Poortwood, Jr., to Alexander H. Stephens, 13 April 1861, AHSLC.

53. Arthur Simkins, *An Address before the State Agricultural Society of South Carolina* (Edgefield, S.C., 1855).

54. Emily P. Burke, *Reminiscences of Georgia* (n.p., 1850), 208–09. This was first published as magazine articles in the 1840s.

55. John H. Cornish Diary, 13 January 1849, 9 and 21 February, 23 and 30 April, 1 May 1855, SHC. For an account of another very poor family, the Randalls, see 20, 24, and 25 May 1853.

56. Ella Gertrude Thomas Diary, 2 April 1856, Perkins Library, Duke University.

57. Fredrika Bremer, *The Homes of the New World; Impressions of America*, 2 vols. (New York, 1864), 1:365–67. *Clay eater* was a term somewhat indiscriminately applied to poor whites because some of them were in the habit of sucking on clay tucked in the roof of the mouth. The origins of this practice are somewhat obscure, but perhaps are related to dietary deficiencies.

58. Frederick Law Olmsted, *A Journey in the Back Country* (New York, 1860), 415–18.

59. John H. Cornish Diary, 9 March 1847 and 5 January 1857, SHC.

60. For a systematic descriptive survey of antebellum housing in this area, see Ava D. Rogers, *The Housing of Oglethorpe County, Georgia, 1790–1860* (Tallahassee, Fla.: State University Press, 1971). I examined inventories for Hart, Glascock, and Taliaferro counties (microfilm, GDAH).

61. The inventory is in the back of the Benton Miller Farm Journal, GDAH.

62. Benjamin Paschal to Martha Shank, 10 September and 19 October 1856, Joseph Belknap Smith Papers, Perkins Library, Duke University. According to the 1850 census, Benjamin Paschal, then age nineteen, owned no property; but listed in the next dwelling was a Dennis Paschal, age fifty-five, owning $9,000 worth of real property. A reasonable guess is that Dennis was the father of Benjamin.

63. Bonner, "Profile," 671, 673.

64. Herbert A. Kellar, ed., *Solon Robinson, Pioneer and Agricultural-ist: Selected Writings* 2 vols. (Indianapolis: Indiana Historical Bu-reau, 1936), 344–49; James H. Hammond Plantation Journal, 12 Oc-tober 1859, JHHSCL. For published portraits of wealthy planters in Augusta's hinterlands, see E. Merton Coulter, "A Century of a Georgia Plantation," *Agricultural History* 3 (1929): 147–59; Mar-ion Alexander Boggs, ed., *The Alexander Letters, 1787–1900* (1910; reprint, Athens: University of Georgia Press, 1980); Drew Gilpin Faust, *James Henry Hammond and the Old South: A Design for Mastery* (Baton Rouge: Louisiana State University Press, 1982).

65. Rogers, *Housing of Oglethorpe*; James C. Bonner, "Plantation Ar-chitecture of the Lower South on the Eve of the Civil War," *JSH* 11 (1945): 370–88, quote on Liberty Hall, 372–73; Chester Destler, "David Dickson's 'system of farming' and the Agricultural Revolu-tion in the Deep South," *Agricultural History* 31 (1957): 30–39. Parker Calloway's house has been restored and opened to the public on the Calloway Plantation, in Wilkes county. His slaveholdings are listed in the slave census for 1850. Liberty Hall, as currently open to the public in a state park in Crawfordville, was rebuilt after a fire in the 1870s.

66. James H. Hammond, Speech in United States Senate, *Congres-sional Globe*, 35th Cong., 1st sess., 6 March 1858.

67. Gavin Wright, *The Political Economy of the Cotton South: House-holds, Markets, and Wealth in the Nineteenth Century* (New York: Norton, 1978), chap. 2, esp. 24–37.

68. The only systematic study comparing wealth distribution among adults in the South with those in other regions concludes that, over-all, the distribution was about the same in the North and the South: Lee Soltow, *Men and Wealth in the United States, 1850–1870* (New Haven, Conn.: Yale University Press, 1975). It should be kept in mind that measures of inequality among whites only, while most relevant to the antebellum debate about the nature of southern so-ciety, ignore the greatest inequality: that black slaves were the prop-erty of others without even rights to their own labor. For a study of wealth distribution in a western area of the slave South, see Ran-dolph B. Campbell and Richard G. Lowe, *Wealth and Power in An-tebellum Texas* (College Station: Texas A&M University Press, 1977).

69. Chancellor [William] Harper, "Slavery in the Light of Social Eth-ics," in Elliot, *Cotton Is King*, 564. This essay first appeared in 1837 as "Memoir on Slavery."

70. **Table 25.** Newcomers in Augusta's Hinterlands, 1860

Category	Glascock County (N = 33)	Hart County (N = 63)	Taliaferro County (N = 45)
Percentage of 1860 sample	20	41	27
Women (%)	21	8	20
Farmers (%)	52	79	47
Slaveowners (%)	9	22	57*
Mean wealth of men ($)	2,188	1,451	4,915

SOURCE: Family Sample from the manuscript returns of the United States Bureau of the Census, 1850 and 1860.

NOTE: See Appendix A for detailed description.

*Excludes three slaveholders without personal property and counted as slave renters.

71. A good introduction to the large literature on the problems, methods, sources, and results of historical studies of social mobility in the United States is Stephan Thernstrom, *The Other Bostonians: Poverty and Progress in the American Metropolis, 1880–1970* (Cambridge, Mass.: Harvard University Press, 1973). For a discussion of the particular sources and methods used in this book, see Appendix A.

    Historians of mobility usually assume that the poor are more mobile than the more wealthy. Since it is very difficult to trace poor people, however, it is possible that geographically mobile people are, like most persisters, getting wealthier.

72. Ella Gertrude Thomas Diary, 2 April 1856, Perkins Library, Duke University.

73. See Appendix B for county-by-county tables.

74. Miller went to Mississippi to get his three slaves shortly after his marriage. From his Farm Journal, however, it cannot be determined whether he had owned the slaves before getting married.

75. Faust, *James Henry Hammond*, chap. 2.

76. Rudolph von Abele, *Alexander H. Stephens: A Biography* (New York: Knopf, 1946).

77. The story of David R. Ware is taken directly from Bonner, "Profile," 667–68. The quotes were taken by Bonner from *Southern Cultivator* 18:266.

78. Overall outmigration, mostly to the West, was greater in the prosperous 1850s than in the depressed 1840s. It is possible, even probable, that the relatively greater upward mobility during the 1850s is exaggerated (as compared with the 1840s) because unsuccessful farmers were more likely to move away in the later decade.

79. Testimony in trial of Richard Cook, Minutes of Taliaferro County Superior Court, term of February 1859, pp. 70–75, GDAH.

80. "A friend" to Alexander H. Stephens, 1 September 1860, AHSLC.

81. J. Henly Smith to Alexander H. Stephens, 7 May 1860, AHSLC.

82. Edgefield *Advertiser*, 28 November 1860.

83. Augusta *Chronicle*, 27 November 1856; Ronald Takaki, "The Movement to Reopen the Slave Trade in South Carolina," *South Carolina Historical Magazine* 66 (1965): 38–54.
84. Letter from "Nothing Laid Up," Augusta *Chronicle*, 5 January 1859. Since this letter, like most, was not signed, we cannot be certain that the writer was poor.
85. James H. Hammond to William Gilmore Simms, 26 March 1850, JHHLC.
86. E. P. Thompson, *The Making of the English Working Class* (New York: Random House, Pantheon, 1963), 9.
87. Linton Stephens to Alexander H. Stephens, 3 February 1860, AHSM.
88. J. Henly Smith to Alexander H. Stephens, 7 May 1860, AHSLC.

4. Ligaments of Community

1. William McKinley to David C. Barrow, 14 April 1857, DCB. In the 1840s and early 1850s, the Whigs had carried Oglethorpe county by overwhelming margins. The remnants of the Whigs, who first joined the American (Know-Nothing) party and then were known simply as the "opposition," were still numerous in the county in 1857. The "old-panel" and "new-panel" Democrats refer to factions based on former party ties and alliances.
2. Augusta *Chronicle*, 8 February 1857.
3. Nathan Gilbert to Alexander H. Stephens, 4 February 1855, AHSLC.
4. R. B. Brodnax to Alexander H. Stephens, 12 January 1861, AHSLC; Elias Allen to Alexander H. Stephens, 1 July 1861, AHSLC.
5. J. H. Spratlin to David C. Barrow, 5 December 1860, DCB.
6. Thomas, Berry, John Smith [*sic*] to David C. Barrow, 9 May 1861, DCB.
7. The best account of the large-scale credit system in the antebellum South is Harold D. Woodman, *King Cotton and His Retainers: Financing and Marketing the Cotton Crop of the South, 1800–1925* (Lexington: University of Kentucky Press, 1968).
8. Thomas Belk to Alexander H. Stephens, 16 April 1852, AHSLC.
9. Linton Stephens to Alexander H. Stephens, 15 February 1860, AHSM.
10. Alex A. Allen to David C. Barrow, 17 March 1853, "cash accounts," in back of David C. Barrow Plantation Diary, 1856, which includes a list of small loans to others, DCB.
11. E. H. Evans to Iveson L. Brookes, 20 September 1858, Iveson L. Brookes Papers, SHC.
12. See, for example, Edward Noble to A. Burt, 25 February 1850, Burt Papers, Perkins Library, Duke University.
13. "Social exchange" as a factor in creating social solidarity has been an important theme in anthropology since the classic work of Bronislaw Malinowski, for example, *Argonauts of the Western Pacific* (London: Routledge & Kegan Paul, 1922), and Marcel Mauss, *The Gift* (1925; English ed., Glencoe, Ill.: Free Press, 1954). Notable among many more recent treatments are Marshall D. Sahlins, "On the Soci-

ology of Primitive Exchange," in *The Relevance of Models for Social Anthropology*, ed. Michael Banton (London: Association of Social Anthropologists of the Commonwealth, 1965); Peter P. Ekeh, *Social Exchange Theory: The Two Traditions* (Cambridge, Mass.: Harvard University Press, 1974).

14. Alexander H. Stephens to Linton Stephens, 23 and 27 December 1860, AHSM; lists of notes due, 1851, 1858, and 1860, Alexander H. Stephens Papers, Perkins Library, Duke University.

15. Edward L. Meadows to Alexander H. Stephens, 25 August 1859, Alexander H. Stephens Papers, Perkins Library, Duke University; Linton Stephens to Alexander H. Stephens, 7 February 1860, AHSM.

16. E. D. Rhodes, at the request of Elizabeth Akins, to Alexander H. Stephens, 1 March 1861, AHSLC.

17. Linton Stephens to Alexander H. Stephens, 6 February 1861, AHSM.

18. See, for example, Benton Miller Farm Journal, 26 January 1858 and 31 January 1859, GDAH; W. I. Brookes to Iveson L. Brookes, 25 January 1848, Iveson L. Brookes Papers, Perkins Library, Duke University; Plantation Account Book, Graves Family Papers, SHC.

19. Glascock County, Estate Inventory Book A, John Cheeley Estate, September 1860, GDAH (microfilm).

20. Ibid., William Seals Inventory, September 1860. Neither the inventories nor, in most cases, the notes or accounts usually mentioned why a debt had been incurred. Notes usually said simply, "for value received."

21. See Appendix A for procedure in selecting inventories.

22. James Z. Rabun, ed., "Alexander H. Stephens's Diary, 1834–1837," *Georgia Historical Quarterly* 36 (1952):71–96, 163–89; entry for 17 June 1834 (p. 92).

23. Thomas Belk to Alexander H. Stephens, 16 April 1852, AHSLC.

24. See, for example, Edgefield *Advertiser*, 20 November 1851, 23 and 30 November 1853.

25. Good recent studies of southern evangelicalism include John Boles, *The Great Revival, 1787–1805: The Origins of the Southern Evangelical Mind* (Lexington: University of Kentucky Press, 1972); Donald G. Mathews, *Religion in the Old South* (Chicago: University of Chicago Press, 1977).

Of the three leading denominations, the Baptist and the Methodist were by far the largest, with the Baptist probably the larger of the two. There were scattered congregations of Episcopalians, Lutherans, Primitive Baptists, Catholics, and smaller sects. A small number of Jews, mostly German immigrants and mostly town merchants, also lived in Augusta's hinterlands. While there were differences in theology and more important ones in governance among the major denominations, they were less striking than were basic similarities. With some exceptions, there was little interdenominational conflict.

26. A partial exception to this generalization was the temperance movement. Also, some of the work among slaves eventually led individual ministers to call for more protection of slave marriages; see Anne Loveland, *Southern Evangelicals and the Social Order, 1800–*

1860 (Baton Rouge: Louisiana State University Press, 1980). On Christianizing slaves as evangelical reform, see Drew Gilpin Faust, "Evangelicalism and the Meaning of the Proslavery Argument : The Reverend Thornton Stringfellow of Virginia," *Virginia Magazine of History and Biography* 85 (1977): 3–17; Jack P. Maddex, "Proslavery Millennialism: Social Eschatology in Antebellum Southern Calvinism," *American Quarterly* 31 (1979): 46–62.

27. James I. Robertson, Jr., ed., *The Diary of Dolly Lunt Burge* (Athens: University of Georgia Press, 1962), entries in 1847 to 1850.

28. Minutes of Goshen Baptist church, 14 November 1857, Goshen Baptist church [Lincoln county] Records, GDAH.

29. Minutes of Long Creek Baptist church, 23 November 1850, 21 April and 24 May 1855, 21 June and 26 July 1856, GDAH.

30. Minutes of Sardis Baptist Church, 6 April, 4 May, 1 June, and 6 July 1850, GDAH (microfilm). This part of Elbert county later became part of Hart county.

31. Based on membership lists in minutes of churches in the GDAH.

32. The exact division of power in churches is not clear in the records. Typically, however, important general committees, such as the one in charge of building a new meeting house for Long Creek Baptist church, and representatives to other churches or local conferences were all male. See Minutes of Long Creek Baptist Church, 22 May 1852, GDAH. Slave church members are discussed on p. 48–49.

33. **Table 26.** Real Estate Owned by White Male Church Members in Augusta's Hinterlands

Church and County	Year	Mean Value ($)	None (%)	(N)
Long Creek Baptist (Warren)	1860	4,101	25	(16)
Williams Creek Baptist (Warren)	1860	2,100	14	(7)
Bethlehem Primitive Baptist (Oglethorpe)	1850	2,175	0	(4)
Sardis Baptist (Elbert/Hart)	1850	1,414	22	(14)
Mt. Zion Presbyterian (Hancock)	1850	1,986	29	(7)

SOURCES: Membership from church records, GDAH; wealth from the manuscript returns of the United States Bureau of the Census, 1850 and 1860.

34. Data are taken from surviving records on microfilm or on deposit in the GDAH. Most of these for Baptist churches. The few Episcopalian churches may have been wealthier than others, but I have found no membership lists.

35. Alexander H. Stephens to Linton Stephens, 24 November 1854, AHSM.

36. Minutes of Williams Creek Baptist Church, Report for 1860, GDAH (microfilm).

37. John H. Cornish Diary, 19 March 1847 and 13 January 1849, SHC. Of course, not all the unchurched were poor or ignorant. James

Henry Hammond held himself aloof from formal religion, although his religious notions had room for a rather idiosyncratic God.

38. Ibid., 19 April 1848. The Graniteville company eventually built churches on its property.

39. Adam L. Alexander to "Dear Child," 27 June 1859, Alexander–Hillhouse Papers, SHC.

40. According to census statistics, fully three-quarters of the population, white and black, in Augusta's hinterlands could have sat down to services every Sunday, but this is, of course, a very imperfect measure of church attendance or membership. Seating capacity is reported in the manuscript schedule for social statistics (microfilm, National Archives and Records Service, Washington, D.C.).

41. Sophia Chapin to Moses Chapin, 31 January 1853 and 21 January 1854, Chapin–Tunnel Papers, SHC.

42. Edgefield *Advertiser*, 22 June 1854.

43. John H. Cornish Diary, 26 July 1846, 9 and 23 March 1856, SHC.

44. The relationship between white churches and slavery is discussed on pp. 48–49.

45. Augusta *Constitutionalist*, 22 April 1864.

46. Standard treatments of sectionalism within South Carolina are William A. Schaper, *Sectionalism and Representation in South Carolina*, American Historical Association Annual Report (1900; reprint, New York: DeCapo Press, 1968), 1:1–237; Chauncey Samuel Boucher, "Sectionalism, Representation, and the Electoral Question in Ante-Bellum South Carolina," *Washington University Studies* 4, pt. 2, no. 1 (1916): 3–62. An important recent study of the social background of the 1808 constitution is Rachel Klein, "The Rise of the Planters in the South Carolina Backcountry, 1767–1808" (Ph.D. diss., Yale University, 1979).

47. Boucher, "Sectionalism"; William W. Freehling, *Prelude to Civil War: The Nullification Crisis in South Carolina, 1816–1836* (New York: Harper & Row, 1964), chap. 1.

48. For discussions of South Carolina's antiparty ideology, see Kenneth Greenberg, "Representation and the Isolation of South Carolina, 1776–1860," *Journal of American History* 64 (1977): 723–43; James N. Banner, "The Problem of South Carolina," in *The Hofstadter Aegis: A Memorial*, ed. Stanley Elkins and Eric McKitrick (New York: Knopf, 1974), 60–93.

49. Taxes in antebellum South Carolina were low. In 1860, according to the census of social statistics, Abbeville's citizens paid $4,557 to keep up roads, $3,347 to support forty paupers, and a little less than $25,000 to the state for all other purposes. This was about $1 per capita, including slaves, or about $10 per white family. In 1857 in Edgefield District, taxes of seventy cents were assessed on each slave, and twenty mills per $100 value on real estate. Thus planters and slaveholders paid most of the taxes. See Edgefield *Advertiser*, 1 July 1857.

50. For a standard treatment of local politics and government in South

Carolina, see David Duncan Wallace, *South Carolina, A Short History* (Chapel Hill: University of North Carolina Press, 1951).

51. To some extent, this was because South Carolina retained a property requirement for legislators; but at $500, it did not prevent many, if any, potential candidates from running. For a state-level comparison of the wealth of legislators in the Deep South, see Ralph Wooster, *The People in Power: Courthouse and Statehouse in the Lower South, 1850–1860* (Knoxville: University of Tennessee Press, 1969). According to Wooster (pp. 39–41), South Carolina's legislators were the richest of all.

52. The successful candidate was Martin W. Gary. If the census was accurate, he was not even eligible for office. However, Gary's parents owned considerable property. Note that the higher median property holding for local candidates shows that the poorest men seldom ran for office.

53. Iveson L. Brookes to C. Wood, Esq., 14 January 1857, Iveson L. Brookes Papers, SHC.

54. This appeal by friends was not entirely a fiction. See, for example, the open letter to A. L. Dearing signed by 125 people in Edgefield *Advertiser*, 20 August 1856; David Lesly to Francis W. Pickens, 16 December 1852, Francis W. Pickens Papers, SCL.

55. Freehling, *Prelude to Civil War*, esp. chap. 7; Drew Gilpin Faust, *James Henry Hammond and the Old South: A Design for Mastery* (Baton Rouge: Louisiana State University Press, 1982).

56. Edgefield *Advertiser*, 1 September 1852.

57. This speech to the legislature was printed in ibid., 9 and 16 January 1856.

58. Ibid., 21 September 1853. The division of Edgefield apparently was preferred by most of the district's population; the contest was more between Edgefield and the low country than within the district.

59. Election results were published each October in the Edgefield *Advertiser*. Of twenty-eight men serving as representatives in the five years mentioned, only three served more than once. In three elections for which all incumbents and candidates are known, seven incumbents or former incumbents stood for office, and four of them were defeated. The delegation had six members, and the results cited include one special election.

60. Edgefield *Advertiser*, 19 and 26 January 1853. Allen supposedly had asked for aid from a tavern keeper who had accused him of having cheated on debts.

61. Ibid., 27 July 1854. Abney, in fact, was not rich; in 1850, he owned neither slaves nor real estate, according to the census.

62. Ibid., 19 December 1855.

63. Ibid., 27 October 1852. Other historians have emphasized the lack of competition in South Carolina elections. Low-country elections were, as Tillman complained, different and probably less hotly contested. Also, competition for local office may have been stronger than that for the United States House of Representatives (there were

no statewide elections). Descriptive evidence on campaigns is scattered, so my interpretation for Edgefield may not be true for other places. For an acerbic comment by James Henry Hammond on the amount of time his son spent campaigning for the state legislature, see James H. Hammond Plantation Journal, 31 August 1858, JHHSCL.

Recent work emphasizing lack of competition includes Greenberg, "Representation and the Isolation of South Carolina"; Banner, "The Problem of South Carolina."

64. According to election returns (Edgefield *Advertiser*, 20 October 1858), 3,263 people voted. According to the census of 1860, there were about 3,350 white males who were age twenty-one and older in the district (after subtracting one-tenth of white males ages twenty to twenty-nine from the total number over age twenty). While there were probably more whites in the district in 1858, the turnout was clearly in the vicinity of 95 percent.

65. Edgefield *Advertiser*, 15 September 1858.

66. Gary was successful in 1860. He *was* poor; see n. 52.

67. Edgefield *Advertiser*, 2 and 9 February 1853. The question of party organization in South Carolina is complex. In the 1850s, moderates wished to attach South Carolina to the national Democratic party. During the decade, some former radicals, including James Henry Hammond and Francis W. Pickens, moved toward or openly joined these "National Democrats." Then, in 1860, secessionists became active in Democratic party politics, some hoping thereby to disrupt the party and precipitate secession. Brooks, a moderate in the context of South Carolina politics, became a national symbol of extremism after beating up Charles Sumner on the floor of the United States Senate. State level politics in the 1850s may be followed in Phillip May Hamer, *The Secession Movement in South Carolina, 1847–1852* (Allentown, Pa.: Haas, 1918); John Barnwell, *Love of Order: South Carolina's First Secession Crisis* (Chapel Hill: University of North Carolina Press, 1982); Harold S. Schultz, *Nationalism and Sectionalism in South Carolina, 1852–1860: A Study of the Movement for Southern Independence* (Durham, N.C.: Duke University Press, 1950); Steven A. Channing, *Crisis of Fear: Secession in South Carolina* (New York: Simon and Schuster, 1970).

68. John L. Tobin to S. S. Evans, 22 May 1857, John L. Tobin Papers, SCL.

69. Votes by place are listed in the Edgefield *Advertiser*, 20 October 1858. These were located using a variety of maps of Edgefield District, several of which are in the South Carolina State Archives. Residences of candidates were located using the manuscript returns of the United States Bureau of the Census, 1860, which lists the nearest post office for each page, and John A. Chapman, *A History of Edgefield County from the Earliest Settlements to 1897* (Newberry, S.C., 1897).

70. An excellent survey of Georgia history is Kenneth Coleman, ed., *A History of Georgia* (Athens: University of Georgia Press, 1977). The

best recent study of local finances and expenditures is Peter Wallenstein, "From Slave South to New South: Taxes and Spending in Georgia from 1850 through Reconstruction" (Ph.D. diss., Johns Hopkins University, 1973). Taxes in Georgia, as in South Carolina, fell mostly on slaveowners and landowners.

71. The most thorough guide to local government and elections is R. H. Clark, Thomas R. R. Cobb, and D. Irwin, *The Code of the State of Georgia* (Atlanta, 1861). See also Melvin Hughes, *County Government in Georgia* (Athens: University of Georgia Press, 1944).

72. Augusta *Constitutionalist*, 27 June 1858.

73. See, for example, Warren County Superior Court, Grand Jury Presentments, Augusta *Constitutionalist*, 24 October 1856; Burke County Superior Court, Grand Jury Presentments, ibid., 27 November 1856.

74. The state government kept records of county officers, which are now in the GDAH. Occupation, wealth, and slaveownership were checked in the manuscript census returns.

75. The election results used were those for the governor's race as reported in the *Tribune Almanac*. They were compared with the number of white men age twenty-one and older as reported in the 1860 census of population. (One-tenth of the men ages twenty to twenty-nine was subtracted from the total over age twenty.) Only in Richmond county was turnout below 75 percent. In some counties, turnout, as calculated by this method, was *more than* 100 percent. Since I have found no charges of fraud, presumably the actual turnout included virtually all those eligible, including a few not eligible and some missed in the census or moved by 1860.

76. On Georgia politics, see Coleman, *History of Georgia*, chap. 10; Ulrich B. Phillips, *Georgia and States Rights, A Study of the Political History of Georgia from the Revolution to the Civil War, with Particular Regard to Federal Relations*, American Historical Association *Annual Report* (Washington, D.C., 1902), 2:3–224; Paul Murray, *The Whig Party in Georgia, 1825–1853* (Chapel Hill: University of North Carolina Press, 1948); Horace Montgomery, *Cracker Parties* (Baton Rouge: Louisiana State University Press, 1950); Donald Arthur DeBats, "Elites and Masses: Political Structure, Communication, and Behavior in Antebellum Georgia" (Ph.D. diss., University of Wisconsin, 1973).

77. Support of slavery by both Whigs and Democrats in the antebellum South is the theme of William Cooper, *The South and the Politics of Slavery 1828–1856* (Baton Rouge: Louisiana State University Press, 1978).

78. Announcements of meetings along these lines ran in the columns of the Augusta papers every election season. I found only one exception—one meeting that proceeded to a secret ballot without nominations. A candidate was chosen on the first ballot.

79. Augusta *Constitutionalist*, 12 July 1853. Probably underlying the complaint was that the writer was a Democrat in a Whig county.

80. Ibid., 13 June 1860. See also ibid., 24 June 1859, for similar complaints. The factions were those supporting and opposing the walk-

out of some Georgia delegates from the national Democratic party convention in Charleston in April.

81. M. M. Landrum to David C. Barrow, 29 April 1859, DCB. In this election, as in the last, I have been unable to determine whether differences between Barrow and Willingham involved differences on major issues.

82. James B. Sims to David C. Barrow, 27 April 1859, DCB.

83. Athens *Banner*, 16 June 1859.

84. C. C. Hammock to David C. Barrow, 9 August 1859, DCB. In the general election, the main issue was whether Joseph E. Brown would be reelected as governor.

85. [James] S[pratlin] to David C. Barrow, 15 August 1859, DCB.

86. On sponsored mobility, see Edward Pessen, "Social Mobility in American History: Some Brief Reflections," *JSH* 45 (1979): 165−84.

87. R. G. Harper to Linton Stephens, 27 August 1855, AHSLC. For similar letters, see, for example, Thomas W. Thomas to Alexander H. Stephens, 5 September 1856, Alexander H. Stephens Papers, Emory University Library; James Cody to Alexander H. Stephens, 24 July 1860, AHSLC; John C. Burch to Alexander H. Stephens, 16 July 1860, AHSLC.

88. Rabun, "Alexander Stephens's Diary," 1 May 1834 (p. 79).

89. Ibid., 27 October 1836 (p. 181).

90. For Stephens's early career, see also Richard Malcolm Johnston and William Hand Browne, *Life of Alexander H. Stephens* (Philadelphia, 1878; reprint, Freeport, N.Y.: Books for Libraries Press, 1971).

91. Colonel R. H. Ward, Address to the Greene County Agricultural Society, Augusta *Chronicle*, 12 February 1851 (delivered 15 November 1850).

92. Letter from "Harper," Edgefield *Advertiser*, 22 March 1854.

93. Augusta *Constitutionalist*, 1 December 1853.

94. Augusta *Chronicle*, 26 April and 3 May 1854. The twenty-four members of the committee on relief were almost all well-to-do planters. The courthouse was less often the actual meeting place in Edgefield district because the district was very big. Meetings were held in neighborhood churches or at crossroads in distant parts of the district. This was, in fact, the complaint of "Harper."

95. Ibid., 25 August 1858. Buck Jeter owned two slaves in 1850.

96. Ibid., 7 October 1851.

Prologue: In the Midst of a Revolution

1. Colonel R. H. Ward, Address to the Greene County Agricultural Society, Augusta *Chronicle*, 12 February 1851 (delivered 15 November 1850).

2. This distinction was not absolute. For example, the Whig *Chronicle* defended the rights of local communities to close down taverns as a part of the right of the majority to rule; see Augusta *Chronicle*, 9 March and 6 September 1853. This position was "Whiggish" in that it assumed the right of the community and its government to legislate to improve public and private morality.

3. Augusta *Constitutionalist*, 7, 16, and 21 September 1853. The bill was introduced into the state legislature in 1842, but it never passed.
4. Augusta *Chronicle*, 10 October 1856, 14 January 1857, 11 April 1860.
5. Augusta *Constitutionalist*, 3 June 1851.
6. See series of letters and editorials on the bank veto message during January 1858 in ibid.
7. Alexander H. Stephens to Thomas W. Thomas, 9 May 1855. This letter was published in the Augusta newspapers and appears in Henry C. Cleveland, *Alexander H. Stephens in Public and Private, With Letters and Speeches, Before, During, and Since the War* (Philadelphia, 1867), 459-71. For similar arguments, see Robert Toombs to T. Lomax, 6 June 1855, in *The Correspondence of Robert Toombs, Alexander H. Stephens, and Howell Cobb*, American Historical Association *Annual Report*, ed. Ulrich B. Phillips (Washington, D.C., 1911; reprint, New York: DeCapo Press, 1970) 2 : 350-53; Augusta *Constitutionalist*, 30 August 1854 and 22 March 1855. I do not wish to argue that this was the sole motive for Stephens's refusal to go along with the new party, for he saw that its national prospects were poor. However, letters to his half-brother, Linton, indicate that he was quite sincere in his denunciation of nativism, and he had to explain his action in terms that were understandable and acceptable to the mass of voters.
8. Cleveland, *Alexander H. Stephens*, 464-65.
9. Letters from "Sydney," Augusta *Chronicle*, 24 May and 2 June 1855.
10. Ibid., 25 June 1857.
11. William W. Freehling, "Spoilsmen and Interests in the Thought and Career of John C. Calhoun," *Journal of American History* 52 (1965): 37. The effect of eighteenth-century republican ideology in South Carolina is most fully explored in Kenneth Greenberg, "The Second American Revolution: South Carolina Politics, Society, and Secession, 1776-1860" (Ph.D. diss., University of Wisconsin, 1976). While I am in basic agreement with most of Greenberg's interpretation, I have found more debate than he indicates. See also James N. Banner, "The Problem of South Carolina," in *The Hofstadter Aegis: A Memorial*, ed. Stanley Elkins and Eric McKitrick (New York: Knopf, 1974), 60-93; Drew Gilpin Faust, *James Henry Hammond and the Old South: A Design for Mastery* (Baton Rouge: Louisiana State University Press, 1982); J. William Harris, "Last of the Classical Republicans: An Interpretation of John C. Calhoun," *Civil War History* 30 (1984): 255-67.
12. James H. Hammond, "Copy from Notes—occasional meditations," 27 March 1852, JHHLC.
13. Edgefield *Advertiser*, 16 May 1849; also several other letters in May and June 1849 issues.
14. Ibid., 1 August 1860. For similar examples see ibid., 6 March 1851, resolutions of a public meeting on 3 March; letter from "Many of the People," 29 June 1854; letter from "John of the People," 5 March 1856.

15. Chauncey Samuel Boucher, "Sectionalism, Representation, and the Electoral Question in Ante-Bellum South Carolina," *Washington University Studies* 4, pt. 2, no. 1 (1916): 3–62.
16. Tillman is discussed in another context on p. 108–09.
17. Tillman's speech appears in the Edgefield *Advertiser*, 9 and 16 January 1856. See also ibid., 21 September 1853, 1 March 1854, 28 November 1855.
18. William C. Moragne, *The Electoral Question. To the Citizens of Edgefield District* (Edgefield, S.C., 1859). This pamphlet reprinted a speech given in February 1856, and first printed in the Edgefield *Advertiser* in several February 1856 issues.
19. See pp. 73–74.
20. James H. Hammond, "Slavery in the Light of Political Science," in *Cotton Is King; And Proslavery Arguments*, ed. E. N. Elliot (Augusta, Ga., 1860), 638.
21. Iveson L. Brookes, *A Defense of Southern Slavery. Against the Attacks of Henry Clay and Alexander Campbell* (Hamburg, S.C., 1851), 45.
22. Augusta *Chronicle*, 15 June 1860.
23. R. Thwealt[?] to Alexander H. Stephens, 11 February 1859, AHSLC.
24. Edgefield *Advertiser*, 17 October 1855.
25. Speech of Joseph Abney, ibid., 26 August 1857.
26. Augusta *Chronicle*, 11 August 1857.
27. Augusta *Constitutionalist*, 16 May 1860.
28. Ibid., 3 and 7 October 1860.
29. Augusta *Chronicle*, 16 September 1860. For a similar comment, see Linton Stephens to Alexander H. Stephens, 21 July 1860, AHSM.
30. Edgefield *Advertiser*, 18 July 1860. Bacon was court clerk in Edgefield District.
31. Ibid., 7 November 1860. A record of the activities of one "Minuteman" association is in the Minutes of the Saluda Association, SCL. On secession in South Carolina, see Steven A. Channing, *Crisis of Fear: Secession in South Carolina* (New York: Simon and Schuster, 1970); Greenberg, "Second American Revolution."
32. Edgefield *Advertiser*, 14 and 21 November 1860.
33. Ibid., 28 November 1860.
34. Robert Toombs, *Speech on the Crisis Delivered before the Georgia Legislature, December 7, 1860* (Washington, D.C., 1860). See also "Substance of Remarks Made by Thomas R. R. Cobb, Esq., Before the General Assembly of Georgia, November 12, 1860," in *CR*, 1 : 157–82; Edward H. Pottle to Alexander Stephens, 8 January 1861, AHSLC.
35. "Special Message of Gov. Joseph E. Brown to the State Legislature, 1 November 1860," in *CR*, 1 : 47.
36. Augusta *Chronicle*, 23 November 1860. For a secessionist version of the conspiracy theory, see Francis W. Pickens, *Speech of Hon. F. W. Pickens Delivered before a Public Meeting of the People of the District, Held at Edgefield S. C., July 7, 1851* (Edgefield, S.C., 1851). Fear of conspiracy in high places, especially English high places, was endemic in eighteenth-century republican thought; see, for ex-

ample, Bernard Bailyn, *The Ideological Origins of the American Revolution* (Cambridge, Mass.: Harvard University Press, 1967), chap. 4.

37. Alexander H. Stephens, "Union Speech of 1860," in *CR* 1:183–205; speech of Benjamin H. Hill, Augusta *Chronicle*, 23 November 1860; speech of H. H. Tucker, ibid., 27 and 29 November 1860.

38. Letter from "Farmer," Augusta *Chronicle*, 23 December 1860.

39. Ibid., 16 February 1861.

40. H. C. Massengale to Alexander H. Stephens, 2 December 1860, AHSLC.

41. Augusta *Chronicle*, 21 November 1860. For an account of a similar split in Warren county, see ibid., 9 December 1860.

42. Linton Stephens to Alexander H. Stephens, 29 December 1860, AHSM.

43. Presidential returns are in the *Tribune Almanac*. For the January 2 vote, I have followed Michael P. Johnson, "A New Look at the Popular Vote for Delegates to the Georgia Secession Convention," *Georgia Historical Quarterly* 56 (1972):259–75. For the campaign in Georgia as a whole, see Johnson, *Toward a Patriarchal Republic: The Secession of Georgia* (Baton Rouge: Louisiana State University Press, 1977); Luke Fain Crutcher, "Disunity and Dissolution: The Georgia Parties and the Crisis of the Union, 1859–1861" (Ph.D. diss., University of California at Los Angeles, 1974).

44. The convention votes are in *CR*, the decisive vote of January 19 is in *CR*, 2:252–56.

45. For a recent survey and introduction to an immense literature, see David M. Potter, *The Impending Crisis, 1848–1861* (New York: Harper & Row, 1976).

46. Channing, *Crisis of Fear*.

47. Johnson, *Patriarchal Republic*.

48. Augusta *Constitutionalist*, 7 December 1860 (emphasis in original).

49. Susan Cornwall Diary, 31 January 1861, SHC.

50. William McKinley to David C. Barrow, 29 March 1861, DCB.

51. James H. Hammond to William Gilmore Simms, 13 November 1860, JHHSCL.

52. Eliza Francis Andrews, *War Time Journal of a Georgia Girl* (1908), 309.

53. Joseph Campbell to Alexander H. Stephens, 3 April 1861, AHSLC.

5. Strains of War

1. Emory Thomas, *The Confederate Nation, 1861–1865* (New York: Harper & Row, 1979), 60–62.

2. John W. Sims to Joseph E. Brown, 14 June 1861, Brown IC. For surveys of Georgia and South Carolina history during the Civil War, see T. Conn Bryan, *Confederate Georgia* (Athens: University of Georgia Press, 1953); Charles Edward Cauthen, *South Carolina Goes to War, 1860–1865* (Chapel Hill: University of North Carolina Press, 1950).

3. Augusta *Constitutionalist,* 3 January 1861.
4. Augusta *Chronicle,* 19 June 1861.
5. James H. Hammond to F. W. Byrdsall, 8 July 1861, JHHLC. Hammond, along with many others, thought at this time that there would be no war; James H. Hammond to M. C. M. Hammond, 1 March 1861, JHHLC.
6. Edgefield *Advertiser,* 24 April 1861; see also ibid., 19 June 1861, for a similar ceremony.
7. See, for example, Augusta *Chronicle,* 18 and 19 May 1861; Alexander H. Stephens to Linton Stephens, 29 April 1861, AHSM.
8. Augusta *Chronicle,* 21 July 1861.
9. Ibid., 11 July 1861.
10. Based on a sample of 271 soldiers from three counties in the Augusta area; see Appendix A for detailed description.
11. Augusta *Constitutionalist,* 9 July 1861.
12. George W. Ray to Alexander H. Stephens, 11 September 1861, AHSLC.
13. Randall Croft to James H. Hammond, 21 November 1861, JHHLC.
14. Edgefield *Advertiser,* 29 May 1861.
15. Augusta *Constitutionalist,* 2 August 1861; Minutes of Hancock County Inferior Court, 1850–1871, 19 August 1862 (p. 190), GDAH.
16. Edgefield *Advertiser,* 11 September 1861; Augusta *Constitutionalist,* 18 May 1861.
17. Minutes of Hart County Inferior Court, 8 June 1861, GDAH; Minutes of Glascock County Inferior Court, 15 July 1861, GDAH; Augusta *Chronicle,* 6 June 1861.
18. James Thomas to Alexander H. Stephens, 2 August 1861, ASHM.
19. B. T. Harris to Alexander H. Stephens, 31 August 1861, AHSLC.
20. D. F. Bardon to Alexander H. Stephens, 11 July 1861, AHSLC.
21. Linton Stephens to Alexander H. Stephens, 1 May 1861, AHSM.
22. **Table 27.** Wealth by Rank at Entry into Service, Soldiers from Augusta's Hinterlands

Rank	Total Wealth* ($)	Slaves*	(N)
Private	2,809	2.3	(242)
Corporal, sergeant	4,628	5.8	(18)
Lieutenant, captain	7,357	4.5	(11)

SOURCE: Samples of men from Glascock, Hart, and Taliaferro counties from the manuscript returns of the United States Bureau of the Census, 1860, whose records were located in service records.
   NOTE: See Appendix A for detailed description.
   *Wealth of a soldier, if a household head or a boarder in 1860; wealth of parent, if living with parents in 1860.

23. G. B. Harben to David C. Barrow, 20 September 1861, DCB.
24. Thomas W. Thomas to Joseph E. Brown, 1 July 1861, Brown IC.
25. Thomas W. Thomas to Linton Stephens, 4 July 1861, Alexander H. Stephens Papers, Emory University Library.

26. Thomas W. Thomas to Alexander H. Stephens, 5 October 1861, in *The Correspondence of Robert Toombs, Alexander H. Stephens, and Howell Cobb*, American Historical Association *Annual Report*, ed. Ulrich B. Phillips (Washington, D.C., 1911; reprint, New York: DeCapo Press, 1970), 579−80.

27. Thomas W. Thomas to Alexander H. Stephens, 10 October 1861, in ibid., 580−81.

28. Thomas W. Thomas to Alexander H. Stephens, 31 December 1861, in ibid., 586−87.

29. Thomas W. Thomas to Alexander H. Stephens, 19 April 1862, Alexander H. Stephens Papers, Emory University Library.

30. Robert Toombs to Alexander H. Stephens, 30? September 1861, in Phillips, *Correspondence*, 577−78.

31. Ulrich B. Phillips, *The Life of Robert Toombs* (New York: Macmillan, 1913), chap. 10.

32. *CR*, 2:43−44.

33. Augusta *Constitutionalist*, 6 June 1861. Disputes between the Davis administration and Governor Brown, as well as other southern governors, have received extensive attention. See, for example, Frank Owsley, *States Rights in the Confederacy* (Chicago: University of Chicago Press, 1925); Louise Biles Hill, *Joseph E. Brown and the Confederacy* (Chapel Hill: University of North Carolina Press, 1939); Joseph Parks, *Joseph E. Brown of Georgia* (Baton Rouge: Louisiana State University Press, 1977). For a treatment of the issue in the context of class divisions in the Confederacy, see Paul David Escott, *After Secession: Jefferson Davis and the Failure of Confederate Nationalism* (Baton Rouge: Louisiana State University Press, 1978), esp. chap. 5.

34. Edgefield *Advertiser*, 15 May 1861.

35. Ibid., 13 November 1861.

36. Ibid., 30 April 1862.

37. Augusta *Constitutionalist*, 6 May 1862.

38. The standard reference on Confederate conscription is Albert Burton Moore, *Conscription and Conflict in the Confederacy* (New York: Macmillan, 1924).

39. Edgefield *Advertiser*, 19 February 1862; see also ibid., 23 April 1862.

40. Augusta *Constitutionalist*, 10 April 1862.

41. Augusta *Chronicle*, 27 May 1862.

42. Ibid., 11 April 1862; see also ibid., 5 April 1862.

43. *CR*, 2:335−44.

44. Augusta *Chronicle*, 5 April 1862; Owsley, *States Rights in the Confederacy*; Hill, *Joseph E. Brown*; Rudolph von Abele, *Alexander H. Stephens: A Biography* (New York: Knopf, 1946); James Z. Rabun, "Alexander H. Stephens and Jefferson Davis," *American Historical Review* 58 (1953):290−321.

45. Linton Stephens to Alexander H. Stephens, 22 August 1862, AHSM.

46. Linton Stephens to Alexander H. Stephens, 29 December 1862, Alexander H. Stephens Papers, Emory University Library.

47. Augusta *Constitutionalist*, 12 November 1862.

48. Ibid., 1 October 1863.
49. John B. Benson to Alexander H. Stephens, 15 October 1861, AHSLC.
50. "CSV" to Alexander H. Stephens, 16 March 1862, AHSLC.
51. Martha Denny to Alexander H. Stephens, 25 July 1863, AHSLC.
52. W. J. Rees to Alexander H. Stephens, 19 September 1861, AHSLC.
53. Thomas C. Butts to Joseph E. Brown, 16 January 1864, Brown IC. For similar pleas, see Paulina S. Wheeler to Joseph E. Brown, 31 October 1864, Brown IC; Polly Tillery to Joseph E. Brown, 27 July 1864, Brown IC; Petition to exempt E. R. Bagby, 25 August 1864, Brown Petitions; Petition to exempt James M. Rowland, July 1863, Brown Petitions; Petition to exempt William A. Paschal, 11 January 1864, Brown Petitions.
54. W. D. Sullivan to Joseph E. Brown, 13 July 1864, Brown IC.
55. Petition to exempt Dr. B. F. Bently, 12 May 1862, AHSLC.
56. O. F. M. Holloday to Alexander H. Stephens, 30 November 1862, Alexander H. Stephens Papers, Emory University Library.
57. William H. Hidell to Alexander H. Stephens, 19 July 1864, AHSLC.
58. J. B. Wooten to Joseph E. Brown, 30 July 1864, Brown IC.
59. Linton Stephens to Alexander H. Stephens, 22 August 1862, AHSM.
60. George Davis to David C. Barrow, 11 March 1862, DCB; David C. Barrow to Colonel W. M. Brown, 31 October 1862, DC3; Affidavit of Samuel Glenn and John G. Wright, 9 January 1864, DCB (copy).
61. James H. Hammond to William Gilmore Simms, 17 May 1862, JHHLC.
62. James H. Hammond Redcliffe Journal, 12 January 1863, JHHSCL.
63. James H. Hammond to James L. Orr, 11 December 1863, JHHLC.
64. James H. Hammond to James L. Orr, 8 January 1864. See also Drew Gilpin Faust, *James Henry Hammond and the Old South: A Design for Mastery* (Baton Rouge: Louisiana State University Press, 1982).
65. Augusta *Constitutionalist*, 23 January 1863.
66. Ibid., 5 March 1863.
67. *CR*, 2:434–35.
68. Richard C. Todd, *Confederate Finance* (Athens: University of Georgia Press, 1954).
69. Charles W. Ramsdell, *Behind the Lines in the Southern Confederacy* (Baton Rouge: Louisiana State University Press, 1944).
70. Elisha Cain to Joseph E. Brown, 25 October 1861, Brown IC.
71. Minutes of Glascock County Inferior Court, 9 January 1862, GDAH; Edgefield *Advertiser*, 12 November 1862. Georgia counties in the Augusta area supported approximately 19 percent of white families from a state appropriation in December 1862. See *CR*, 2:403–06, for a list of the number of widows and dependent women supported in each county. The number of families in each county in 1860 is listed in U.S. Bureau of the Census, "Population," in *Eighth Census, 1860* (Washington, D.C., 1865).
72. Peter Wallenstein, "Rich Man's War, Rich Man's Fight: The Civil War and the Transformation of Public Finance in Georgia," *JSH* 50 (1984):15–42; Escott, *After Secession*, chap. 5.
73. James H. Hammond Redcliffe Journal, 1 November 1861, JHHSCL;

James H. Hammond Account Book, 1834–1865, p. 234, JHHSCL; Edgefield *Advertiser*, 4 December 1861.

74. Edgefield *Advertiser*, 19 November 1862.

75. Letter from "Greene County," Augusta *Chronicle*, 31 July 1863.

76. Augusta *Constitutionalist*, 18 April 1862.

77. See, for example, Emily M. Farrar to David C. Barrow, 21 February 1865, DCB.

78. J. H. R. to Joseph E. Brown, 29 June 1864, Brown IC. This was despite a pledge by Washington county farmers to sell corn to the poor in 1864 at one-third of current wholesale prices; Augusta *Constitutionalist*, 6 February 1864.

79. Emma Partridge to Alexander H. Stephens, 14 January 1864, AHSLC.

80. "An Appeal," Edgefield *Advertiser*, 4 December 1861.

81. Ibid., 5 March and 12 November 1862. The wholesale price of corn in Augusta averaged about $1.50 a bushel during 1862; Augusta *Chronicle*, 25 February and 2 December 1862.

82. Edgefield *Advertiser*, 12 November 1862. The corrosiveness of inflation is symbolically highlighted by an entry in John H. Cornish Diary. In February 1864, his wife died, and the congregation donated $800 just to buy cloth for mourning dresses for his daughters. But that amount was enough to clothe only three of them.

83. James H. Hammond to William Gilmore Simms, 29 August 1862, JHHLC.

84. Edgefield *Advertiser*, 25 September 1861.

85. L. R. A. Harper to Alexander H. Stephens, 25 September 1861, AHSLC; A. G. Foster to Alexander H. Stephens, 20 September 1861, AHSLC.

86. Letter from E. Penn, Edgefield *Advertiser*, 9 October 1861.

87. Augusta *Chronicle*, 7 December 1861.

88. James Thomas to Alexander H. Stephens, 11 February 1862, AHSLC.

89. Augusta *Chronicle*, 2 February 1861; see also Minutes of the Beech Island Farmers Club, 1 June 1861, SCL.

90. *Southern Cultivator* 20 (1862):65.

91. Edgefield *Advertiser*, 22 January 1862.

92. *Southern Cultivator* 20 (1862):68.

93. Ibid., 83.

94. Augusta *Constitutionalist*, 19 March 1862.

95. *Southern Cultivator* 20 (1862):83.

96. James I. Robertson, Jr., ed., *The Diary of Dolly Lunt Burge* (Athens: University of Georgia Press, 1962), entries of 26 March, 6 May 1862.

97. Augusta *Constitutionalist*, 7 June 1862. See Toombs's haughty reply in Phillips, *Correspondence*, 595.

98. Bryan, *Confederate Georgia*, 118–22; David Duncan Wallace, *The History of South Carolina*, 4 vols. (New York: American Historical Society, 1934), 3:193.

99. *CR*, 2:369.

100. Robertson, *Diary*, 6 May 1862.

101. Tax Statement for David C. Barrow, Greene county, 6 December 1864, DCB; Tax Statement for Alexander H. Stephens, 19 Novem-

ber 1863, AHSLC. James H. Hammond claimed that his 1862 crop was one-tenth of normal; James H. Hammond to Christopher C. Memminger, April 1862, JHHLC.

102. Edgefield *Advertiser*, 10 September 1862.
103. Minutes of Hancock County Superior Court, Grand Jury Presentments, 14 October 1862, GDAH.
104. Augusta *Chronicle*, 9 July 1862.
105. John H. Cornish Diary, 8 November 1862 and 25 March 1863, SHC.
106. Bryan, *Confederate Georgia*, 38–40; Cauthen, *South Carolina Goes to War*, 150.
107. Minutes of Glascock County Superior Court, 10 April 1863, GDAH.
108. Edgefield *Advertiser*, 1 April 1863.
109. Minutes of Hart County Inferior Court, 11 May 1863, GDAH.
110. Edgefield *Advertiser*, 14 January 1863; see also letter from "Spirit of Sixty-Two," ibid., 26 November 1862.
111. Augusta *Chronicle*, 20 April 1862.
112. Augusta *Constitutionalist*, 5 and 7 February 1863.
113. Kate Rowland (Mrs. Charles A. Rowland) Diary, 10 November 1863, Emory University Library (microfilm).
114. James H. Hammond Redcliffe Journal, 4 February and 5 April 1863, JHHSCL.
115. Edgefield *Advertiser*, 12 August 1863.
116. Augusta *Constitutionalist*, 12 November 1863; reprinted in Edgefield *Advertiser*, 9 December 1863.
117. Augusta *Chronicle*, 25 November 1863.
118. Ibid., 18 September 1863.
119. Cauthen, *South Carolina Goes to War*, chap. 13; Rebecca Christian, "Georgia and the Confederate Policy of Impressing Supplies," *Georgia Historical Quarterly* 28 (1944): 1–33.
120. James H. Hammond to Willis B. Grant, 3 March 1862, JHHLC.
121. James H. Hammond to Major General J. C. Pemberton, 28 April 1862, JHHLC; James H. Hammond to General R. S. Ripley, 8 May 1862, JHHLC; Hammond to Pemberton, 29 May 1862, JHHLC.
122. Augusta *Constitutionalist*, 5 and 14 August 1862.
123. Linton Stephens to Alexander H. Stephens, 8 August 1862, AHSM.
124. Linton Stephens to Alexander H. Stephens, 6 September 1862, AHSM.
125. Augusta *Constitutionalist*, 11 and 26 August 1863.
126. Edgefield *Advertiser*, 17 February 1864.
127. Augusta *Chronicle*, 7 February 1864.
128. Ibid., 31 May 1864.
129. James H. Hammond to B. Howard, 16 January 1864, JHHLC.
130. Receipt for ninety-day Note for $60,000 for sale of 6,000 bushels of corn to the Graniteville Company, 8 July 1864, JHHSCL; Notice of Impressment, 18 July 1864, JHHSCL; James H. Hammond Redcliffe Journal, 20 July 1864, JHHSCL.
131. James H. Hammond Redcliffe Journal, 2 August 1864, JHHSCL.

132. James H. Hammond to William Gilmore Simms, 24 August 1864, JHHLC.
133. Augusta *Constitutionalist*, 23 and 25 October 1863.
134. See n. 33 and n. 44, above.
135. James H. Hammond to William Gilmore Simms, 7 May 1861, JHHLC.
136. James H. Hammond to M. C. M. Hammond, 24 March 1862, JHHLC.
137. James H. Hammond to Lewis H. Ayer, 15 December 1863, JHHLC.
138. James H. Hammond to L. T. Wigfall, 15 April 1864, JHHLC.
139. James H. Hammond to William Gilmore Simms, 12 June 1864, JHHLC.
140. Alexander H. Stephens to Thomas W. Thomas, 23 June 1862, AHSLC.
141. Augusta *Chronicle*, 23 September 1862.
142. Linton Stephens to Alexander H. Stephens, 6 April 1863, AHSM.
143. Linton Stephens to Alexander H. Stephens, 12 October 1863, AHSM.
144. Alexander H. Stephens to Richard Malcolm Johnston, in Richard Malcolm Johnston and William Hand Browne, *Life of Alexander H. Stephens* (Philadelphia, 1878; reprint, Freeport, N.Y.: Books for Libraries Press, 1971), 453.
145. *CR*, 2 : 335–44.
146. Henry C. Cleveland, *Alexander H. Stephens in Public and Private, With Letters and Speeches, Before, During, and Since the War* (Philadelphia, 1867), 785.
147. Alexander H. Stephens to H. V. Johnson, 22 June 1864, Alexander H. Stephens Papers, Emory University Library.
148. For a stark argument in these terms, see the editorial in Augusta *Constitutionalist*, 18 October 1864.
149. Linton Stephens to Cosby Connel, 11 March 1864, AHSLC. See also Linton Stephens to Alexander H. Stephens, 14 July 1863, AHSM.
150. C. P. Culver to Alexander H. Stephens, 23 July 1863, AHSLC. For Toombs's public denunciations of the Confederate government, see Augusta *Constitutionalist*, 26 June 1863; Phillips, *Life of Robert Toombs*, chap. 10.
151. See, for example, Augusta *Chronicle*, 11 August 1864, in which an editorial compares Davis with Louis XIV.
152. See, for example, letter from "X," Augusta *Constitutionalist*, 15 March 1864.
153. Ibid., 3 June 1863.

6. The Captives Set Free

1. Linton Stephens to Alexander H. Stephens, 3 October 1863, AHSM.
2. William McKinley to David C. Barrow, 20 October 1863, DCB; Linton Stephens to Alexander H. Stephens, 6 October 1863, AHSM.
3. Linton Stephens to Alexander H. Stephens, 6 October 1863, AHSM;

Minutes of Hancock County Superior Court, 1858–1870 (pp. 399–414), GDAH.

4. William McKinley to David C. Barrow, 20 October 1863, DCB.
5. Linton Stephens to Alexander H. Stephens, 6 October 1863, AHSM; minutes of Hancock County Superior Court, 1858–1870 (pp. 399–414, quote on p. 411), GDAH.
6. Alexander H. Stephens to Linton Stephens, 23 November 1863, AHSM.
7. Linton Stephens to Alexander H. Stephens, 4 November 1863, AHSM; Alexander H. Stephens to Linton Stephens, 23 November 1863, AHSM.
8. Minutes of Hancock County Inferior Court, 1850–1871 (p. 233), GDAH.
9. Advertisement in Augusta *Chronicle*, 5 December 1863.
10. Minutes of Hancock County Inferior Court, 1850–1871 (pp. 238–39), GDAH.
11. Cosby Connel to Alexander H. Stephens, 6 and 13 February 1864, AHSLC.
12. Alexander H. Stephens to James Thomas, 31 January 1864, James Thomas Papers, Emory University Library.
13. Cosby Connel to Alexander H. Stephens, 20 February 1864, AHSLC.
14. Augusta *Constitutionalist*, 8 October 1863.
15. William McKinley to David C. Barrow, 20 October 1863, DCB.
16. Thomas W. Thomas to James Thomas, 21 October 1863, James Thomas Papers, Emory University Library.
17. Augusta *Constitutionalist*, 29 January 1861.
18. Augusta *Chronicle*, 7 February 1861.
19. Edgefield *Advertiser*, 17 April 1861.
20. Augusta *Constitutionalist*, 27 April and 21 May 1861.
21. James H. Hammond, "Slavery in the Light of Political Science," in *Cotton Is King; And Proslavery Arguments*, ed. E. N. Elliot (Augusta, Ga., 1860), 639–40.
22. James H. Hammond to W. D. Parker, 16 June 1861, JHHLC.
23. Edgefield *Advertiser*, 17 July 1861.
24. Ibid., 15 May 1861.
25. See, for example, ibid., 22 May 1861, on the formation of the Mountain Creek Home Guards.
26. Augusta *Chronicle*, 31 July 1861.
27. Edgefield *Advertiser*, 26 June 1861.
28. Ibid., 7 August 1861.
29. James Thomas to Alexander H. Stephens, 23 July 1861, AHSM.
30. J. H. Taylor to David C. Barrow, 16 June 1861, DCB.
31. George Davis to David C. Barrow, 21 June 1861, DCB.
32. See, for example, James Filey to David C. Barrow, 26 August 1861, DCB, which criticizes the vigilance committee that "discovered" one of these insurrections.
33. Edgefield *Advertiser*, 20 November 1861.
34. Ibid., 27 November 1861.
35. E. R. Carswell to Joseph E. Brown, 11 December 1861, Brown IC.

36. James H. Hammond Redcliffe Journal, 2 May 1862, JHHSCL.
37. James H. Hammond to A. B. Allen, 2 February 1861, JHHSCL (draft).
38. Jacob Stroyer, "My Life in the South," in *Five Slave Narratives: A Compendium* (1898; reprint, New York: Arno Press and the New York Times, 1968), 99.
39. Rawick, *Ga. Narr.*, 12(1):161–67.
40. Ibid., 12(2):1–10.
41. Ibid., 13(4):161–67.
42. Ibid., 12(1):251–64.
43. Linton Stephens to Alexander H. Stephens, 27 December 1862 and 8 May 1863, AHSM.
44. G. F. Bristow to Alexander H. Stephens, 11 September 1861, AHSM; Alexander H. Stephens to Linton Stephens, 28 and 29 March 1864, AHSM.
45. J. H. Taylor to David C. Barrow, 27 October 1861, DCB.
46. James C. Filey to David C. Barrow, 14 December 1862, DCB.
47. James Spratlin to David C. Barrow, 24 January 1864, DCB.
48. Baker Daniel to David C. Barrow, 6 October 1864, DCB.
49. James H. Hammond Redcliffe Journal, 10 November 1861, JHHSCL.
50. Ibid., 13 April 1863.
51. Ibid., 28 June 1863.
52. Ibid., 30 August 1863. See also Drew Gilpin Faust, *James Henry Hammond and the Old South: A Design for Mastery* (Baton Rouge: Louisiana State University Press, 1982), chap. 17, for an illuminating discussion.
53. Rawick, *Fla. Narr.*, 17:24.
54. Augusta *Chronicle*, 17 March 1864.
55. Augusta *Constitutionalist*, 4 May 1864.
56. Ibid., 12 August 1864.
57. Ibid., 24 August 1864.
58. W. I. Brookes to Iveson L. Brookes, 8 June 1863, Iveson L. Brookes Papers, SHC.
59. Edgefield *Advertiser*, 3 February 1864.
60. Augusta *Constitutionalist*, 4 May 1864.
61. Edgefield *Advertiser*, 15 October 1862 and 9 March 1864.
62. Augusta *Constitutionalist*, 28 May 1863. Just three weeks earlier (3 May 1863), the editor had pointed to a "negro ball" as evidence of how well off Augusta's slaves were and how this was a rebuke to the abolitionists.
63. Armstead Robinson, "In the Shadow of Old John Brown: Insurrection Anxiety and Confederate Mobilization 1861–1863," *Journal of Negro History* 55 (1980):279–97. Brown was the abolitionist who had seized the federal arsenal at Harper's Ferry in 1859.
64. William C. Wright to Alexander H. Stephens, 16 July 1864, AHSLC.
65. David C. Barrow to J. A. Spratlin, 10 February 1864, DCB.
66. J. M. Rowland to Joseph E. Brown, 27 February 1863, Brown IC.
67. Petition to exempt Dr. L. L. Clark, 4 August 1864, Brown Petitions.
68. Petition to exempt Michael Wiggins (Jefferson county), 21 July 1864, Brown Petitions.

69. Petitions to exempt Walker Hawes, 21 January and 10 June 1864, Brown Petitions.
70. Petition for detail for Augustus J. Pugsley, 28 December 1863, Brown Petitions.
71. Petition to exempt Eli A. Veazey, undated, Brown Petitions.
72. Petition for release of Private John H. Boyd, undated, Brown Petitions.
73. *CR*, 2:483–86.
74. Augusta *Constitutionalist*, 2 April 1863.
75. *CR*, 2:440; Augusta *Chronicle*, 4 April 1863.
76. Edgefield *Advertiser*, 10 June 1863.
77. Augusta *Constitutionalist*, 20 August 1863.
78. Ibid., 14 November 1863.
79. Letter from "Mary," Edgefield *Advertiser*, 11 February 1863.
80. Ibid., 8 April 1863.
81. Linton Stephens to Thomas W. Thomas, 15 July 1863, Alexander H. Stephens Papers, Emory University Library.
82. Thomas W. Thomas to Joseph E. Brown, 18 July 1863, Brown IC.
83. Linton Stephens to Alexander H. Stephens, 26 July 1863, AHSM.
84. Hattie Young to Alexander H. Stephens, 16 July 1863, AHSLC.
85. Linton Stephens to Alexander H. Stephens, 25 September 1863, AHSM. The wording of the proclamation calling out the militia had specified that each county would decide on a specific territory, such as a congressional district, it would be required to defend.
86. Augusta *Constitutionalist*, 19 August and 3 September 1863.
87. Athens *Southern Banner*, 20 May 1863.
88. **Table 28.** Reason Given for Last Appearance in Service Records, Soldiers from Augusta's Hinterlands

	(%)
War-related death	36
Captured	8
Disabled, disease	16
TOTAL	60
Deserted, AWOL	3
Other, none	19
Surrendered, 1865	17
(N)	(269)

SOURCE: Samples of men from Glascock, Hart, and Taliaferro counties from the manuscript returns of the United States Bureau of the Census, 1860, whose records were located in service records.
NOTE: See Appendix A for detailed description.

89. Minutes of Glascock County Inferior Court, 7 July 1862, GDAH.
90. List of Edgefield residents reported AWOL, Edgefield *Advertiser*, 12 April 1865. Occupations and wealth from manuscript schedules of the 1860 census.

91. **Table 29.** Entering and Leaving Service, Soldiers from
Augusta's Hinterlands

Year	Entering	Leaving
1861	90	9
1862	145	62
1863	18	43
1864	10	45
1865	0	105

SOURCE: Samples of men from Glascock, Hart, and Taliaferro counties from the manuscript returns of the United States Bureau of the Census, 1860, whose records were located in service records.
NOTE: See Appendix A for detailed description.

92. James I. Robertson, Jr., ed., *The Diary of Dolly Lunt Burge* (Athens: University of Georgia Press, 1962), 1 January 1864.
93. James H. Hammond to George A. Trenholm, 11 August 1864, JHHLC.
94. Augusta *Chronicle*, 2 June 1864.
95. Edgefield *Advertiser*, 21 September 1864.
96. Ibid., 7 December 1864.
97. Kate Rowland Diary, 29 November 1864, Emory University Library.
98. Ibid., 3 December 1864. For contrasting interpretations of the responses of slaves to Sherman's troops, see Paul David Escott, "The Context of Freedom: Georgia's Slaves During the Civil War," *Georgia Historical Quarterly* 58 (1974): 79–104; Edmund L. Drago, "How Sherman's March Affected the Slaves," *Georgia Historical Quarterly* 57 (1973): 361–75.
99. Augusta *Chronicle*, 7 December 1864.
100. Ibid., 2 December 1864.
101. "Letter From Warrenton," ibid.
102. Ibid., 29 December 1864.
103. Minutes of Richmond County Superior Court, Grand Jury Presentments in ibid., 29 January 1865; see also Florence Corley, *Confederate City: Augusta, Georgia, 1860–1865* (Columbia: University of South Carolina Press, 1960), chap. 6.
104. *Southern Cultivator* 23 (1865): 14.
105. Minutes of Hancock County Superior Court, 1858–1870, 13 April 1865 (p. 449).
106. John H. Cornish Diary, 10 February 1865, SHC.
107. While there is no single starting point for this aspect of policy of the *Chronicle*, which was regularly critical of the Davis administration, the call for negotiations became quite insistent in its editorial columns after Sherman entered Atlanta in September, 1864; see Augusta *Chronicle*, 17 September 1864.
108. Stephens was a member of the southern delegation to the abortive negotiations in February 1865, at Hampton Roads, Virginia. He afterward became convinced that Davis had purposely intended

the negotiations to fail; see Rudolph von Abele, *Alexander H. Stephens: A Biography* (New York: Knopf, 1946), chap. 4.

109. Augusta *Chronicle*, 20 January 1865.
110. Ibid., 16 February 1865.
111. Ibid., 9 April 1865.
112. Robert F. Durden, *The Gray and the Black: The Confederate Debate on Emancipation* (Baton Rouge: Louisiana State University Press, 1972).
113. Augusta *Constitutionalist*, 24 June 1863.
114. Ibid., 29 July 1864.
115. Ibid., 2 and 7 August 1864.
116. Ibid., 13 and 20 October 1864.
117. Ibid., 9 and 10 December 1864.
118. Ibid., 2 February 1865.
119. Ibid.; see also ibid., 31 December 1864 and 6 January 1865, for similar arguments from "Harry South."
120. Ibid., 24 January and 22 February 1865.
121. Ibid., 1 March 1865.
122. Ibid., 31 December 1864.
123. Quoted in Durden, *Gray and Black*, 183–85.
124. Augusta *Constitutionalist*, 31 December 1865.
125. Edgefield *Advertiser*, 23 November 1864.
126. Ibid., 30 November 1864 and 18 January 1865.
127. Augusta *Constitutionalist*, 26 January 1865.
128. Ibid., 14 February 1865.
129. Ibid., 10 and 12 March 1865.
130. Edgefield *Advertiser*, 19 April 1865.
131. Augusta *Chronicle*, 10 January 1865. These words were used in an editorial specifically on a related plan to emancipate slaves in return for recognition and assistance from England and France.
132. Ibid., 12 March 1865.
133. Ibid., 22 and 23 March 1865.
134. Ibid., 29 March 1865.
135. Augusta *Constitutionalist*, 26 January 1865.
136. Augusta *Chronicle*, 1 February 1865.
137. Ibid., 15 April 1865.
138. Ibid., 18 April 1865.
139. Ibid., 12 April 1865.
140. Augusta *Constitutionalist*, 4 January 1865.
141. Robertson, *Diary*, 15 November 1864.
142. Ibid., 29 April 1865.
143. Edgefield *Advertiser*, 26 April 1865.
144. Eliza Francis Andrews, *War Time Journal of a Georgia Girl* (1908), 198.
145. Manuscript description of "Last Moments of James H. Hammond," JHHLC, largely from E. Spann Hammond to Harry Hammond, 13 November 1864, JHHLC.
146. Linton Stephens to Alexander H. Stephens, 28 May 1865, AHSM.

147. Rawick, *Ga. Narr.*, 13(4): 230–35.
148. Paul Fussell, *The Great War and Modern Memory* (New York: Oxford University Press, 1975), 7.

✵ ESSAY ON SOURCES

Here I would like to comment briefly on the most important sources used, as well as mention some works whose importance may not be reflected in the Notes. For a full bibliography, see the chapter notes.

Unpublished Manuscripts

Of special importance for the social history of the Augusta area are the various papers of Alexander H. Stephens. There are large Stephens collections in the Library of Congress (LC) and at Manhattanville College of the Sacred Heart, Purchase, New York, and smaller collections in the Perkins Library at Duke University and in the Emory University Library. The LC collection is valuable not only as a record of Stephens's own views and political correspondence, but also of the many letters from poorer white Georgians asking for favors or advice, or simply making their opinions known to an important public official. The Manhattanville collection consists almost completely of letters between Alexander and his half-brother, Linton. At times, these two corresponded daily, or even more frequently; their long letters often include observations of daily life in rural Georgia.

The large James Henry Hammond collections in the Library of Congress and in the South Caroliniana Library (SCL) at the University of South Carolina contain much of interest to the social historian, including Hammond's detailed plantation journals. The David C. Barrow Papers in the University of Georgia Library include many boxes of material left by the family and overseers of this substantial Georgia planter. The Ella Gertrude (Clanton) Thomas Diary in the Perkins Library at Duke University records the lively observations and commentary of a perceptive and intelligent plantation mistress. The Benton Miller Farm Journal in the Georgia Department of Archives and History (GDAH) is a rare detailed record of operations on the farm of a small slaveowner during an eighteen-month period.

Other collections with significant material include the E. Spann Hammond Papers, Hammond–Bryan–Cummings Papers, and Iveson L. Brookes Papers in the SCL; the Nathan B. Moore Farm Journal and Iveson L. Brookes Papers at Duke; the Alexander–Hillhouse Papers,

Iveson L. Brookes Papers, and John H. Cornish Diary in the Southern Historical Collection (SHC) of the University of North Carolina Library; and the Burge–Gray Papers, Kate Rowland Diary, and James Thomas Papers at Emory.

Several types of organizational records were helpful at points. The GDAH has microfilmed or typescript copies of church minutes. The Stephen D. Heard Papers in the SHC contain the business records of an important Augusta cotton factor, and helped me to define the limits of Augusta's economic hinterlands. The Dun & Bradstreet Collection in the Baker Library at the Harvard University Business School contains observations on stores and manufacturing establishments in every county, made by the credit reporters of the Dun Company. A typescript of the minutes of the Beech Island Farmers Club in the SCL records the economic and social ideas of large planters in South Carolina and Georgia.

Several of these collections are at least partly accessible in published form. Much Stephens material has been printed in four volumes: Henry C. Cleveland, *Alexander H. Stephens in Public and Private* (Philadelphia, 1867); Richard Malcolm Johnston and William Hand Browne, *Life of Alexander H. Stephens* (Philadelphia, 1878; reprint, Freeport, N.Y., 1971); James D. Waddell, ed., *Biographical Sketch of Linton Stephens* (Atlanta, 1877), which includes much of the Manhattanville correspondence; and Ulrich B. Phillips, ed., *The Correspondence of Robert Toombs, Alexander H. Stephens, and Howell Cobb*, American Historical Association *Annual Report* (Washington, D.C., 1911; reprint, New York, 1970). A few of Hammond's letters are in Carol Bleser, ed., *The Hammonds of Redcliffe* (New York, 1982). Some of the letters in the Alexander–Hillhouse Papers are in Marion Alexander Boggs, ed., *The Alexander Letters, 1787–1900* (1910; reprint, Athens, Ga., 1980). The diary of a plantation mistress, in the Burge–Gray Papers, is printed in James I. Robertson, Jr., ed., *The Diary of Dolly Lunt Burge* (Athens, Ga., 1962).

Unpublished Government Records

Microfilms of most surviving local-government records for Georgia counties are in the GDAH. County Tax Digests were helpful in assessing the wealth of some individuals. Probate records inventoried wealthholdings of and debts owed to deceased persons. Minutes of the inferior courts recorded county business, and minutes of the superior courts contain records of criminal and important civil cases, as well as Grand Jury Presentments.

The Executive Officers Books and the records of the Secretary of State list all locally elected officials. Especially valuable for the Civil War years are the Incoming Correspondence and the Petitions Received in the Governor Joseph E. Brown Papers. Many of these are requests for help of various kinds from ordinary citizens throughout the state.

The original returns of the United States census for various years, the source of most of the statistical information, are discussed in Appendix A. Of great assistance in using these records is the series of county-by-county indexes of the 1850 census compiled by Mrs. Walter W. Otto of Savannah.

Published Primary Sources

Newspapers were invaluable sources for many kinds of information: reports on county-level politics; advertisements; local stories; and current opinions, in the form of editorials and letters, on political or other public matters. Newspapers also reprinted many speeches and lectures. Augusta was served throughout the period before emancipation by two daily papers, the *Daily Chronicle and Sentinel* and the *Daily Constitutionalist*. These newspapers usually were controlled by different parties or factions. They circulated throughout the hinterland area in Georgia, and together they provide excellent coverage of affairs and opinions. The weekly Edgefield *Advertiser*, the originals of which are in the Mims Library in Edgefield, South Carolina, was unusually conscientious in opening its pages to conflicting opinions on most current affairs. The *Southern Cultivator*, a monthly published in Augusta, concentrated on plantation economics, but contained information on political and social issues as well.

Contemporary books and pamphlets of special interest for the Augusta area include several published in or near Augusta: E. N. Elliot, ed., *Cotton Is King; And Proslavery Arguments* (Augusta, 1860), a compendium that includes essays previously published by South Carolinians James H. Hammond and William Harper; Iveson L. Brookes, *A Defense of Southern Slavery* . . . (Hamburg, S.C., 1851) and *A Defense of the South Against the Reproaches of the North* . . . (Hamburg, S.C., 1850); Christopher C. Memminger's proslavery *Lecture . . . before the Young Men's Library . . .* (Augusta, 1851); William C. Moragne, *The Electoral Question. To the Citizens of Edgefield District* (Edgefield, S.C., 1859); Francis W. Pickens, *Speech of Hon. F. W. Pickens . . .* (Edgefield, S.C., 1851); and Arthur Simkins, *An Address before the State Agricultural Society of South Carolina* (Edgefield, S.C., 1855). Several of James H. Hammond's speeches and writings are collected in *Selections from the Letters and Speeches of the Hon. James H. Hammond* (New York, 1866). A copy of "Brutus," *An Address to the Citizens of South Carolina* (n.p., ca. 1849), is in the Hammond Papers in the SCL.

Many of Alexander H. Stephens's important addresses are included in

Cleveland, *Alexander H. Stephens in Public and Private*. George Mc-Duffie's proslavery message to the South Carolina legislature in 1835 is in Albert B. Hart and Edward Channing, eds., *American History Leaflets, Colonial and Constitutional*, no. 10 (New York, 1893). R. H. Clark, Thomas R. R. Cobb, and D. Irwin compiled *The Code of the State of Georgia* (Atlanta, 1861), which provides the best guide to the structure of local government in late antebellum Georgia. Allen D. Candler, ed., *The Confederate Records of the State of Georgia*, 3 vols. (Atlanta, 1909–11), contains several of the most important pro- and antisecession speeches in Georgia, the official correspondence and messages of Governor Brown during the Civil War, and a selection of resolutions sent by county public meetings during the secession crisis. Robert Toombs, *Speech on the Crisis* (Washington, D.C., 1860), is printed in pamphlet form.

Among important primary works that circulated in the Augusta area, but did not originate there, mention should be made of Hinton Rowan Helper, *The Impending Crisis of the South. How to Meet It* (n.p., 1857), and Thomas R. R. Cobb, *An Historical Sketch of Slavery* (Philadelphia and Savannah, 1858). A modern edition of Helper, with an illuminating introduction by George Fredrickson, was published by Harvard University Press in 1968.

Several travelers and visitors left accounts or observations of the Augusta area. Mark Van Doren, ed., *The Travels of William Bartram* (n.p., 1928), includes a description of the land as it was before major white settlement. Solon Robinson's observations of several farms and plantations are included in Herbert A. Kellar, ed., *Solon Robinson, Pioneer and Agriculturalist: Selected Writings*, 2 vols. (Indianapolis, 1936). Fredrika Bremer, *The Homes of the New World; Impressions of America*, 2 vols. (New York, 1864), and Emily P. Burke, *Reminiscences of Georgia* (n.p., 1850), describe visits to the homes of plain folk in the 1840s and 1850s. Scottish mechanic William Thomson visited the Augusta area and described his encounters in *A Tradesman's Travels . . . in . . . 1840, 1841, and 1842* (Edinburgh, 1842). Fredrick Law Olmsted visited the Augusta area only briefly, but many of his observations, especially in *A Journey in the Back Country* (New York, 1860), are relevant to any study of southern classes. Mrs. Irby Morgan described life as a Civil War refugee near Augusta in *How It Was: Four Years Among the Rebels* (Nashville, 1892).

Two accounts by slaves who lived just outside the Augusta area provide rare insights into slave society in the Piedmont. Jacob Stroyer recounted his first two decades in "My Life in the South," in *Five Slave Narratives: A Compendium* (1898; reprint, New York, 1968). Stroyer lived near Columbia, South Carolina, and was freed at emancipation. John Brown escaped from a DeKalb county, Georgia, farm in the 1840s, and described his harsh life in *Slave Life in Georgia: A Narrative of the*

Life, Sufferings and Escape of John Brown, A Fugitive Slave (London, 1855; reprint, Savannah, 1972). F. Nash Boney, editor of the modern edition, painstakingly documented the accuracy of Brown's story.

The single best source for slave life and culture in the area is the compilation of interviews with former slaves by the Works Progress Administration in the 1930s: George Rawick, ed., *The American Slave: A Composite Autobiography*, 19 vols., with Supplement 1, 12 vols., and Supplement 2, 10 vols. (Westport, Conn., 1972–79). Rawick's "General Introduction" to Supplement 1 provides an excellent discussion of the limitations of these sources: they are accounts by elderly black people, given usually to white interviewers, and most of the people interviewed were children during the slavery period. Fortunately for my purposes, the Georgia interviews are, by scholarly consensus, among the best. Many are quite long, and they show relatively little evidence of manipulation of fact or tone by interviewers trying to whitewash the history of slavery. Many Augusta residents were interviewed. There are also some excellent interviews of former slaves who had spent time in the Augusta area as slaves, and subsequently moved to other states. Altogether, some 130 of the interviews had useful material for this study.

Secondary Sources

The questions treated in this study have been the subject of historical inquiry for generations. For a discussion of the interpretive literature on the South as a whole, see the Introduction.

Biographies of public figures in the Augusta area were helpful in many places. Of special importance is Drew Gilpin Faust, *James Henry Hammond and the Old South: A Design for Mastery* (Baton Rouge, 1982). Faust's attention to social, as well as personal, political, and intellectual, matters allows her to throw light on many of the topics discussed here. On Alexander H. Stephens, in addition to the works cited above, see Rudolph von Abele, *Alexander H. Stephens: A Biography* (New York, 1946). Robert Toombs has been the subject of books by Ulrich B. Phillips, *The Life of Robert Toombs* (New York, 1913), and William Y. Thompson, *Robert Toombs of Georgia* (Baton Rouge, 1966). Joseph Parks, *Joseph E. Brown of Georgia* (Baton Rouge, 1976), covers Brown's political career in detail. Louise Biles Hill, *Joseph E. Brown and the Confederacy* (Chapel Hill, 1939), is largely critical of Brown's opposition to Jefferson Davis. Both books on Brown have much to say about his wartime political allies, the Stephenses. Mary Elizabeth Massey's article on Ella Gertrude Thomas, "The Making of a Feminist," *Journal of Southern History* 39 (1973): 3–22, gives an excellent analysis of the life of a fascinating woman.

Arguments about the economics of slavery have largely been framed by a pioneering essay by Alfred H. Conrad and John R. Meyer, "The Economics of Slavery," in *The Economics of Slavery and Other Studies in Econometric History*, ed. Conrad and Meyer (Cambridge, Mass., 1965). Their contention that slavery produced handsome profits for owners has not been successfully challenged. The January 1970 issue of *Agricultural History*, separately published as William N. Parker, ed., *The Structure of the Cotton Economy of the Antebellum South* (Berkeley, 1970), contains much of the fruits of the research stimulated by Conrad and Meyer. Gavin Wright, *The Political Economy of the Cotton South: Households, Markets, and Wealth in the Nineteenth Century* (New York, 1978), is especially valuable because Wright's mastery of contemporary sources enables him to analyze economic decision making from the point of view of nineteenth-century cotton farmers and planters. Lewis Cecil Gray, *History of Agriculture in the Southern United States to 1860*, 2 vols. (Washington, D.C., 1933; reprint, Gloucester, Mass., 1958), is still unsurpassed on many subjects. On special economic topics, see Fred Bateman and Thomas Weiss, *A Deplorable Scarcity: The Failure of Industrialization in the Slave Economy* (Chapel Hill, 1980); James C. Bonner, *A History of Georgia Agriculture, 1732–1860* (Athens, Ga., 1964); Robert E. Gallman and Ralph V. Anderson, "Slaves as Fixed Capital: Slave Labor and Southern Economic Development," *Journal of American History* 64 (1977): 24–46; Sam B. Hilliard, *Hogmeat and Hoecake: Food Supply in the Old South, 1840–1860* (Carbondale, Ill., 1972); Julius Rubin, "The Limits of Agricultural Progress in the Nineteenth-Century South," *Agricultural History* 49 (1975): 362–73; and Harold D. Woodman, *King Cotton and His Retainers: Financing and Marketing the Cotton Crop of the South, 1800–1925* (Lexington, Ky., 1968).

Research on the role of republican ideology in the nineteenth-century United States has grown from a discovery of its importance in the eighteenth century. See, especially, Bernard Bailyn, *The Ideological Origins of the American Revolution* (Cambridge, Mass., 1967), and J. G. A. Pocock, *The Machiavellian Moment: Florentine Political Thought and the Atlantic Republican Tradition* (Princeton, N.J., 1975). Republicanism's legacy in South Carolina is addressed in James N. Banner, "The Problem of South Carolina," in *The Hofstadter Aegis: A Memorial*, ed. Stanley Elkins and Eric McKitrick (New York, 1974), and Kenneth Greenberg, "The Second American Revolution: South Carolina Politics, Society, and Secession, 1776–1860" (Ph.D. diss., University of Wisconsin, 1976). Eugene Genovese places proslavery thought at the center of southern ideology in *The World the Slaveholders Made: Two Essays in Interpretation* (New York, 1969). On the role of race in white thought, see George Fredrickson, *The Black Image in the White Mind: The Debate on Afro-American Character and Destiny, 1817–1914* (New York, 1971). Of special merit on religious belief and practice is Donald G. Mathews, *Religion in the Old South* (Chicago, 1977).

Among the major works that have led to a revision in our understanding of slavery are John Blassingame, *The Slave Community: Plantation Life in the Antebellum South*, rev. and enl. ed. (New York, 1979); Eugene Genovese, *Roll, Jordan, Roll: The World the Slaves Made* (New York, 1974); Herbert G. Gutman, *The Black Family in Slavery and Freedom, 1750–1925* (New York, 1976); Lawrence Levine, *Black Culture and Black Consciousness* (New York, 1977); and Leslie Howard Owens, *This Species of Property: Slave Life and Culture in the Old South* (New York, 1976). Still unsurpassed in many respects as a study of the slave regime is Kenneth Stampp, *The Peculiar Institution* (New York, 1955). Ralph B. Flanders, *Plantation Slavery in Georgia* (Chapel Hill, 1933), is outdated in interpretation but still contains useful information. Of special relevance for the Augusta area are Drew Gilpin Faust, "Culture, Conflict, and Community: The Meaning of Power on an Antebellum Plantation," *Journal of Social History* 14 (1980): 83–97, a study of the Hammond plantations; Michael S. Hindus, "Black Justice Under White Law: Criminal Prosecutions of Blacks in Antebellum South Carolina," *Journal of American History* 63 (1976): 575–99; Clarence Mohr, "Slavery in Oglethorpe County, Georgia," *Phylon* 33 (1972): 4–21; and Ulrich B. Phillips, "Origin and Growth of the Southern Black Belts," *American Historical Review* 11 (1906): 798–816.

Class conflict and community among southern whites are discussed in many of the general works cited above and in the Introduction. Historians are just beginning to probe these topics at the local level. A pioneering essay, still valuable, is James C. Bonner, "Profile of a Late Ante-Bellum Community," *American Historical Review* 49 (1944): 663–80. Steven Hahn, *The Roots of Southern Populism: Yeoman Farmers and the Transformation of the Georgia Upcountry, 1850–1890* (New York, 1983), is a study of an area with relatively few slaves or plantations, but contains much of interest to any social historian of the South. Vernon O. Burton, "Unfaithful Servants? Edgefield's Black Reconstruction: Part I of the Total History of Edgefield County, South Carolina" (Ph.D. diss., Princeton University, 1976), includes important material on the antebellum period. Vernon O. Burton and Robert McMath, eds., *Class, Conflict, and Consensus: Antebellum Southern Community Studies* (Westport, Conn., 1982), includes a wide range of local studies.

On state-level politics, William W. Freehling, *Prelude to Civil War: The Nullification Crisis in South Carolina, 1816–1836* (New York, 1964), is especially valuable in placing South Carolina's politics in its social and economic context. Rachel Klein, "The Rise of the Planters in the South Carolina Backcountry, 1767–1808" (Ph.D. diss., Yale University, 1979), does much the same for an earlier period. Other studies of South Carolina politics include John Barnwell, *Love of Order: South Carolina's First Secession Crisis* (Chapel Hill, 1982); Chauncey Samuel Boucher, "Sectionalism, Representation, and the Electoral Question in

Ante-Bellum South Carolina," *Washington University Studies* 4 (1916): 3–62; William A. Schaper, *Sectionalism and Representation in South Carolina*, American Historical Association *Annual Report* (1900; reprint, New York, 1968); and Harold S. Schultz, *Nationalism and Sectionalism in South Carolina, 1852–1860: A Study of the Movement for Southern Independence* (Durham, N.C., 1950).

On Georgia politics, see Donald Arthur DeBats, "Elites and Masses: Political Structure, Communication, and Behavior in Antebellum Georgia" (Ph.D. diss., University of Wisconsin, 1973); Horace Montgomery, *Cracker Parties* (Baton Rouge, 1950); Paul Murray, *The Whig Party in Georgia, 1825–1853* (Chapel Hill, 1948); and Ulrich B. Phillips, *Georgia and States Rights*, American Historical Association *Annual Report* (Washington, D.C., 1902).

There are recent studies of secession in both Georgia and South Carolina. Steven A. Channing, *Crisis of Fear: Secession in South Carolina* (New York, 1970), stresses racial fears as a cause. Michael P. Johnson, *Toward a Patriarchal Republic: The Secession of Georgia* (Baton Rouge, 1977), believes that internal conflict among whites was most important in precipitating secession in Georgia.

The war years are surveyed in T. Conn Bryan, *Confederate Georgia* (Athens, Ga., 1953), and Charles Edward Cauthen, *South Carolina Goes to War, 1860–1865* (Chapel Hill, 1950). Important special topics are treated in Clarence Mohr, "Georgia Blacks During Secession and Civil War, 1859–1865" (Ph.D. diss., University of Georgia, 1975), and Peter Wallenstein, "Rich Man's War, Rich Man's Fight: The Civil War and the Transformation of Public Finance in Georgia," *Journal of Southern History* 50 (1984): 15–42.

Emory Thomas, *Confederate Nation* (New York, 1979), is an excellent recent survey of the Confederacy. On the Confederate home front, see Paul David Escott, *After Secession: Jefferson Davis and the Failure of Confederate Nationalism* (Baton Rouge, 1978), which emphasizes Davis's failure to prevent class cleavages among southern whites and includes a helpful discussion of Davis's disputes with Governor Brown of Georgia; Albert Burton Moore, *Conscription and Conflict in the Confederacy* (New York, 1924); James L. Roark, *Masters Without Slaves: Southern Planters in Civil War and Reconstruction* (New York, 1977), which emphasizes most planters' commitment to slavery above all else, including southern independence; Bell Wiley, *The Plain People of the Confederacy* (Baton Rouge, 1943); Charles W. Ramsdell, *Behind the Lines in the Southern Confederacy* (Baton Rouge, 1944), which stresses economic hardships; and Robert F. Durden, *The Gray and the Black: The Confederate Debate on Emancipation* (Baton Rouge, 1972).

Finally, I would like to mention some works that influenced my treatment at particular places: on ideologies, Clifford Geertz, "Ideology as a Cultural System," in Geertz, *The Interpretation of Cultures* (New York,

1973), and J. G. A. Pocock, "Languages and Their Implications: The Transformation of the Study of Political Thought," in Pocock, *Politics, Language, and Time: Essays on Political Thought and History* (New York, 1971); on the interplay of class, race, and ideology, Edmund S. Morgan, *American Slavery, American Freedom: The Ordeal of Colonial Virginia* (New York, 1975), and E. P. Thompson, *The Making of the English Working Class* (New York, 1963); on slave "underlife," Erving Goffman, "The Underlife of a Public Institution," in Goffman, *Asylums: Essays on the Social Situation of Mental Patients and Other Inmates* (Garden City, N.Y., 1961); and on debt, Marshall D. Sahlins, "On the Sociology of Primitive Exchange," in *The Relevance of Models for Social Anthropology*, ed. Michael Banton (London, 1965).

☘ INDEX

About the Author

J. William Harris has written a number of journal articles on Southern studies. A native of Jacksonville, Florida, he is a graduate of the Massachusetts Institute of Technology (B.S., 1968) and of Johns Hopkins University (M.A., 1976; Ph.D., 1982), and has received a summer stipend from the National Endowment for the Humanities. He has taught at Boys' Latin School in Baltimore, at Pennsylvania State University, at Harvard University, and since 1985 as assistant professor of history at the University of New Hampshire. This is his first book.

About the Book

Plain Folk and Gentry in a Slave Society has been composed in Trump Mediaeval by G & S Typesetters of Austin, Texas. It was printed on 60 lb. Warren's Olde Style and bound by Thomson-Shore of Dexter, Michigan. Design by Joyce Kachergis Book Design and Production of Bynum, North Carolina.
Wesleyan University Press, 1985.